Hezekiah Butterworth

Young folks' History of Boston

Hezekiah Butterworth

Young folks' History of Boston

ISBN/EAN: 9783744778824

Printed in Europe, USA, Canada, Australia, Japan

Cover: Foto ©ninafisch / pixelio.de

More available books at **www.hansebooks.com**

History of Boston.

BY

HEZEKIAH BUTTERWORTH,

AUTHOR OF "ZIGZAG JOURNEYS IN EUROPE," "ZIGZAG JOURNEYS IN
CLASSIC LANDS," "ZIGZAG JOURNEYS IN THE ORIENT,"
"YOUNG FOLKS' HISTORY OF AMERICA," ETC.

FULLY ILLUSTRATED.

BOSTON:
PUBLISHED BY ESTES AND LAURIAT,
301-305 WASHINGTON STREET.
1881.

Copyright, 1881,
BY ESTES AND LAURIAT.

UNIVERSITY PRESS:
JOHN WILSON AND SON, CAMBRIDGE.

PREFACE.

SOME ten years ago the writer of this volume came to Boston, a stranger, for the purpose of reading in the Public Library and obtaining work as a journalist. Becoming deeply interested in works of local history, especially in those of Drake, and being unacquainted with society, he resolved to visit all the old historic places in and about Boston, in hours needed for exercise, and to study their associations.

About a year ago the publishers asked him to prepare a young people's history of Boston, and to seek to make it popular and entertaining, after the methods of the "Zigzag" books. It was a pleasure to attempt this work, as it revived the memories of the solitary walks ten years ago, and brought into use the material then collected.

This book does not seek to follow the common historic methods, but to be as entertaining as possible while imparting information. The elaborate works of Drake, Shurtleff, Quincy, and the noble "Memorial History" fully cover the subject for the scholar and the adult reader of means and leisure, but hardly meet the wants of popular reading and the young. Hence stories, incidents, poems, and pictures have been freely used. We hope that the reading of this volume may at least create an interest for the study of the larger works we have named, and tend to develop that honest pride in our local history which is essential to the best citizenship.

28 *Worcester Street.*

CONTENTS.

CHAPTER		PAGE
I.	WHEREIN IS GIVEN SOME ACCOUNT OF ST. BOTOLPH	15
II.	WHEREIN IS GIVEN SOME ACCOUNT OF ST. BOTOLPH'S CHURCH IN LINCOLNSHIRE	31
III.	WHEREIN IS GIVEN AN ACCOUNT OF WILLIAM BLACKSTONE, A RECLUSE, WHO WAS THE FIRST SETTLER OF BOSTON	39
IV.	WHEREIN IS CONTAINED THE STORY OF LADY ARBELLA JOHNSON	47
V.	WHEREIN ARE RELATED SOME INCIDENTS OF THE LIFE OF GOVERNOR JOHN WINTHROP, THE FOUNDER OF BOSTON	57
VI.	WHEREIN IS GIVEN SOME ACCOUNT OF SIR HENRY VANE, ANNE HUTCHINSON, AND THOSE RELIGIOUS PERSECUTIONS OUT OF WHICH GREW LIBERTY OF CONSCIENCE AND OPINION	85
VII.	WHEREIN ARE RELATED SOME STORIES OF A NERVOUS DISEASE CALLED WITCHCRAFT	109
VIII.	WHEREIN IS SHOWN HOW THE COLONY BECAME A PROVINCE	137
IX.	WHEREIN ARE TOLD SOME STORIES OF OLD COLONY TIMES	151
X.	WHEREIN IS GIVEN SOME ACCOUNT OF THE TIMES OF THE ELEVEN ROYAL GOVERNORS AND OF THE OLD PROVINCE HOUSE	169

CHAPTER		PAGE
XI.	THE TIMES OF THE ELEVEN ROYAL GOVERNORS AND OF THE OLD PROVINCE HOUSE, CONTINUED	189
XII.	THE EVE OF REVOLUTION	205
XIII.	BUNKER HILL	243
XIV.	THE SIEGE OF BOSTON	253
XV.	THE STORY OF HOLLIS STREET MEETING-HOUSE AND CURIOUS OLD MATHER BYLES, THE ROYALIST	283
XVI.	FREEDOM AND PROSPERITY	293
XVII.	THE ANTISLAVERY STRUGGLE	309
XVIII.	THE BOSTON OF TO-DAY	323
XIX.	THE PLEASURE RESORTS AND THE BEAUTIFUL SUBURBS OF BOSTON	349
XX.	THE OLD BOSTON SCHOOLS	369
XXI.	THE ASSOCIATIONS OF BOSTON POETRY	389
XXII.	ASSOCIATIONS OF WHITTIER'S POETRY	421
XXIII.	THE CONCORD AUTHORS AND THE ASSOCIATIONS OF THEIR WORKS	439
XXIV.	MOUNT AUBURN	455
	INDEX	475

LIST OF ILLUSTRATIONS.

	PAGE
Dorothy Hancock's Reception	*Frontispiece*
Monks at Study	16
Lincoln Cathedral	17
Preaching the Gospel to the Saxons	21
Ruins of an Ancient Abbey	25
A Saxon Priest destroying an Idol	27
St. Botolph's Church	33
Charles I.	35
Cotton Memorial Chapel	36
William Blackstone's House	39
Trimountain	40
On the Banks of the Charles	41
Sailing from England	48
Sir Richard Saltonstall	49
The First King's Chapel	51
Winthrop's Fleet in Boston Harbor	53
John Winthrop	59
Winthrop and Dudley	63
First Meeting-House	65
Winthrop fording a Stream	67
Revels at Merry-Mount	68
Miles Standish discovers the Revellers at Merry-Mount	69
Endicott cutting down Morton's May-pole	73
A Lost Settler found	77
Indians returning a Lost Child	80
The Harbor of Boston	81
Henry Vane	86
Burial of the King	88
Execution of Charles I.	89

List of Illustrations.

	PAGE
Oliver Cromwell	91
Roger Williams appealing to the Indians	93
Cutting out the Red Cross	95
The Stocks	96
John Endicott	97
The Pillory	99
Whipping Quakers at the Cart's Tail in Boston	101
Old Elm and Quakers' Graves	105
Witches	109
Witchcraft at Salem Village	113
Cotton Mather	117
Martha Corey and her Persecutors	121
The Old Elm	125
A False Alarm	129
Increase Mather	133
Governor Leverett	138
The Old Feather Store	139
Charles II.	141
Sir Edmund Andros	143
Governor Andros a Prisoner	147
Nix's Mate	152
Massacre at Bloody Brook	153
Charles chasing the Moth	157
Old-time Courtesies	163
Elder Brewster's Chair	166
Queen Anne	171
The Province House	175
Franklin	178
King's Chapel, Tremont Street	179
George I.	183
Franklin's Birthplace	185
Faneuil Hall	191
The Old South Church	193
Revocation of the Edict of Nantes	195
The Frankland House	198
The Liberty Tree	200
Map of New England about 1700	201
Bostonians reading the Stamp Act	207
The Hancock House	210
Adams opposing the Stamp Act from the Old State House	211

List of Illustrations.

	PAGE
Destruction of the Tea	217
Provincials rallying at Concord	221
Conflict at the North Bridge	223
Section of Bonner's Map, 1722	227
John Hancock	231
Christ Church	235
From Bonner's Map, 1722	237
Plan of the Battle of Bunker Hill	245
The Battle of Bunker Hill	249
The Washington Elm	254
View from Beacon Hill, Boston	255
The Holmes House	258
Plan of the Investment of Boston	259
Pine-Tree Flag	262
Washington's Treasure-chest	263
George III.	269
Plan of the Town of Boston, 1775	273
Boston with its Environs, 1775-76	277
The Old Hollis Street Church	283
From Bonner's Map, 1722	285
Mather Byles	288
Lafayette	297
Daniel Webster	300
Washington Irving	304
Mr. Garrison in the Hands of the Mob	311
Theodore Parker	314
First Subscriptions for Soldiers' Families	315
Fort Sumter	317
Massachusetts Sixth in Baltimore	318
State House	325
Corner of Washington and Milk Streets, before the Great Fire	328
"Summer Street a Wall of Flame"	329
"The Old South stands"	333
Henry Wilson	335
Soldiers and Sailors' Monument	336
Map of Boston in 1838	337
Skeleton of Mammoth	343
Statue of Edward Everett	351
Northmen on an Expedition	357
The French King troubled at the Approach of the Northmen	363

List of Illustrations.

	PAGE
The Old Pedagogue	370
Ear Pincers	371
John Lovell	377
Charles K. Dillaway	379
First Latin School, School Lane	380
The English High and Latin School	381
Benjamin Franklin	391
Charles Sprague	392
The "Old Brick" Church	395
"Elmwood," the Home of Lowell	407
James Russell Lowell	409
Oliver Wendell Holmes	411
John G. Whittier	421
The Carwitham View of Boston, about 1730	425
An Old-time Husking Frolic	433
Ralph Waldo Emerson	439
Nathaniel Hawthorne	442
The Old Manse	443
Thoreau's Hut	444
Margaret Fuller (Countess Ossoli)	449
Ossoli Memorial	456
Entrance to Mt. Auburn Cemetery	457
Spurzheim Monument	459
Bronze Statue of Dr. Nathaniel Bowditch	460
The Chapel	461
The Story Statue	462
Charles Sumner's Sarcophagus	465
Louis Agassiz	467
The Agassiz Boulder	468
The Tower	470
Jared Sparks	471

" Kind hearts are more than coronets,
　And simple faith than Norman blood."
　　　　　　　　　　　　Tennyson.

YOUNG FOLKS'
HISTORY OF BOSTON.

CHAPTER I.

WHEREIN IS GIVEN SOME ACCOUNT OF ST. BOTOLPH.

IF you will look at the map of England, you will see on the right hand the great maritime county of Lincolnshire. Its shores are washed by the North Sea. The coast from the river Humber to the Wash is low, and embankments are built as a protection against the stormy tides.

It is a district of wonderful fertility, bountiful gardens, luxuriant meadows, and rich grazing-lands, whereon are seen the finest horses and cattle of England. The people here from the time of the Norman Conquest have been remarkable for their intelligence and heroic and independent spirit. The Wesleys lived here, and most of the leaders of the Massachusetts Bay Colony came from this place.

The capitol of the county is Lincoln, famous for its beautiful cathedral, which has three great towers, one of which is three hundred feet high. The celebrated old bell, "Tom of Lincoln," once rang sweetly from one of the towers.

The coast is very dangerous, and in early times a good abbot who befriended people in peril became a patron saint.

This benefactor was St. Botolph. He was the good abbot of Ikanho,[1] and became very favorably known for his pious and benevolent deeds about the year 655.

The name Botolph or Botulph is made up of two Saxon words, *boat* and *ulph*, meaning *boat help*, an inspiring sound

MONKS AT STUDY.

to storm-tossed mariners. One of the churches in Aldersgate, London, was dedicated to this saint, also a church at Colchester, the ruins of which are now seen.

After a life of beneficence in the rude times when Christianity was being established in England, the "holy man"

[1] Ancient name of Boston.

LINCOLN CATHEDRAL.

died, and his remains were entombed in St. Edmund's Monastery, Bury.

The abbot was so good in his life that it was supposed that his remains would be of equally good influence after he was entombed.

We have a curious story to tell you about this founder of Old Boston, whose piety and charity gave the name to our city.

There were dry seasons at Bury. The wells became low, the lowing of cattle for water was heard in the pastures, the gardens withered, the fields turned brown. At these dry seasons the people called upon the monks to do something to bring rain.

What could the poor monks do?

The monks of St. Edmund's Monastery remembered the sanctity of St. Botolph. They resolved to take his coffin from the tomb and carry it about the streets in a procession, and see if that would not bring rain.

The pious experiment was entirely successful: rain came, and so the saint was even more highly esteemed than before his decease, and whenever it began to be a little dry the monks of Bury in early times would carry about the streets, in a long, dark procession, the coffin of good St. Botolph.

There must have been occasions when the clouds did not promptly respond to the attractions of the good saint's bones, and possibly in some such way the relics lost credit. We cannot tell. St. Botolph has been allowed to rest in peace for a thousand years. Whatever we may think now of the influence of the ceremony in bringing rain, we cannot but respect the faith in God and in the power of a pious and benevolent character that underlay the pleasant fancy, for it was this confidence that made men morally strong in Saxon times, and helped our ancestors to be what they were in a more enlightened age.

"The History and Antiquities of Boston" (England), by Pishey Thompson, published in 1856, a copy of which may be found in Harvard College Library, contains long extracts from the Chronicles of John of Tynemouth, in which are given many beautiful incidents of the life of St. Botolph. John of Tynemouth was rector of St. Botolph's Church, Boston, in 1518.

Mr. Thompson, in his History of Boston, thus speaks of the saint: —

"St. Botulph and his brother, St. Adulph, flourished about the middle of the seventh century. They were of noble family, and were sent very young into Belgic France, where, according to the testimony of Bede, our ancestors in those days usually sent their children to be educated. The brothers Botulph and Adulph, having been initiated in the discipline and austerity of a monastic life, took the religious habit, and became famous for their learning, zeal, and spiritual labors. The fame of St. Adulph having reached the French king, he was by that monarch exalted to the government of the church of Maestricht in Belgium, the duties of which station he filled with such ability as to attract the most unqualified eulogies of the writers of his time."

The Chronicles of John of Tynemouth thus continue the story: —

"But the blessed father Botulph was disposed to return to Britain. Now there were in the same monastery in which he was staying two sisters of Ethelmund, King of the East Angles (having been sent thither for the sake of the monastic discipline), who, understanding that the blessed man was wishing to return to his own country, impose upon him certain commands to be carried to the king, their brother. Having passed over the sea, he is honorably entertained by the king, who, having heard the pious petitions of his own sisters that he should grant Botulph a piece of ground to

PREACHING THE GOSPEL TO THE SAXONS.

build a monastery for the love of the divine reward, he gave his kind consent. . . . The venerable father chose a certain uncultivated place, deserted by man, called Ykanho."

The story is a charming one, and goes on with an innocence truly Herodotean: —

"Now that region was as much forsaken by man as it was possessed by demons, whose fantastic illusion by the coming of the holy man was to be immediately put to flight, and the pious conversation of the faithful substituted in its place, so that where up to that time the deceit of the devil had abounded, the grace of our beneficent founder should more abound. Upon the entry, therefore, of the blessed Botulph, the blackest smoke arises, and the enemy, knowing that his own flight was at hand, cries out, with horrid clamor, saying: 'This place which we have inhabited for a long time we thought to inhabit for ever. Why, O Botulph, most cruel stranger, dost thou try to drive us from these seats? In nothing have we offended you, in nothing have we disturbed your right, what do you seek in our expulsion? What do you wish to establish in this region of ours? After being driven out of every corner in the world, do you expel us wretched beings even out of this solitude?'"

But the blessed St. Botolph was not to be entreated by evil spirits. He made the sign of the cross, and addressed them heroically, and put them all to flight, — a scene worthy of a painter.

The Chronicles give a series of charming incidents illustrating the humility of the saint, his beautiful sympathies, and harmony of character.

Say the Chronicles, in regard to the time of his decease: —

"At last, when God called, he was delivered from the prison of the body on the 15th of the kalends of June, A. D. 680, and is buried in the same monastery which he had erected."

Of the stories of miracles performed at his tomb, here is a beautiful one from the Chronicles, which, if it were true, would indicate that saints have a care for their bodies after death : —

"In the time of Edgar (959-975), St. Ethelwold, the repairer of monasteries, obtained leave of the king to transfer the bodies of saints from the places and monasteries destroyed by the pagans, to the monasteries erected in his own time.

"Now the Monastery of Ykanho (Ikanhoe-Boston) had been left destitute as an abode of monks, and destroyed by the persecutors of St. Edmund, the king, but it was by no means deserted by the devotion of the faithful. The place known to the inhabitants was held in great reverence, but it was saved in the divine offices of a single priest.

"Now when a certain monk, with many others at the command of St. Ethelwold, had come to the tomb of St. Botulph, and had collected his precious bones and wrapped them in fine linen, and, having raised them on their shoulders, were endeavoring to carry them away, they are fixed with so great a weight that by no effort can they move a step.

"The cloisters of the altar resound with a loud noise, as if to intimate the teaching of God's grace.

"The monk aforesaid recollects of the things he has heard, that the blessed Adulph, the bishop, was buried with his brother.

"They raised this brother's body out of the earth; they then were relieved of the weight, and carried both bodies with them to St. Ethelwold, rejoicing.

"He assigned the head of St. Botulph to the monastery of Ely, but reserved for himself and his cabinet of royal relics a portion of the rest of his body; and what was left he conceded to the Church of Thorney, together with the body of the blessed Adulph."

RUINS OF AN ANCIENT ABBEY.

The accounts of St. Botolph (or Botulph) are as beautiful as fairy stories, and would be a pleasing subject for a more extended article than we give here. My readers, I am sure, will be pleased to know that Boston received its name from one so greatly beloved and esteemed.

"Though ages long have passed
   Since our fathers left their home,
   Their pilot in the blast,
   O'er untravelled seas to roam, —
Yet lives the blood of England in our veins!
   And shall we not proclaim
   That blood of honest fame,
   Which no tyranny can tame
             By its chains?

"While the language, free and bold,
   Which the bard of Avon sung,
   In which our Milton told
   How the vault of heaven rung,
When Satan, blasted, fell with all his host;
   While this, with reverence meet,
   Ten thousand echoes greet,
   From rock to rock repeat
             Round our coast;

"While the manners, while the arts,
   That mould a nation's soul,
   Still cling around our hearts,
   Between let ocean roll,
Our joint communion breaking with the sun;
   Yet, still, from either beach,
   The voice of blood shall reach,
   More audible than speech,
           'We are One!'"

                    WASHINGTON ALLSTON.

CHAPTER II.

WHEREIN IS GIVEN SOME ACCOUNT OF ST. BOTOLPH'S CHURCH, IN LINCOLNSHIRE.

The city of Boston was founded by gentlemen; not sons of a decayed aristocracy; not persons using wealth to gain wealth; not adventurers in search of gold; not romantic dreamers in quest of a fountain that would restore to them their lost youth. It was indeed founded by gentlemen of wealth, but they were men who turned their backs on luxury for moral principle and peace of soul.

The American traveller who reaches Liverpool in an Atlantic steamer may take the Manchester, Lincoln, and Sheffield Railway, and in a few hours find himself in the town of Boston, from which the founders of our Boston came.

The borough resembles Holland in many respects. Here red-tiled roofs, like those of Rotterdam, are seen; and quaint gables and small windows. Dutch-looking vessels lie in the harbor. It contains about fifteen thousand inhabitants. St. Botolph's Church is its principal architectural ornament. *Our* Boston contains nearly four hundred thousand inhabitants and two hundred churches. Old Boston is proud of her daughter, and the traders love to speak of her on market days. She has a right to be proud, for the daughter grew strong by following the instructions of a wise and worthy mother.

The ancient name of Old Boston was Ikanho, or Icanhoe. St. Botolph was abbot of Ikanho. America has named her towns and public buildings for nearly all the interesting places in the Old World mentioned in history, song, and fable, but Ikanho does not appear among them.

The town is situated on the river Wytham. The church was begun in 1309. Its tower, which can be seen forty miles at sea, is three hundred feet high.

This tower was anciently used as a lighthouse. For hundreds of years the sailors on the North Sea saw it blazing over the coast, and blessed the memory of St. Botolph.

The old church, as tested by the funeral services of the Princess Charlotte, would hold more people than any single church in New Boston. Five thousand people assembled there on the occasion of the memorial service for the princess.

Here John Cotton, vicar of Boston, preached twenty years. Here Isaac Johnson and Lady Arbella listened to his fervid preaching.

John Cotton was born in the town of Derby, 1585. His father was a lawyer. He was graduated at Trinity College. He was descended from noble families, and received the most thorough training for whatever duty he should be called to fulfil.

He was one of the independent spirits who refused to conform to the ritual imposed upon the Church by Archbishop Laud. He regarded the ritual as superstition, and he appealed to the Bishop of Lincoln and Earl of Dorset to protect him from persecution. He pleaded his unselfish and blameless life. The Earl of Dorset told him that "if his crime had been drunkenness or uncleanness or any lesser fault," he could be pardoned; but *non-conformity* could not be overlooked. He advised him to fly. Charles I. was on

ST. BOTOLPH'S CHURCH.

the throne at this time. Archbishop Laud was filling the English gaols with Non-conformists. Cotton would not discrown his manhood by yielding to what he believed to be

CHARLES I.

wrong; he therefore fled from Old Boston to found a new church " in the wilderness."

The people used to say, " The old lantern in St. Botolph's Church went out for ever when Cotton left the town."

But the lamp of religious freedom that was kindled in St. Botolph's shines to-day in thousands of sanctuaries whose influence fills the Western world!

COTTON MEMORIAL CHAPEL.

Some years ago Edward Everett and a number of liberal American people restored a chapel of St. Botolph's Church, at a cost of about three thousand dollars, and placed in it a tablet, with an inscription in Latin by Mr. Everett, to the memory of John Cotton.

"OUR ancestors have left no Corinthian temples on our hills, no Gothic cathedrals on our plains, no proud pyramid, no storied obelisk, in our cities. But mind is there. Sagacious enterprise is there. An active, vigorous, intelligent, moral population throng our cities, and predominate in our fields; men, patient of labor, submissive to law, respectful to authority, regardful of right, faithful to liberty. These are the monuments of our ancestors. They stand immutable and immortal, in the social, moral, and intellectual condition of their descendants. They exist in the spirit which their precepts instilled, and their example implanted." — PRESIDENT QUINCY.

CHAPTER III.

WHEREIN IS GIVEN AN ACCOUNT OF WILLIAM BLACKSTONE, A RECLUSE, WHO WAS THE FIRST SETTLER OF BOSTON.

WILLIAM BLACKSTONE'S HOUSE.

This picture does not bear much resemblance to the houses on Beacon Street, to the Hotels Brunswick or Vendome. It looks small indeed as compared with the new Post Office or City Hall, yet it was the first house ever built in Boston.

The house stood on the west side of Beacon Hill, and a lovely situation it must have been in summer time, looking out upon the forests on the river Charles, the harbor, and the pine-shadowed hills of the Mystic. There were very pure springs of water here, one near the place where is now Louisburg Square, another where is now Spring Lane.

Its sole inhabitant was William Blackstone. He was a hermit, or at least he loved solitude better than society. He was a royalist, a firm Episcopalian, and believed, as did King

Charles and Archbishop Laud, in the divine right of kings to rule, without any parliaments to vex them or share the responsibility. He did not like the Puritans, their principles, or ways, but he was still a very kind-hearted and benevolent man, as you shall presently be told.

He was a graduate of Emanuel College, Cambridge. Nearly all of the first settlers of Boston had received a collegiate education. He began life as an Episcopal clergyman. He came to America soon after the Pilgrims, and settled at Shawmut, as Boston was then called, in 1623. Here he lived in seclusion, having only Indians for neighbors, for nearly seven years. He was at this period between thirty and forty years of age.

TRIMOUNTAIN.

A part of the emigrants who came to Salem formed a settlement at Charlestown. Shawmut, now Boston, then presented the appearance of three high hills. The settlers at Charlestown called it Trimountain.

In the summer of 1630, a great sickness broke out among the settlers at Salem and Charlestown. Many died. The sickness was attributed to unwholesome water.

When William Blackstone heard of the distress, he invited Winslow and his friends to remove to Boston, telling them how pure and healthful were the springs at that place. The invitation was accepted, and settlers from Salem and Charlestown began to build around the three pleasant hills.

ON THE BANKS OF THE CHARLES.

But William Blackstone did not like his new neighbors, whom he had so cordially invited to the healthful springs in their distress. He was so ungracious as to sneer at them as "my lord neighbors," and he sold all his land to them, except six acres, and removed again into the wilderness in 1633. He settled at Rehoboth, Rhode Island. Blackstone River received its name from this pioneer.

The Common was a part of Mr. Blackstone's farm, and Washington Street and Tremont Street are said to follow "the windings of William Blackstone's cow." We could readily believe this even were it not further stated that the new dwellings were erected upon the paths through the woods made by Blackstone in his journeys about his farm. The cow must have picked out easy paths, without much regard to directness. She did not know what illustrious people would follow her ways.

The six-acre lot that Mr. Blackstone reserved extended from the top of Beacon Hill to the Charles River. Beacon Street and Mt. Vernon Street run through the place now. Upon it what eminent people have lived! Copley, Phillips (the first mayor), Harrison Gray Otis, Channing, John Hancock, Prescott, Motley, Parkman, and others of equal or nearly equal eminence.

Mr. Blackstone married late in life. He died at Cumberland, Rhode Island, in May, 1675, aged about eighty years. He was always a lover of solitude, and this taste led him to Shawmut.

The settlements on the Charles River were Arcadias in comparison with other places. The Indians were friendly, and never stained the peaceful banks with white people's blood. The colonists were generally exempt from sickness, famine, or any great calamities. Thus the settlements grew, stretching away along the banks of the winding river, that led them ever on to fertile fields and happy homes.

"THEY rejected with contempt the ceremonious homage which other sects substituted for the pure worship of the soul. Instead of catching occasional glimpses of the Deity through an obscuring veil, they aspired to gaze full on the intolerable brightness, and to commune with Him face to face. Hence originated their contempt for terrestrial distinctions. The difference between the greatest and meanest of mankind seemed to vanish, when compared with the boundless interval which separated the whole race from Him on whom their own eyes were constantly fixed. They recognized no title to superiority but His favor; and confident of that favor, they despised all the accomplishments and all the dignities of the world." — MACAULAY, — "*The Puritans.*"

CHAPTER IV.

WHEREIN IS CONTAINED THE STORY OF LADY ARBELLA JOHNSON.

THOSE were dark times in England when good George Herbert, the gentle prophet, wrote: —

> "Religion stands on tiptoe in our land,
> Ready to pass to the American strand."

Charles I. was entering upon a course of tyranny that brought him to the block. Illegal taxes were imposed upon the people. Laud ruled the Church with a rod of iron, and thought it heresy for any man to think differently from the king and himself. The king dissolved the Parliament, and announced his intention of ruling without one. The Star Chamber made personal liberty and private rights everywhere unsafe. Injustice prevailed in the Court, in the Church, everywhere. Men even feared to call upon God for help.

The Puritan churches, or Dissenters, as those who differed from the Established Church were called, were persecuted on every hand.

"'The Church hath no place left to fly into but the wilderness," said good John Winthrop; and into the wilderness John Winthrop, and some of the noblest and most heroic men and women of England, determined to fly, and to dare any danger rather than violate the principles of their faith.

They engaged a ship to take them to New England. It was called the Eagle.

"Let us name it the Arbella," said one of these Christian pioneers, "for we have with us the daughter of an earl."

The daughter of the earl was Lady Arbella Johnson. Her father was Thomas, the third Earl of Lincoln. She was a woman of great strength and beauty of character. Mather says, "She took New England on her way to heaven."

She had married Isaac Johnson, a gentleman of wealth, the owner of landed estates in the counties of Rutland, Northampton, and Lincoln.

Lady Arbella's pastor was good John Cotton, of St. Botolph's Church, Boston. Mr. Johnson had been led to the exercise of strong faith in God by the influence of this Dissenting minister. Just before leaving England he made a will in which he remembered his pastor as one from whom he had received "much help and comfort in his spiritual state."

SAILING FROM ENGLAND.

This gentleman was indignant at the oppression and injustice that he saw his church suffering, and was one of those resolute men who were willing to sacrifice luxury and ease for religious freedom.

The Lady Arbella joined him in his views and purpose. She went, according to Hubbard, "from a paradise of plenty and pleasure, which she enjoyed in the family of a noble earldom, into a wilderness of wants." She left England in April, 1630.

The ship Arbella led the way of a great emigration to New England. Ten other ships followed, among them the Mayflower that had brought the Pilgrims to Plymouth.

And now the Arbella is upon the sea. The storms of spring toss her about like a thing of air. Storm succeeds storm, and the voyage is slow. But a high purpose inspires the company amid all the perils. The colonists pray, sing, read the word of God, and encourage each other with pious conversation.

John Winthrop is among them, who has sold the estate of his forefathers, and is going forth over the waters to plant a free church "in the wilderness." He has the king's charter in his keeping. He is a person of grave

SIR RICHARD SALTONSTALL.

but benevolent countenance; he dresses in black, with a broad ruff around his neck, when on land, and he makes a very handsome picture, which we present to the reader. Sir Richard Saltonstall is also here, one of the first five projectors of the new colony.

It was the month of June when the Arbella sailed into the harbor of Salem.

In 1626 Peter Palfrey, Roger Conant, and one or two other gentlemen settled in Salem. In 1628 they were joined by John Endicott and a small company, and thus a plantation was begun at the place.

There were six or eight dwellings in the town when the Arbella arrived. The new land must have looked cheerful to the sea-weary colonists, for it was clothed with the verdure of summer time, and the days were the longest and fairest of the year.

Lady Arbella, looking very pale and feeling very much exhausted, becomes the guest of John Endicott. Some of the company go away to form a settlement at Charlestown.

Her husband makes a journey to Boston with Governor Winthrop and others. He thinks the three green hills overlooking the sheltered harbor very lovely, and he decides that he will there make his abode and provide a home for his beautiful wife.

He began to prepare the ground where the Court House stands to-day, near the City Hall. The lot he selected extended to where King's Chapel now lifts its low tower, and reminds all who pass of the generations that are gone. He marked it out, dreamed bright dreams of the future, and returned to Salem to tell Lady Arbella what a lovely spot he had found.

He returned on foot, through the summer forests that stretched away from the blue harbor.

When he arrived at Salem he found Lady Arbella suddenly reduced to the mere shadow of a woman; he saw that she was not long for this world, and his heart sank within him.

The settlers shook their heads and said, "The Lady Arbella will not be with us long. We will make her life as happy as we can."

She looked out upon the new settlement, and saw the men at work on their houses; she saw at times dusky forms in paint and feathers come to the town. She heard the settlers talk of their plans for the future, but she felt that she would

THE FIRST KING'S CHAPEL.

not long enjoy the sight of the pleasant harbors and green forests, but would soon be at rest.

And so it was. She was after a little time unable to sit up in her chair, and in about one month from the time of the landing she died.

They made her a grave amid the oaks and pines. The

city of Salem sprang into life around it, and at last, after two hundred years, they have erected a stone church on the spot.

Her husband returned to Boston a broken-hearted man. He, too, began to waste away. He lived but a few weeks after the death of Lady Arbella.

"Bury me," he said, "in the spot I had marked out for *our* house."

They did so. His was the first grave in the field that is now known as King's Chapel Burying-ground.

In July the Arbella, the admiral of the little fleet, a vessel of three hundred and fifty tons, manned with fifty-two seamen, and furnished with twenty-eight pieces of ordnance, dropped anchor in Boston harbor, accompanied by the Talbot, the vice-admiral, and the Jewell, the captain of the fleet.

These were probably the vessels into which Lieutenant-Governor Dudley says "we unshipped our goods, and with much cost and labour brought them in July to *Charles Towne*."

WINTHROP'S FLEET IN BOSTON HARBOR.

"Month after month passed away, and in autumn the ships of the merchants
Came with kindred and friends, with cattle and corn for the Pilgrims.
All in the village was peace; the men were intent on their labors,
Busy with hewing and building, with garden-plot and with merestead,
Busy with breaking the glebe, and mowing the grass in the meadows,
Searching the sea for its fish, and hunting the deer in the forest."

CHAPTER V.

WHEREIN ARE RELATED SOME INCIDENTS OF THE LIFE OF GOVERNOR JOHN WINTHROP, THE FOUNDER OF BOSTON.

THE traveller in England, who goes down to Groton, in the county of Suffolk, in summer, will there see an ancient, fortress-like church, standing serenely in the sun, and overlooking a quiet landscape of matchless verdure. Close to to the church, under the windows as it were, may be seen the old tomb where rest the remains of the Winthrop family. In this dreamy old town Governor John Winthrop was born on the 22d of January, 1588.

Few of my readers will ever go to Groton, England, to see the old tomb of the Winthrops, but nearly all may go to King's Chapel Burying-ground and there see the tomb where Governor John Winthrop, one of the most noble men and certainly the most useful member of the Massachusetts Bay Colony, sleeps. The slender trees shade it, the sun pencils it lightly in summer through the green leaves, beyond it busy men are seen going to and coming from the City Hall.

Governor John Winthrop was the founder of Boston.

He was educated at Cambridge, England, in Trinity College.

He was elected governor by the Massachusetts Bay Company of London. He sailed in the Arbella, as we have told you, and he brought the charter of Massachusetts with him. He landed at Salem, removed to Charlestown, and thence to

Boston, and was twelve times re-elected governor of the Colony, and three times chosen deputy-governor.

His residence was on Washington Street, just opposite the foot of School Street; the Old South Church stands on the ground that was a part of his garden. There was a natural spring of water near by, cool and very healthful. This spring gave the name to a once famous, but now almost neglected street, called Spring Lane.

In his youth he was the subject of a somewhat remarkable religious experience, which formed his views and directed his aims for life. We will give you a glance at this powerful change, as it will show you what kind of men the Puritans were, and how firmly they believed themselves led and inspired by the Spirit of God: —

"I began," he says, "to come under strong exercises of conscience. I could no longer dally with religion. God put my soul to sad tasks sometimes, which yet the flesh would shake off and outwear still. Notwithstanding all my stubbornness and kind rejections of mercy, He left me not till He had overcome my heart to give itself up to Him and to bid farewell to all the world.

"Now came I to some peace and comfort in God. I loved a Christian and the very ground he went upon. I honored a faithful minister in my heart, and could have kissed his feet. I could not miss a sermon, though many miles away."

In his journal, passing over a period of many years, he has left an account of his inward struggle with besetting sins. He was one of the most blameless of men, but one would suppose from this account that he was a most dreadful evil-doer. When he was about thirty years of age he was taken very sick. During this sickness he gained that experience of faith which every Puritan believed essential to a Christian life.

JOHN WINTHROP.

He says: —

"The good Spirit of the Lord breathed upon my soul and said I should live. Now could my soul close with Christ and rest there in sweet content, so ravished with his love, as I desired nothing and feared nothing, but was filled with joy unspeakable and glorious, and with the spirit of adoption."

This language reads like that of an ancient prophet. We might quote pages of similar narrative as simple and sublime. But these pictures will show you the kind of man the father of our city was. You may perhaps look with more veneration on the bronze statue in Scollay Square, after getting this view of his inner life.

But it was the stern battles of his public career that history most records. The journal of his life in Boston lies before me; it reads like a long story; we hope our young friends may read it.[1]

Here is an extract of the events of a single week, written soon after his arrival at Salem: —

"*Thursday, July* 1 (1630). The Mayflower and the Whale arrived safe in Charlton (Charlestown) harbor. Their passengers were all in health, but most of their cattle dead.

"*Friday*, 2d. The Talbot arrived there. She had lost fourteen passengers.

"My son, Henry Winthrop, was drowned at Salem.

"*Saturday*, 3d. The Hopewell and William and Francis arrived.

"*Monday*, 5th. The Trial arrived at Charlton, and the Charles at Salem.

"*Tuesday*, 6th. The Success arrived.

"*Wednesday*, 7th. The Lion went back to Salem.

"*Thursday*, 8th. We kept a day of Thanksgiving in all plantations."

---

[1] "The History of New England from 1630 to 1649," by John Winthrop, Esq., from his original manuscripts. Edited by James Savage.

What heroic modesty appears in this simple journal: "*My son, Henry Winthrop, was drowned at Salem.*" He would have considered it selfish to have said more of his boy. Were there not stricken hearts all around him? What were his griefs more than another's! Yet this son was a most interesting and promising young man, and beloved by all the colonists.

This journal of a week shows also how rapidly emigrants began to arrive. These emigrants had intended to settle in one place. But this was not so to be. "We were forced," says Deputy-Governor Dudley, in a letter to the Countess of Lincoln, "to change counsel, and for our present shelter to plant dispersedly; some at Charlestown, which standeth on the north side of the mouth of Charles River; some on the south side thereof, which place we named BOSTON, as we intended to have done the place we first resolved on; some of us upon the Mistick, which we named Medford; some of us westward on Charles River, which place we called Watertown; others of us two miles from Boston in a place we named Roxbury, and the western men four miles south from Boston, at a place we called Dorchester."

Cambridge, which included within its limits the territory where are the present towns of Brighton, Newton, Arlington, Lexington, Bradford, and Billerica, had its beginning in an agreement between Governor Winthrop and his assistants to build a protected town for the seat of government between Roxbury and Boston. The location proved unsuitable, and they finally determined to build "at a place a mile east of Watertown, on the Charles River." Here Cambridge was founded in 1631. Deputy Governor Dudley and his son-in-law, Bradstreet, were the first inhabitants. Governor Winthrop built a house there, but was called by duty to Boston. For this, Dudley, who was a fiery-minded man, accused him of violating his promise, and called him many hard names, which caused Winthrop much sorrow.

WINTHROP AND DUDLEY.

Governor Winthrop's settlement in Boston rapidly grew, and drew to it some of the ablest men that came to New England at the beginning of the great emigration. A church was formed, and John Wilson, a saintly man, became the first pastor. It was called the First Church. The simple covenant of this church is now inscribed on one of the windows of the First Church on the Back Bay. You may like to go and see it some day.

Mr. Wilson preached at times in private houses and under the boughs of great trees. A meeting-house was at last erected. Here is a picture of it.

Should you go to the Back Bay to see the covenant of the First Church, look around you upon the splendid edifices of religion, art, and education that rise on every hand, then think of this picture, and of good Mr. Wilson preaching under the trees.

FIRST MEETING-HOUSE.

The new colonists decided that Boston would be the most appropriate place to hold public meetings and the General Court. Of course, Mr. Dudley thought it should be Cambridge, and he became very angry over the decision and said more hard things about Governor Winthrop.

We have given you some incidents of Winthrop's religious feelings, let us now give you a few anecdotes of his conduct under severe trial. Dudley once wrote him a hard, insulting letter. He returned it calmly, saying : —

" I am not willing to keep such an occasion of provocation by me."

Afterwards, when Winthrop did Dudley a great kindness, the latter gracefully said: —

"Your overcoming yourself hath overcome me."

The two men were reconciled at last. We will tell you one of the ways by which it was brought about. It reads like a passage from the ancient Scriptures. Says the chronicler: —

"'The Governor and Deputy-Governor went down to Concord to view some lands for farms.

"'They offered each other the first choice, but because the Deputy's was first granted, and himself had store of land already, the Governor yielded him the choice.

"So at the place where the Deputy's land was to begin there were two great stones which they called Two Brothers.

"'They did this in remembrance that they were brothers by their children's marriage and did so brotherly agree.

"A little creek near those stones was to part their lands."

Salem, Charlestown, Boston, Roxbury, and Cambridge now began to receive large additions by emigration, and the persecuted Dissenters in England looked to this promising colony as their place of refuge.

A settlement had been made near Boston some years before the coming of Winthrop. In 1625 Captain Wollaston had led a company to Braintree, and called the place Mount Wollaston.

The settlement was a happy and prosperous one for a time, but Captain Wollaston and a part of the company left it at last to make a voyage to Virginia.

Among the men left behind was one Thomas Morton, a noisy, riotous fellow, who seems to have believed that the object of life was to enjoy one's self, and not to live with definite aims as the Puritans did.

One night after the captain's departure Morton called the people together and gave them plenty of punch, and when they had become merry and excited he said, —

"The captain is gone; let us turn out the lieutenant, and then we can all do as we please."

This would be freedom, indeed. The men consented, and the poor lieutenant was obliged to relinquish his authority.

The company now began to do as they pleased, and a great change passed over the settlement at Mount Wollaston. The men spent their days in idleness, or dancing with the Indians, and their nights in drinking and carousing. They erected a May-pole to mark the place for their dances and carousals. They called the place Merry-Mount.

The Indians liked Merry-Mount, and the Indian women joined in the merry-makings. Morton began to sell arms to the Indians.

This was unlawful. Captain Miles Standish was accordingly sent from Plymouth to arrest Morton, which he did, and the colony at Merry-Mount was thus broken up. Soon after the settlement of Salem, Endicott visited Mount Wollaston, and cut down the May-pole of the roystering pioneer. Morton says that this May-pole was "a goodly pine-tree, eighty feet long, with a pair of buck horns nailed somewhat near the top of it." The drunken and licentious revels at Merry-Mount proved a calamity to the colonies, in that it put the Indians in possession of the deadly weapons of the whites.

WINTHROP FORDING A STREAM.

The journal of Governor Winthrop is full of interesting

stories. One of them relates to his visit to Plymouth when he forded streams by being carried on a stout man's back.

REVELS AT MERRY-MOUNT.

Here is a touching story of a misfortune that happened in the cool October weather of 1630.

MILES STANDISH DISCOVERS THE REVELLERS AT MERRY-MOUNT.

THE LOST FAMILY.

On the 28th of October, Richard Garrett, a shoemaker of Boston, and one of his daughters, and four other persons went towards Plymouth in a shallop. Mr. Garrett started against the advice of his friends, as cold weather was at hand.

They were driven out to sea by a high wind, and the boat took in much water, which began to freeze.

They gave themselves up for lost, commended themselves to God, and waited for death.

At last one espied land near Cape Cod. They hoisted a part of their sail and were driven through the rocks to the shore.

A part of the company landed, but some of them found their feet frozen into the ice so that they could not move them until cut out.

They kindled a fire, but having no hatchet they could secure but little wood to feed it, and were forced to lie in the open air all night. The weather was severely cold for the season, and their sufferings were extreme.

The next morning two of them set out on foot for Plymouth, which they supposed to be near, but which was really fifty miles distant.

On their way they met two Indian squaws. These, in going to their wigwam, said to the braves, —

"We have seen Englishmen."

"They are shipwrecked," said the Indians. "Let us go in search of them, and bring them to our wigwam."

The company was soon overtaken by the friendly Indians, and returned with them to their wigwam, where they were provided with warmth and food.

One of the Indians offered to lead the two men to

Plymouth, and another started to find the members of the company left behind, and to relieve them, if possible.

This faithful Indian found the lost travellers at last in great distress, at a distance of some seven miles.

"I will go back and get a hatchet," he said, "and I will build you a wigwam."

Back, a seven miles' walk, on that cold day plodded the Indian, and returned as soon as he could with the hatchet. He built a shelter for the sufferers, and got them wood to feed the fire.

They were so weak and frozen as to be scarcely able to move.

Garrett, the leader of the adventure, was one of the disabled party left behind at this place. In two days he died.

The ground was frozen so hard that they could not dig a grave for him, but the good Indian succeeded in cutting a hole about half a yard deep, and in this he laid the body and covered it with boughs to protect it from the wolves.

What hours of anguish were these, and what a messenger of mercy proved that one faithful Indian!

After a time a party arrived from Plymouth to rescue them. Another of the company died, his legs being "mortified with frost." The two men who went towards Plymouth died, one of them on his journey thither, and the other soon after his arrival. But the Indian guide led the English to the surviving sufferers. The girl escaped with the least injury. The survivors were taken back to Boston in a boat. They were supposed by the colonists there to have been lost.

It was not an uncommon thing for some member of the colony to get lost. The governor himself lost his way at one time, and passed a most uncomfortable night alone.

He had a farm on the west side of Mystic River, which he called Ten Hills. One evening in October, 1631, he

ENDICOTT CUTTING DOWN MORTON'S MAY-POLE.

took his gun and walked away from his farmhouse, thinking he might meet a wolf. The wolves were very plenty between the Charles and the Mystic at that time. He was overtaken by darkness, and was unable to tell the direction of his house. He at last came to a deserted Indian wigwam elevated upon posts. He built a fire outside to keep away the animals, and lay down on some mats he found within, but could not sleep.

He arose, and passed the night feeding the fire and singing psalms.

A little before day it began to rain. The governor crept into the wigwam. Presently he heard a noise outside. He looked out, and saw an Indian squaw climbing up.

He shut the door and fastened it against her, which seems rather ungracious treatment. The squaw went away from her poor home in the rain, and the governor gladly sought his own home as soon as it was light.

The white people of both the Plymouth and Massachusetts Bay Colonies always found friends in the Indians in their troubles at this early period, and when any one lost his way, a good Indian guide would be found to leave his own way and lead him home. We will close this chapter with one of the many stories of Indian friendliness that at this time were told by the winter firesides of the two colonies: —

THE LOST BOY.

Aspinet, sagamore of the Nausets, was the first open enemy encountered by the Pilgrims of Plymouth Colony.

He had suffered a grievous wrong at the hands of the English, before the Pilgrims came, and this was the cause of his hostility.

In 1614 one Hunt, a trader, sailing along the coast in search of fish, kidnapped twenty-four Indians belonging to Patuxet or Plymouth. He enticed them to his vessel by false pretences and promises, and caused them to be secured in a very brutal manner. Twelve of these Indians were Nausets, under the sachemship of Aspinet.

In the summer of 1621, a little boy belonging to one of the families of Plymouth Colony strayed into the forests that then covered Massachusetts, and lost his way.

He at last met an old Indian, and indicated his distress to him by his gestures and his tears. The Indian treated him kindly, and gave him food, and took him along with him, till they came to a most lovely expanse of water that lay by the sea.

There was great excitement in Plymouth Colony when it became certain that the boy was lost. The colonists were very suspicious of the Indians, well knowing how much cause for hostile feeling towards the English had been given them by Hunt and by other early adventurers.

A company of colonists, under the leadership of Edward Winslow, set out from Plymouth in search of the lost boy. They hoped to find him among the friendly natives near the settlement, but much feared that he had fallen into the hands of Aspinet, who, they believed, would kill him, in retaliation for the injuries that the coast Indians had suffered.

The party sailed along the coast until they came to Cummaquid, where they anchored in a sheltered body of water, near the fishing huts of the Mattakees. The chief of this territory was a young man named Gyanough. His manners were so courteous and gentle, and his disposition so amiable and pacific, that he made himself greatly beloved by his own people and by the neighboring tribes. The English, who were his neighbors, bestowed upon him the appellation, "The Courteous Sachem of Cummaquid." His sachemship extended over the Indians inhabiting the country known now as the eastern part of Barnstable, and the western part of Yarmouth, in Massachusetts.

A LOST SETTLER FOUND.

During the night, the tide fell so low as to leave them aground. In the morning they discovered some of Gyanough's Indians on the shore, and they sent Squanto, an Indian interpreter, to them, to inform them of the object of their visit, and of their friendly disposition.

"Have you any tidings of a lost English boy?" asked Squanto.

"We have heard of him. He was found wandering in the woods by a fisherman. He is well."

"Where is he now?"

"At Nauset, with Aspinet."

The English now thought it prudent to land, and to make Gyanough a visit. The Indians seemed greatly delighted with the proposal, and a part of them voluntarily remained with the boatmen as hostages, while the others conducted the strangers to the rural palace.

Gyanough received them in a very courteous manner, and ordered a feast to be spread for them. He assured them of the safety of the missing boy, and did not seem to doubt that Aspinet would receive the English kindly, and deal with them justly.

The English spent a few hours with Gyanough, and then sailed for Nauset, to recover the missing boy.

Nauset, or Namskeket, was a favorite resort of the Wampanoag Indians, who came there to gather shell-fish from the immense quantities that filled the picturesque shores. As soon as the English arrived, which was on a lovely summer afternoon, they sent Squanto to the royal residence of Aspinet, to acquaint the chief with their errand, and to ask the favor of a friendly interview.

Aspinet received Squanto kindly, and, as he was too noble an Indian to take advantage of an accident or a misfortune for the purpose of revenge, he at once promised to pay the English a friendly visit at a place near the coast.

It was sunset, and the fair summer light was fading on the calm sea. Just as the shadows were growing dark on the eastern slopes of the hills, Aspinet appeared, followed by a

INDIANS RETURNING A LOST CHILD.

great train of warriors. He was richly ornamented, and his followers were bedecked with all the insignia of barbarian splendor. Upon his great shoulders, glittering with beads and wampum, the noble-hearted chief carried the little boy.

The child's heart was filled with joy, and he held his hands aloft with emotion; when he saw from the glimmering hill-top the English sail on the beautiful sea.

Aspinet came down to the water's edge, bearing the delighted child, and followed by a hundred braves. The English were waiting to receive him in their boat, that was anchored in the shallow water near the shore. The chieftain did not stop for a canoe to convey him to them. He came wading through the water until he reached the English, then taking the boy from his shoulders, he placed him upon the deck. The boy wore on his neck a most beautiful ornament of Indian beads.

"THE hand that cut
The Red Cross from the colors of the king,
Can cut the red heart from this heresy."

CHAPTER VI.

WHEREIN IS GIVEN SOME ACCOUNT OF SIR HENRY VANE, ANNE HUTCHINSON, AND THOSE RELIGIOUS PERSECUTIONS OUT OF WHICH GREW LIBERTY OF CONSCIENCE AND OPINION.

BOSTON grew. All of the settlements on the borders of Massachusetts Bay rapidly increased. Ships bringing emigrants came constantly into Boston harbor.

Stores and inns were opened in Boston. Boats were built on the Mystic. Ferry-boats were run between Boston and Charlestown.

John Cotton, the learned Dissenter of St. Botolph's Church, preached to the people. The Church governed politics, and the ministers to a large extent governed the Church.

In 1635 a notable event happened in Boston. It was the arrival of Mr. Henry Vane, a young man about twenty-three years of age. He has been called "one of the greatest and purest men that ever walked the earth."

He was the son of Sir Henry Vane, was educated at Oxford, and had become an enthusiastic republican in politics, and a Non-conformist in religion. He had travelled in France and Switzerland, and was well schooled in politics and the knowledge of statesmanship.

He was received in Boston with public demonstrations of joy, and in a few months after his arrival, when only twenty-four years of age, was chosen governor of the colony.

About this time dissenters from the Puritans' doctrines began to agitate the colony. The Puritans dissented from the rituals of the Episcopal Church. The new dissenters objected to the Levitical Law, which was virtually made the

HENRY VANE.

government of the church and colony. They were called Antinomians. They taught that Christians were no longer under the *law* but under *grace*, and should be governed by the Holy Spirit in all things, and whatever they did or might do was right. Each man was a law unto himself.

The leader of this dissension was an accomplished and brilliant woman, the daughter of an English clergyman and the wife of an influential colonist. Her name was Anne Hutchinson.

She was accustomed to hold religious meetings for women. These were attended by some seventy or eighty persons. She prayed, gave expositions of Scripture, and lectures on the sermons of Wilson and Cotton.

The leading men of the colony resolved to silence this woman, but Governor Vane had no sympathy with the attacks on Mrs. Hutchinson. The gallant Sir Henry espoused her cause, and was the first person to lay down with precision the doctrine that religious opinion ought to be exempted from all civil authority.

This position of Vane made him unpopular, and the next year he failed of an election as governor. He returned to England in disappointment. Mrs. Hutchinson, being banished, went to Rhode Island, and afterwards to New York, where she was killed by the Indians in one of the attacks on the Dutch colonies. She was a good woman, but the tendency of her doctrines, as the reader can see, was towards too great freedom in government and religious conduct. In the matter of the rights of conscience, she was in the main correct, but the people were not quite prepared for this new principle.

Sir Henry Vane became a leader in England in the struggle for civil and religious liberty. He carried into the House of Peers the articles of impeachment against Archbishop Laud, whose persecutions had driven the Puritans to Boston. He helped bring Charles I. to the block, but he was jealous of the rising power of Cromwell. On the establishment of the Commonwealth in 1649, he became one of the Council of State.

He criticised the ambition of Cromwell so severely as to cause the Protector much vexation and chagrin.

88   *Young Folks' History of Boston.*

"The Lord deliver me from Sir Harry Vane!" exclaimed Cromwell on one occasion, after having been assailed by the fiery-minded republican.

After the restoration of the Stuarts to the throne, this apostle of liberty, this "thorn in the flesh to kings and to Cromwell," lost his influence. He was accused of high treason, tried, condemned, and executed on Tower Hill.

BURIAL OF THE KING.

His deportment at the hour of execution was full of dignity. His last prayer was wonderful. He died like a martyr and a victor. The principles that he taught have their best memorial in the political and religious freedom of our own country, and the republican sentiment of the world.

In February, 1631, there had come to Boston from Wales a Non-conformist minister, by the name of Roger Williams. He had been educated at Pembroke College, Cambridge.

EXECUTION OF CHARLES I.

He was chosen assistant to Mr. Skelton in the ministry at Salem. Here he asserted the principle that the Church

OLIVER CROMWELL.

should be separated from the State, and that a man's conscience should not be subject to the civil law. For these opinions, which all true Americans hold to-day, he was obliged to leave Salem. He went to Plymouth, but afterwards returned to Salem, and became the pastor of the church. In 1635 he was banished, for again asserting his views of religious toleration and freedom. He went to Rhode Island; was sheltered by the good chief Massasoit, who showed himself as much a Christian at heart as the magistrates of Salem had shown themselves bigots in spirit and conduct; he founded the State of Rhode Island, the happiest and most prosperous of all the early New England Christian Commonwealths, and one of which the civilization of the world has never been ashamed. Rhode Island is the smallest State in the Union, and the richest, according to the number of inhabitants, and it has, perhaps, the fairest history of all.

Roger Williams studied the Indian language, and endeavored to teach the Indians. As he was a man of peace, his influence over them was great. Hearing that a council of war was to be held by the leaders of the tribes for the destruction of the towns that had sent him into exile, he suddenly appeared among the Indians, and tried to prevent the alliance.

He visited England, and was a friend of Milton, Cromwell, and Sir Henry Vane. He died at Providence in 1683.

In 1649 Governor Winthrop died. He was succeeded by John Endicott, the founder of Salem, a very stern, resolute, inflexible man.

There were strange doings in Governor Endicott's day, as you shall presently be told. He felt that it was his prerogative as governor to make all the people think as he did, and to punish any who should not. What was the use of a governor if it were not to control the opinions of men?

Endicott had left England because he differed in opinion from the state Church, but it does not seem to have occurred

ROGER WILLIAMS APPEALING TO THE INDIANS.

to him that any one had the right to be so perverse as to dissent from *him* and from *his* church, and for this reason he left a very dark history, as we shall see. He cut the red cross out of the English flag one training-day, because he regarded it an emblem of idolatry; and he was unwilling to march his company of soldiers under it, — an act which much disturbed Governor Winthrop, whose heart was loyal to the banner associated with England's historic greatness and glory.

CUTTING OUT THE RED CROSS.

In 1656 Governor Endicott learned with surprise that some Quaker books had been brought into the colony; his surprise was soon after doubled by hearing that a vessel from Barbadoes had landed two Quaker women in Boston.

Two Quaker women! What was to be done? Endicott summoned Deputy-Governor Bellingham, a man of a cloudy, severe, and quick temper, and Rev. John Norton, the Boston pastor, a man of austere and melancholy temperament, to a consultation. The three were not long in deciding that the two women should be arrested and sent to jail until they could be carried out of the jurisdiction of the colony.

There was an open space before the meeting-house which contained some corrective implements that would look rather odd in an open space before a meeting-house to-day. There were the stocks and pillory and whipping-post, and we know not what other means of discipline and grace. Here a pile of fagots was made, and the dangerous Quaker books were burned, after which the magistrates for a short time rested from their resolute efforts to secure uniformity of opinion.

But not long: another vessel came, bringing *eight* Quakers, four men and four women. Here was trouble, indeed. The officers, however, were not delinquent; they arrested them

THE STOCKS.

all as soon as they arrived, and marched them off to jail. What an interesting procession that must have been! They were sent back in the same vessel that brought them, and judicial old Governor Endicott had time to breathe freely once more.

He must have been glad when they were gone, for one Sunday, when he was returning from church in great dignity, and had reached the place opposite the jail, he heard a sharp voice exclaiming, —

JOHN ENDICOTT.

"Woe, woe to the oppressor! Woe, woe!" or words to this import.

He was greatly shocked that his office was not more respected. The voice was one of the imprisoned Quakers.

THE PILLORY.

"Have her silenced," he ordered, and then proceeded on his way, wondering that there were such unreasonable people in the world.

The General Court now passed an act forbidding Quakers to come into the colony. But they continued to come. The magistrates had them whipped and sent away, and when they returned had them whipped again. Whipping at the cart-tail was a common mode of punishment. The clothes of the Quaker were stripped down to the loins, and the lash was applied to his bare back. We give a picture of one of these unhappy scenes.

A number of Quakers in England, hearing of the persecutions of their sect in New England, thought they were bound in duty to come to America, and after the manner of the ancient prophets to denounce the "bloody magistrates" for laying hands on the "people of the Lord." Governor Endicott, as you may well believe, attended to their cases as fast as they arrived; he caused them to be imprisoned, whipped, and some of the more persistent ones to lose their ears. It was at last enacted that any Quaker who returned to the colony three times should have his "tongue burned through with a hot iron." We must confess that we do not very greatly love Governor Endicott, and should not be inclined to urge one to subscribe over-liberally for a monument to him. He is not one of the characters that improve with history.

Yet he thought he did right. The Quakers themselves were sometimes to blame; some of them sought martyrdom, and they often said and did unwise things, — interrupting meetings and disturbing the public peace, calling the clergy "hypocrites," the "seed of the serpent," "hirelings," and other names disagreeable to hear.

Some of them were executed. Three of a company who had been banished returned to suffer, one of the women bringing "winding-sheets" with them. What a strange spectacle that must have been!

But the people at last sickened of scenes like these. Governor Endicott and the melancholy Norton were compelled by public sentiment to pause and consider what they were doing. The General Court repealed the law for capital punishment of Quakers, and the excitement gradually died away.

WHIPPING QUAKERS AT THE CART'S TAIL IN BOSTON.

THE STORY OF MARY DYER.

The people have gathered on Boston Common to witness an execution. From the jail to the Common the highway is full of excited men, some sullen, some indignant, that people who have committed no crime should be condemned to die; some upholding the magistrates, others excusing them; all is rancor; every one's heart is moved.

Soldiers are distributed here and there to preserve order, and prevent an outbreak. There are a hundred soldiers about the jail.

Three condemned Quakers come forth from the prison. Look at them. They walk hand in hand, — two men, one woman.

They pass firmly along, a great crowd following.

On the Common there was a gallows; some say that the Old Elm was used for the purpose. It was near the "end of the Common," and the great tree marked the end of the Common then.

The victims go up to it, and bow their necks calmly to the hangman's nervous hands.

A shudder passes through the crowd. The two men are swung into the air, — a dreadful sight, — but the woman stands unharmed, as though still awaiting her doom.

The men die; then the magistrates order the woman to be taken away.

The crowd are joyful that she is spared. There is a feeling of relief in the hearts of the people surging under the trees.

"Why dost thou not let me die with my brethren?" she demands.

"Your son has come to the city, and has interceded for your life. We made you stand by the condemned and witness their death that you might see their sufferings and your peril, and never return to Boston again."

She went away with her son. But she was sorry she could not have been a martyr. Her dissatisfaction grew.

Not long after she returned to Boston, and denounced the magistrates for their unholy deeds.

"Woe, woe, woe!" she said, and followed it with the awful language of the prophets, when condemning the bloody cities of old for their sins.

She was again condemned to death.

Again a great crowd gathered on the Common. It was not then the beautiful park that it is now. The Charles River marshes came almost to the hill where the Soldiers' Monument now stands. The Great Elm stood at the end of the town, on the border of the marshes.

"We will release you," said the magistrates, "if you will promise to go away, and never return again."

"No. In obedience to the will of God I came, and in obedience to His will I will now remain, faithful unto death."

The executioner performed his office, and Mary Dyer died the death she had sought, as though it was the greatest blessing the heart could desire. In her own view she was thus enabled to surrender her life to the Lord.

The people turned away from the Common, sick at heart, wondering if, indeed, Governor Endicott or Mary Dyer was right, or both alike wrong.

The Quakers who were executed were buried "in an enclosed place" on the Common. If we knew where the spot is, we would tell you. We think it was near the place of the Old Elm.

OLD ELM AND QUAKERS' GRAVES.

" No one is so accursed by fate,
   No one so utterly desolate,
        But some heart, though unknown,
        Responds unto his own."

CHAPTER VII.

WHEREIN ARE RELATED SOME STORIES OF A NERVOUS DISEASE, CALLED WITCHCRAFT.

WITCHES.

The belief in witches was common in Europe at the time of the early settlement of the towns of New England. The Puritan fathers brought it with them, and the severity of their lives and the awful mysteriousness of the forests, peopled by wild men, and made perilous by wild beasts, favored the impression that there were spirits of evil in the air, earth, and sea, and in the very hearts of men.

The strange picture at the head of this chapter represents not a reality, but the unseen world, as it sometimes appeared to the Puritans' disordered fancy.

Much has been said about the witchcraft delusion of Boston and Salem, as though it was a thing peculiar to the colonies. The same delusion was prevalent in both England and Scotland at the same time as in New England. Witch-finding became a profession in England, and witch-finders were regarded as people of remarkable genius and spiritual insight, and the office was held in honor.

More than two hundred years ago there lived in England a rough, brutal old man, who took for his name, "Witch-Finder General."

His real name was Matthew Hopkins. He lived when there were numerous prosecutions for witchcraft in England, during 1645 and 1646.

The title, by which he was generally known, indicates the part he acted. He seems to have been a privileged agent under the protection of the government. The expenses he incurred in travelling over the country were paid from the public treasury, and he also received a specified sum for every witch he found.

You may be certain he discovered many, when such encouragement was given him.

It was a favorite practice with the witch-finders of those days, to prick the body of the suspected person with some sharp instrument, like an awl or penknife, to find the "witch-mark," as it was called.

Suspected persons were obliged to have their bodies pricked over with this instrument, by those chosen for the purpose, and if a callous or hard place was found, which was most often the case with hard-working or aged persons, they were at once condemned as witches.

"Does not Satan always make his mark upon those who sell themselves to him?" argued the witch-finder.

Hopkins was not satisfied with this test, but contrived others far more cruel.

For instance, he compelled his aged and decrepit victims to sit on high stools with their limbs crossed, and would not allow them to go to sleep till they had confessed their intimacy with the devil.

He would also take some worn-out old man, and compel him to walk barefoot over rough ground until the wretched victim fell dead from exhaustion and exposure.

Hopkins's most common mode of torture was this: having tied the thumb of the right hand to the great toe of the left foot, he threw the miserable victim into a pond or river, and caused her to be dragged to and fro. If the accused persons floated, as they probably would in this position, he said it was proof of their guilt. If they sank, they died in innocence. It must have been a dreadful misfortune to incur the suspicion of such a man.

It has been said, on good authority, that he caused to be put to death, in one county in England, in one year, more than three times as many as suffered at Salem, during the whole delusion, half a century later.

You may find reference to this monster, Hopkins, in the following lines from Butler's Hudibras: —

> "Has not this present Parliament
> A leiger to the devil sent,
> Fully empowered to treat about
> Finding revolted witches out,
> And has he not within a year
> Hanged threescore of them in one shire?"

His success was accounted for, by believing that in an encounter with Satan he had wrested from him *his private memorandum book*, in which were kept the names and addresses of those in his employ.

Among those put to death was an aged man named Lewis. He had been a minister of the Established Church for fifty years, and was over eighty when he was brought to trial, or rather to torture, for witchcraft.

He was subjected to the cruel tortures of the day, even to being dragged through the pond.

The intrepid old man maintained his innocence through the whole, but was at last condemned to die the death of a felon, without the rite of burial. He was obliged to read his own burial service on the scaffold.

Imagine this old, gray-haired minister standing on the fatal drop, about to be launched into eternity, repeating, with tremulous voice, the simple but beautiful words of his own funeral service.

The witch-finder at last came to a miserable end. He was himself accused of being a wizard. He was seized one day and tied, just as his many victims had been, and dragged through a pond. Subjected to his own test, he sank, and that was the end of his long career of deception and wickedness.

These facts, which we gather from a curious article on Hopkins, are more dark and cruel than anything that happened in Salem, although even there an innocent man was pressed to death with weights because he would not acknowledge himself to be a wizard.

In June (15th), 1648, the first execution for witchcraft took place in Boston. The victim was Margaret Jones. For her good offices in trying to heal the diseases of the people, she fell under suspicion and was hung. She was a doctor, and dealt in roots and herbs. We are told that her medicines "had extraordinary violent effects," not an uncommon result of the use of botanic remedies. It was thought she had bewitched them. If she used lobelia or like plants freely in her prescriptions, as most "root and herb doctors" did in those days, we can easily see that the patients could hardly have believed that anything growing out of the earth could produce such surprising effects. We are further told that she would tell certain persons that they could never be healed, and these always grew worse. The same influence is quite noticeable to-day. Quacks succeed because they assure the

WITCHCRAFT AT SALEM VILLAGE.

patient of the cure. The imagination acting powerfully on the nervous system is one of the surest means of healing or destruction.

After she had been imprisoned, we are told that "a little child was seen to run from her into another room, and, being followed by an officer, vanished." But this foolish story was not all. At her trial she told the witnesses against her that they lied, — an awful instance of depravity. She was adjudged a witch, of course. How could such witnesses lie?

But the trouble that these foolish accusations made did not end with the victim. Her husband, disheartened at the loss of his wife, took passage for Barbadoes. The ship lay in the harbor. One day she began to "roll," in calm weather; the effect of some undercurrent, perhaps. The sailors said that it was bewitched, and attributed it to the ghost of poor Margaret. The magistrates had Mr. Jones arrested and imprisoned, after which the ship was quiet. Margaret's ghost must have possessed wonderful physical power to cause a ship to "roll."

Most extraordinary things were believed of witches. They could do anything through the power of the devil, who was their servant. On the day of the execution of Margaret Jones in Boston, there was a tempest in Connecticut, a not uncommon thing in June, and this was attributed to either the wrath of the devil at the execution, or his joy at securing poor Margaret's soul.

If the reader will visit the Public Library and read Cotton Mather's "Magnalia," he will be amazed at the stories of gross superstition he will there find. How any man of intelligence could have for a moment credited such things as are there stated is a mystery hard to explain. To Mather's fancy unseen evil spirits followed men like an army, and life was a deadly contest with dark inhabitants of the air.

From time to time a supposed example of witchcraft disturbed the peace of the colonies. In 1692 the delusion known as the Salem witchcraft began, and spread like a disease. Among the victims were a number of unfortunate people of Boston.

THE STORY OF OLD GOODY GLOVER.

In 1688 the children of Mr. John Goodwin began to behave very strangely. Their bodies were drawn out of shape, as in a case of rickets. Their tongues were sometimes drawn in out of sight, and at other times thrust out of their mouths. They evidently suffered from some nervous disease that spreads by imitation.

They *mewed* like cats, and *barked* like dogs. We are told that they flew through the air like geese, which would indeed have seemed a proof of actual witchcraft if the statement had ended here. But it is added, " their toes *barely* touched the ground." They did touch the ground, you may be sure, and the flying part was all in the excited fancy of the witnesses.

The parents said, "The children are bewitched."

They called in excitable old Cotton Mather, whose love of the marvellous exceeded anything in colonial history. One of the children played a number of ungracious pranks upon him, as she found little difficulty in doing.

She would read the Prayer-Book, but could not be induced to read the Bible, as though the Prayer-Book were for the most part anything but the Bible rearranged for public service. This pleased Cotton Mather, who was violently opposed to Episcopalianism, for he thought it indicated the manner in which the devil regarded the two books, which was quite in accordance with his own views.

When the credulous minister showed his "Food for Babes," a religious book that he highly commended, and of course immensely superior in his own view to the Book of Common

COTTON MATHER.

Prayer, the child became silent. We do not wonder at this. The bewigged doctor was greatly pleased, and thought it an uncommon compliment, — did it not indicate the great displeasure of the devil with his " Food for Babes " ?

The ministers of Boston and Charlestown held a fast at the house where the "bewitched" children lived, and one of the sufferers pretended to find relief from the occasion.

There was an infirm old woman in the town, called Goody Glover. She was a Catholic, and the Puritans regarded Catholics with as much disfavor as the Catholics were wont in earlier times of history to regard them.

This weak old woman had offended Dame Goodwin, and what more natural solution of the mystery could there be than that Goody Glover was a witch?

"She used threatening language to me," said Dame Goodwin.

Here was evidence indeed. Goody Glover was arrested.

She was taken to jail, and her house was searched.

They found dreadful things there, — those magistrates. There were images, or puppets, made of rags and covered with fur.

They brought these into the court-room.

She acknowledged that they were the implements of the devil. She said that she had only to stroke the fur on one of these rag babies, and something evil would happen.

She took up one of them, and drew her hand across it, and just then one of the children who was present, and who expected something evil to happen, fell down in a fit.

Poor, weak, old woman! They told her she was a witch, and she believed it. She confessed everything they wanted her to confess, even to an alliance with the Evil One.

"Have you any one standing by you now?" asked one of the magistrates.

"No," said she, peering into the air; "he is gone."

"Who is gone?"

"My prince."

"What prince?"

"The Evil One."

Witnesses can always be found to testify against one accused of crime.

At the trial a witness appeared, by the name of Hughes. He testified that six years before Goody Glover had bewitched a woman to death.

He was asked how he knew.

"I have myself seen Goody Glover come down the chimney of the house where the woman lived."

Goody Glover received little pity for her gray hairs after such testimony as that. Mather says he prayed with her, and adds, "If it were a fault it was an excess of pity." We fear "an excess of pity" was not one of Dr. Mather's besetting sins.

Goody Glover was condemned and hung. We fancy we see her now, the poor old creature, followed by a jeering mob, and stretched up by her neck under the fair green leaves of the great tree on the Common. And this in *our* city only about two hundred years ago.

The children continued to suffer after Goody was buried. Mather took one of them home with him. He tells us that an invisible horse was brought to her, and that she would ride on it about the room, and on one occasion rode upstairs. Just how large a horse it could have been to have carried a child up a flight of stairs in an old-time house he does not state. It was, however, an *invisible* horse. Probably the child in her nervous paroxysms pretended to canter about, after the manner of children at play. And her motion suggested the horse to the Doctor's vivid imagination, when it became to him a horse indeed.

Cotton Mather regretted the part that he had acted in the witchcraft delusion before he died. But he said he was sincere

in his belief at the time of his errors, and that he did what he thought to be his duty as a conscientious man.

During the prevalence of this moral disease, *nineteen* persons in the colony were hanged; one was pressed to death; one hundred and fifty were thrown into prison, and some two hundred accused.

One Martha Corey, when visited in prison by Mr. Parris and other clergymen, rebuked her persecutors in language of terrible sternness, and was excommunicated before being hanged. Mary Easty, who is said to have been a woman of deep piety, and of a very sweet disposition, conscious of her innocence, firmly denounced the cruelty and falseness of the testimony upon which she and others had been condemned to death, and petitioned her judges and the ministers to make further inquiry, not into her own case, but into those of the others, that no more innocent blood might be shed, for, said she, "I know you are in the wrong way."

You will ask, "What brought it to an end?"

In the beginning, only the poor, the infirm, and unfortunate were accused of witchcraft. As the delusion spread, people in better estate began to be accused. At last the governor's wife[1] was accused. Every household then was filled with terror.

The magistrates began to whisper among themselves, "Some of *our* families may be accused."

Then they began to doubt if, indeed, there were witches.

"What credit is to be given to the *spectre* testimony?" was asked in the court one day, after the leading families began to be in danger.

"None whatever," said the judge.

If this had been the decision at the beginning, no one would have been sacrificed. It was *spectre* testimony that produced these evils, and nothing else.

[1] Mrs. Phipps.

When this *spectre* testimony began to threaten the homes of the magistrates, the executions for witchcraft ceased.

The sad story of witchcraft in New England shows that good men may entertain wrong opinions, and, if their opinions are wrong, their conduct will be wrong. Men of greater virtue than these magistrates never lived. Each of them would have sacrificed his life, rather than have done an act of dishonor. Like Saul, when persecuting the church, they thought they were maintaining truth.

In ancient times in the Hebrew nations there were witches. They dealt in poisons; they had "familiar spirits;" they engaged in dark plots; were the accessaries of crime, and thus dangerous to the community. The Bible said to the Hebrews: "Suffer not a witch to live." Endicott and his followers attempted to govern the colony by the Levitical law. They misinterpreted the Scripture. They applied "Suffer not a witch to live" to any unfortunate old creature whom an enemy or child might accuse. They did it all to sustain a pure morality. It was a terrible error. Never do anything for the cause of virtue or religion, the influence of which is against virtue and religion, and if you must act severely for the sake of justice, be sure your opinions are correct.

THE OLD ELM ON BOSTON COMMON.

Among the historic trees in this country, perhaps none have had so great prominence as the Old Elm on Boston Common, on which, it is supposed, condemned witches were hung. It was almost the only well-preserved living relic of early colonial times, and historically was as famous as the Royal Oak was in England. Boston Common, on which it stood, is, even apart from its historic associations, one of the most delightful places in New England.

THE OLD ELM.

It is full of quiet beauties, with its shaded walks, playground, deer-park, fountains, birds, and grand old trees.

Some of these trees antedate the city's charter. They were planted by hands that long ago crumbled to dust; and the Old Elm broke ground while Boston was yet Shawmut, an Indian village, situated on three bare hills, with the smoke-wreaths of its conical wigwams crowning their summits. This was the Great Tree, as it was called one hundred years ago, but was afterwards known as the Old Elm.

It grew green in spring, and golden in autumn, through all the green springs and golden autumns of New England's early history. The tree was the true American elm, so much admired for its spreading shade, its massive foliage, and drooping, roof-like limbs. It was seventy-two feet high, and twenty-three feet six inches in circumference at the base.

This cherished relic stood nearly in the centre of the Common, at the edge of the rising ground, where was placed the old Liberty Pole, of historic fame. It was surrounded by an iron fence, on the gate of which is the following inscription : —

"*This tree has been standing here for an unknown period. It is believed to have existed before the settlement of Boston, being full grown in* 1722. *Exhibited marks of old age in* 1792, *and was nearly destroyed by a storm in* 1832. *Protected by an enclosure in* 1854.

"J. V. C. SMITH, MAYOR."

Near where the Old Elm stood is the Frog Pond, also of historic fame. It does not look now as it did when the British soldiers prevented the boys from sliding and skating there, and the delegation of young Americans waited upon General Gage, and laid before him the story of their wrongs. It is now surrounded by a granite margin, and is shaded by young trees. In the pleasant summer and autumn weather a spreading fountain throws its sparkling jets of water far above its surface. But in winter it is still a skating pond, as in the old Revolutionary days.

On the rising ground near the Old Elm stood the old Powder-house. There also was fought the first duel in Boston. The victim of the unfortunate combat was a young man, twenty years of age, whose grave may yet be seen in Granary Burying-ground, near the Tremont House. His antagonist fled to Rochelle, France, where he died of a broken heart.

The historical associations of the Old Elm would fill a volume, like that of Hawthorne's "Grandfather's Chair," and a very interesting volume it might be made.

Shawmut, the Indian name of the promontory on which a part of Boston stands, was very barren of trees. The Old Elm, being the most conspicuous tree in the time of our forefathers, was used for the purpose of executions. Tradition tells us that Indian prisoners were executed there.

The story of the Indian wars does not form a part of the history of Boston. The town was never attacked by the Indians. But the people were often terrified by the massacres of the settlers by the Indians in other places, and in neighboring towns. Hostile Indians were sometimes believed to be approaching, but such reports were false alarms.

But while Boston did not suffer from the Indians, many noted Indians were brought here for execution. Philip's great warrior, Annawon, was one of these.

We have no space to tell all of the interesting historical traditions of the Indian troubles which are associated with the old tree. The stories of old Matoonas, of Sagamore Sam, and the Sagamore Quabaog, are among the most interesting of an early date.

The story of old Jethro is, perhaps, less known than most of the others that have been related in connection with the ancient elm. This Indian was among the first to attach him-

A FALSE ALARM.

self to the interests of the English at Boston. He possessed more than ordinary intelligence. Under the teaching of the English, he professed to have embraced Christianity, and associated himself with the praying. men of his tribe. His Indian name, Tantamous, was changed by the colonists after he became associated with them.

In 1674 he was appointed missionary to the Nipmucks, living at Weshakin, since Sterling.

On Sunday, Aug. 22, 1675, the colony was startled by the murder of a family, consisting of a man, his wife, and two children, at Lancaster. It was evident that the deed had been done by Indians; and the praying Indians, of whom old Jethro was one, fell under suspicion. Captain Mosely, their principal accuser, found "much suspicion against them for singing, dancing, and having much powder and many bullets and slugs hid in their baskets."

For this offence, eleven of them, among whom was old Jethro, were sent to Boston to be tried.

Captain Mosely seems to have been a stern man, who used relentlessly the ordinary modes of torture common in those days. One of the Indians, named David, he bound to a tree. Then guns were levelled at him, and his life was threatened, unless he made a full confession. The Indian, to save his life, accused the "praying Indians" of the murder, and among them was old Jethro.

There is an island near Boston, dividing the sea as it flows into the harbor, called Deer Island, and to this the accused Indians were sent. A short time after the real perpetrator of the Lancaster murder was discovered, and the complete innocence of the "praying Indians" proved. They were released, and it will hardly accord with our modern ideas of penalty when we state that David, who had made the false confession to save his life, was sold into slavery as a punishment for the act.

About a year afterward the Indian hostilities were resumed, and the English resolved to send the "praying Indians," among the most prominent of whom was old Jethro, to Deer Island, both for their own security and to keep them away from any temptation to join the enemy. The men who were sent to take them to the island were very overbearing in their conduct, and so insulted old Jethro that he escaped while on the way, and fled into his native wilds. His hiding-place was at last discovered to the English by his own son, Peter Jethro, an act which caused Increase Mather to say, "that abominable Indian, Peter Jethro, betrayed his own father unto death."

Old Jethro was captured and brought to Boston. He was tried and sentenced to be hanged.

It was Sept. 26, 1676, when the first colorings of autumn were on the leaves. The Old Elm then stood at the "end of the town," near the waters of the Charles River, whose marshes, covered deep with earth, are now occupied by costly houses. The tree was in its full strength and beauty then, and we can imagine its low branches, with their tinged leaves, spreading themselves over the lonely hollow. Here old Jethro was hanged, according to tradition.

During the Revolution effigies of Tories were hanged upon the branches of the tree. A young tree has been planted on the spot where the Old Elm stood, and stands in the same enclosure.

It is not certain that all the executions that old-time stories associate with the tree actually took place there. Other trees may have been used for such a purpose, and there seems to have been a gallows erected there during the colonial period. Of this we shall give a sad story in another chapter.

INCREASE MATHER.

"Here rest the great and good, — here they repose
After their generous toil. A sacred band,
They take their sleep together, while the year
Comes with its early flowers to deck their graves,
And gathers them again, as winter frowns.
Theirs is no vulgar sepulchre, — green sods
Are all their monument; and yet it tells
A nobler history than pillared piles,
Or the eternal pyramids. They need
No statue nor inscription to reveal
Their greatness. It is round them; and the joy
With which their children tread the hallowed ground
That holds their venerated bones, the peace
That smiles on all they fought for, and the wealth
That clothes the land they rescued, — these, though mute
As feeling ever is when deepest, — these
Are monuments more lasting than the fanes
Reared to the kings and demigods of old."

J. G. Percival.

CHAPTER VIII.

WHEREIN IS SHOWN HOW THE COLONY BECAME A PROVINCE.

THE picture on the next page represents one of the most popular governors under the charter that the colony ever had, — John Leverett. He was governor from 1673 to 1678, and he rendered efficient aid to Plymouth Colony in the struggle with the Indians, known as King Philip's War. He, too, was born in Old Boston, and was one of the congregation of St. Botolph's. He returned to England for a time during the Commonwealth, and was on intimate terms with Cromwell. His house stood at the corner of Court and Washington Streets, where the Sears Building now stands.

In 1679 there was a great fire in Boston. Eighty dwelling-houses and seventy warehouses were consumed. The people now began to build of brick. Some of these brick houses at the North End may still be seen.

Perhaps you would like a view of some of the houses of Boston during the early colonial period. Here is the old Feather Store, built in 1680, and taken down in 1860. It stood in Dock Square.

There is a very ancient wooden house in Salem Street, which at the time we write (1881) may still be seen.

About the year 1676, just one hundred years before the Declaration of Independence, the people of Massachusetts Bay Colony began to be alarmed at the prospect of losing their charter, and with it their liberties.

Charles II. was now on the throne. He had been proclaimed king in Boston in 1661 with much public ceremony. A writer of the times thus describes the scene: "After our

GOVERNOR LEVERETT.

ordinary lecture, the soldiers being all in arms, viz., our four companies and the country troop, the magistrates mounted on horseback, the ministers being present, and a great number of people, King Charles II. was proclaimed by Edward

THE OLD FEATHER STORE.

Rawson, secretary of state, all standing with uncovered heads, and ending with 'God save the king.' The guns in the castle, fort, and on the ships were fired, and the chief officers feasted that night at the charge of the country."

CHARLES II.

The people under the charter were very independent. They elected their own governor and members to the General Court, and the government of the colony was but little different from that of the state to-day. The colonists were subjects of the English Crown in name, but in reality were the masters of their own public affairs.

Under the reign of Charles II. an attempt was made to impose the English laws of trade upon the colony. The magistrates resisted. They said: "Such acts are an invasion of the colony's rights, since *we are not represented in parliament.*" Thus was begun the resistance to a government without representation, which in one hundred years resulted in the independence of the colonies.

In 1680 King Charles gave the province of Maine to Sir Ferdinando Gorges. The government of Massachusetts soon afterwards purchased it of Gorges, thus exercising the right of an independent power. This brought the colony under the displeasure of the king.

About this time there appeared a man in the colony whom the people came to hate. Hawthorne has given a very dark picture of him in the "Legends of the Province House." Perhaps you may like to take down from your library shelf "Twice Told Tales," and read in this connection "Edward Randolph's Portrait."

Randolph has been called "the evil genius of New England." He was an enemy to the Puritan idea of government, a firm friend of King Charles, and he crossed the ocean again and again, bearing evil reports to the king, and making mischief as often as he came and went. Randolph made many complaints to the king, but some of them were reasonable. He said the Puritans tolerated no religion but their own, and that they had even enacted a law against the observance of Christmas.

The controversy was a long one. The colonists would not surrender their rights under the charter. Said Increase Mather, one of the principal men of the colony: "If we make a submission, we fall into the hands of men; but if we

SIR EDMOND ANDROS.

do not, we still keep ourselves in the hand of God." The king sent commissioners to the colony, but their authority was ignored. In his remonstrance against the treatment of his commissioners, the king said: "In opposition to our authority, it was proclaimed by the sound of the trumpet within the town of Boston *that the General Court was the Supreme Judicature in that Province.*" It was, certainly, the wish of the colony that the General Court, or Legislature, should be the governing power.

The king, finding his efforts to regulate the affairs of the colony under the old charter fruitless, at last lost patience, and determined to take the charter away. He sent Randolph to Boston with a letter, which thus pronounced the doom of liberty. He said: "We are fully resolved in Trinity term next ensuing, to direct our Attorney-General to bring a Quo-Warranto in our Court of King's Bench, whereby our charter granted unto you, with all the powers thereof, may be legally evicted and made void. And so we bid you farewell."

In 1684 the charter of Charles I., which had left the government of the colony almost wholly to the people, was rolled up and put away, a precious, but worthless, piece of parchment.

What next?

Charles II. died on the 6th of February, 1685. He has been called the "Merry Monarch." His life was devoted to pleasure. It is said that when the Dutch fleet was threatening the very gates of London, sailing proudly up the Thames, the king was attending a party at Lady Castlemaine's, and was amusing his favorites by chasing a moth that had strayed into the house.

James II. succeeded Charles. He was a Catholic. Protestant England had little love for him, and New England had none; but it was under him that Massachusetts was compelled to tolerate all religious beliefs. Strange as it may seem, it was thus that the Episcopal Church sprang into life in Boston.

James appointed a provisional government for the colony, and commissioned Joseph Dudley as president. Dudley was soon succeeded by Sir Edmund Andros, who was appointed viceroy of all the New England colonies. He was a haughty, brusque, choleric man, bigoted, and determined to crush out the spirit of independence in New England, wherever it might be found.

The Boston people hated Andros, and were ripe for revolt. Early in the spring of 1689 news was received that William, Protestant Prince of Orange, who had married the Princess Mary, had landed in England, and driven James from the throne. Boston was filled with joy, and Andros was smitten with chagrin. He issued a proclamation, charging the people to hold themselves in readiness to resist any forces that the Prince of Orange might send. But the people raised a company of men for quite a different purpose. These seized Andros, and made him their prisoner. King William soon ordered that Andros and Randolph should be sent to England, and the people were glad to have them go.

In 1692 a new charter was granted the colony, and Sir William Phips was appointed governor by the Crown.

Under the new charter, the governor was to be appointed by the king, and he was to have the appointment of all military officers. The General Court was to be elected by the people, as formerly, but the governor could prorogue it, and no act was to be valid without his consent. No money could be paid from the public treasury except upon his warrant, approved by his council. This new charter brought the government of the colony directly under the power of the king.

So the colony became a province, and thus remained for nearly one hundred years.

This is a sad history, and this chapter is not an interesting one. We hope you may find the next more entertaining.

GOVERNOR ANDROS A PRISONER.

"'T is sweet to remember! When storms are abroad,
We see in the rainbow the promise of God:
The day may be darkened, — but far in the west,
In vermilion and gold, sinks the sun to his rest;
With smiles like the morning he passeth away:
Thus the beams of delight on the spirit can play,
When in calm reminiscence we gather the flowers
Which Love scattered round us in happier hours."

W. G. CLARK.

CHAPTER IX.

WHEREIN ARE TOLD SOME STORIES OF OLD COLONY TIMES.

In few communities have such marvellous stories been told as in the Massachusetts Bay Colony in the days of John Cotton and the Mathers. The reader will readily believe this if he will consult Mather's "Magnalia," or the "Wonders of the Invisible World." But these stories, for the most part, were associated with Indians, ghosts, and awful judgments. Many families had escapes from Indians to relate. All had their ghost stories. Instead of the "Arabian Nights" wonder tales, or fairy stories, incidents like the Indian attack at Bloody Brook, or like the Salem witches, made the young shudder, as they left the evening fireside for the cold, dark chamber.

There were, however, some fireside stories other than those of Indians and ghosts. We give a few of them here.

THE STORY OF NIX'S MATE.

There lies a low, black island in the harbor, treeless, shrubless, herbless. There is no green thing upon it, not so much as a weed. The very sea-mosses seem to have forsaken it. The sea dashes upon it incessantly, wearing it away, and it seems to grow blacker, and certainly does become smaller, every year.

The excursionists pass it on the bright summer days, as the gay boats drop down to Nahant, Nantasket, Downer Landing, Hull, and Hingham. The ocean passengers see it as they leave the havened waters, dotted with islands, for the open sea. Strangers look at the black pyramid that stands upon it and warns the pilot, and ask, —

"What is that?"

"'That,' says the old Bostonian, "is Nix's Mate."

NIX'S MATE.

The stranger thanks his informant, but does not quite understand. The strip of rock and the pyramid are so black and so mysterious, that they hold his eye, as the boat glides on amid the summer towns and the green isles on either side.

The black island was green once, like other islands in the harbor. It was a place of execution for pirates. The island was selected for this purpose, because the sea robber, dangling in air, in his chains, could be seen by all the sailors as they passed into or out of the harbor. It must have been a grim sight, with the wind whistling around the gibbet.

There was in the early days of the colony a ship-master, named Nix. He was mysteriously murdered, and his body was buried on this island, more than two hundred years ago, when the island was green. His mate was accused of the murder, and was sentenced to be hanged. He declared his innocence.

When the time for execution came, he said, —

"I am not guilty of the crime with which I am charged. Before God, I did not the deed. God bear witness of my innocence. That the people may know that I am a guiltless man, may this island wholly disappear!"

He was executed, and soon the sailors began to say, —

MASSACRE AT BLOODY BROOK.

"The island is withering. Nix's mate was an innocent man."

Time passed, and the people said, —

"The green earth has been washed away, and only the rocks remain. Nix's mate was surely an innocent man."

A century passed, and the hard rocks themselves seemed slowly shrinking away, under the action of the sea, and the old story-tellers told the new generation that the island was disappearing, as a witness to the innocence of Nix's mate.

> "The mate murdered Nix
> And was executed,
> And, though the fact
> Seems much disputed,
>
> " He informed his friends
> Both far and near,
> Were he innocent the island
> Would disappear.
>
> "The island is gone;
> And the mate is free
> Of this cruel charge
> Made by history."

THE STORY OF REBECCA RAWSON.

The Puritan communities had their romances that, as in the case of gayer societies, became fireside tales. The Charlotte Temple of Boston, although her history has never been made the subject of a popular novel, was Rebecca Rawson.

Her father, Edward Rawson, was a distinguished man in the colony, and was for a long time secretary to the General Court. For thirty-six years his name appears in all the principal legal affairs of the colony. He died in 1693.

He lived on a pleasant, green street, called Rawson's Lane. It is now Bromfield Street.

To his home the noblest men in the colony came, and there the most eminent visitors from abroad were sometimes entertained.

It was a pleasant neighborhood. Near it was the Winthrop House, where the Old South Church now stands, with its beautiful garden and flowing spring. The stately mansion, afterwards bought for the Province House, was near, with its broad yard and bowery trees. The new King's Chapel, then a wooden building, was but a few steps away, and where are now blocks and warehouses, on Tremont and Washington and Winter and School Streets, were green lawns, and behind the fine houses rose three hills, two of which have since been almost levelled, and cast into the sea, to make new land.

Secretary Rawson had a daughter, who was the delight of his home. Her name was Rebecca. She was famous for her loveliness and accomplishments. She received great attention from society, and young men sought her hand in marriage.

Sometime about the year 1678 there came to the colony a fascinating young man, who said he was the nephew of Lord Chief Justice Hale, of England. He claimed to be a knight, and was known as "Sir Thomas Hale." He was invited to the house of the Colonial Secretary, and there met the lovely Rebecca. He pretended to be enamored of her, and she returned his proffered affection with girlish trust and simplicity.

There was much rejoicing in the town when the wedding of "Sir Thomas" and Rebecca Rawson was announced. All were glad that the Secretary's beautiful daughter was to be connected with the wealthy and powerful English family.

Secretary Rawson, as was the custom of wealthy men of the period, gave the bride a rich outfit. Full of happiness, and with the most glowing anticipations, Rebecca left with her husband for England.

The ship had no sooner arrived in London than the bridegroom disappeared. The endowment that the Colonial

CHARLES CHASING THE MOTH.

Secretary had bestowed upon his daughter, to make her suited to her high position, was carried away by him. Rebecca Rawson found herself among strangers, deserted, and with the dreadful suspicion she had been deceived.

Days of grief and crushing disappointment followed. She found that the man whom she had married was not a knight at all, but a mere adventurer, and that he had a deserted wife still living in Canterbury.

A child was born to her. Hope almost faded out of her young life. Her beauty withered, but her youthful pride remained.

Should she return to Boston? No; she said in her heart she could not do that. She could not meet her family and old friends, with the story of her great disappointment.

The abandoned wife, and the daughter of the rich and honored Provincial Secretary, determined to support herself and child by the industry of her own hands. She was skilled in needlework and painting, and by these arts she lived for some thirteen years.

But the memory of her old home in the bowery town haunted her; the thought of her father, whose hair was now whitening with years, led her affections back over the sea. She resolved to return.

She embarked for Boston in a ship bound thither by the way of the West Indies. She arrived safely at Port Royal, in Jamaica. Being ready to proceed on the voyage, the ship again was preparing to spread sails to the winds.

It was a day in June, 1692. The sun had arisen, glimmering in splendor over the thin mists of the ocean. Suddenly a subterranean thundering began. The crust of the earth was upheaved and shaken. There was a great vortex in the sea, and into this the ship was drawn, and went down to deeps unknown. Such was the melancholy history and sad end of Rebecca Rawson. Her father died soon after receiving the news of the loss of the ship in the great earthquake at Jamaica.

THE FIRST DUEL.

Some years ago we used to linger in summer-time under the delicious shade of the old Paddock elms that once stood on Tremont Street, in front of an ancient historic enclosure, called the Granary Burying-ground. The sights and scenes of the city were new to us, and we loved to watch the tide of travel that incessantly poured through the busy avenue.

Near the iron fence stands an old gravestone, whose inscription can be read from the street, and that used to be not unfrequently deciphered by people waiting for the horse-cars, under the elms. It is as follows: —

"*Here lies the body of Benjamin Woodbridge, son of Hon. Dudley Woodbridge, who died July 3, 1728, in the twentieth year of his age.*"

We have already alluded to young Woodbridge. He was the son of a wealthy gentleman in Barbadoes, and was sent to Harvard College to be educated. He seems to have had an ardent, kindly nature, spirited, social, and keenly susceptible to friendship. He had an intimate friend by the name of Samuel Phillips, a graduate of the college, and connected with the best colonial families.

Never did life open with fairer prospects before two young men. But their warm, social nature led them to the gaming-table, and gambling to the free use of wine, and their lives were suddenly eclipsed by an act that sent a thrill of excitement and terror through the town of Boston.

A dispute arose between them, and young Phillips killed Woodbridge in a duel on Boston Common, on a summer's night in July, more than one hundred and fifty years ago.

Phillips, conscience-smitten, fled to Rochelle, France, that charming city of the waters. He sought to gratify his æsthetic taste amid historic scenes; but neither the refinements of art nor the morning and evening splendors of the bay could efface the memory of the stain of blood. He died of a broken heart exactly one year from the death of his victim.

The Puritans made mistakes at times, but their principles were in the main correct. Had that young man learned the principles of the good people about him, and practised them, his gravestone would have had a different date. We have often recalled, as we have seen a young man beginning a course of dissipation, this solitary grave here, and another in far Rochelle.

JOHN SHENHAN.

A STORY OF 1676.

"O Johnny, my boy, be spry! Don't you see
The morning sun hangs o'er the vale of the Lee?
Hear the birds singing sweet in the tops of the trees,
And the bells of old Cork swinging light in the breeze.
O Johnny, O Johnny, you are dear unto me,
But an idler lad ne'er was seen on the Lee."

"O mither, ne'er mind, for my spirit is bold,
And I'm going away to the country of gold.
I long on the breast of the billows to rock,
And sink in the ocean the harbor of Cork.
O mither, be aisy, for soon you will see
Of me nothing more in the vale of the Lee."

"O Johnny, be steady, and listen no more
To the tales that they tell in the inn on the shore.
Be honest and steady, and you will find gold
In Ireland's soil. My boy, I am old.
My hair is fast changing; hey, boy, don't you see?
Oh, stay wi' me here in the vale of the Lee."

He sat with his mother that eve 'neath the tree,
The moon hanging low on the wave of the Lee.
"Oh, stay wi' me, boy, and ne'er mind the gold!"
"I'll come back to ye, mither, to cheer ye when old."
He kissed her next morn on an ocean-swept rock,
And sunk in the ocean the harbor of Cork.

He worked a hard passage across the wide main,
Till hilltops arose from the ocean again, —
Till a town in the wilderness glanced on the seas
From three beautiful heights overshadowed with trees.
He hailed the new land with a shout of delight,
And slept in the inn near the harbor that night.

He arose the next morn with a gold-haunted brain,
He walked near the town in a sun-sprinkled lane;
He saw the new houses uplifting their walls,
And the cottages cool on the banks of the Charles;
And he saw, dismal sight! with a shudder of pain,
The *gallows* that hung mid the trees in the lane.

He at last met a Puritan, stately and old,
And asked him the way to the region of gold.
"By the sweat of thy brow," the grave Puritan said,
And he looked on the boy with a shake of the head.
And all that he questioned the same story told
Of the Puritan way to the region of gold.

Time passed; he worked hard, with a resolute will,
But felt the sharp pinches of poverty still.
His language was thick; they were loath to employ
At wages, like others, the poor Irish boy.
And Johnny grew heavy at heart in the end,
And wished, but in vain, for a pitying friend.

'T was June — a calm night — the moon hung o'er the walls
Of the houses that stood on the banks of the Charles.
It silvered the lane and the pastures beyond;
It silvered the roses that margined the pond;
It silvered the ringlets of Johnny's light hair,
As he sat 'neath the elm in the cool summer air.

OLD TIME COURTESIES.

O Johnny Shenhan, what's the matter with thee?
Are thy thoughts far away on the banks of the Lee?
Oh, why dost thou start at each step passing by?
And why does that stealthy look fall from thy eye?
He leans his young brow on his trembling palms,
And hears in the distance the music of psalms.

He creeps towards a house, — it stands on the hill,
The windows are open, the rooms are all still.
On the top of the desk there are papers unrolled,
In the till of the desk, it may be, there is gold.
He climbs through the casement, he opens the till,
Then flies like a ghost o'er the brow of the hill.

Gold! gold! he has gold, but, his innocence gone,
Sleep flies from his eyes and he trembles till morn.
He has gained what was never a Shenhan's before,
He has lost what eternity cannot restore.
No lad in the town is as wretched as he,
He wishes him back in the vale of the Lee.

When the moonlight again on the summer trees fell,
It reached not poor Johnny, — he lay in a cell.
He was brought into court, the men held their breath,
While the judge pronounced slowly his sentence, — 't was death!
He stood like one smitten, tears rolled from his face
And he bitterly said as he turned from the place, —

"My sentence is hard, oh, how dreadful to hear!
But, sheriff, 't is less for myself that I care
Than for her who looks out from the ocean-swept rock
For the sails that come home to the harbor of Cork!
Oh, the ships will come back o'er the foam-covered sea,
But bring not her boy to the vale of the Lee!"

'T was autumn, — a coolness came down with the breeze,
The gold and vermilion hung light on the trees,
The scaffold was ready, — it stood where to-day
The boys of the city have freedom to play,
O'erlooking the Common, o'erlooking the pond,
O'erlooking the river that rippled beyond.

A multitude gathered, as people now go
To see the odd sights at a fair or a show,
And Johnny was brought, — he looked on the air,
And the river that rolled in the full sunlight there,
He looked on the faces upturned like a sea,
And his thought wandered back to the vale of the Lee.

"Forgive me," he said, and the tears gathered fast
When he saw that the hour of man's mercy was past,
"Though just is the sentence my error receives,
'T is hard to die thus while a poor mother lives.
The ships will return o'er the fair sunny sea,
And a heart will be broke in the vale of the Lee."

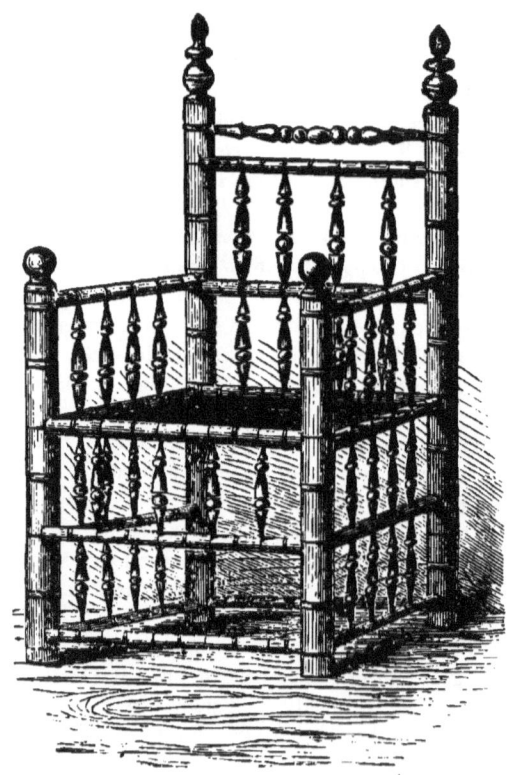

ELDER BREWSTER'S CHAIR.

"What constitutes a state?
Not high-raised battlements, or labored mound,
   Thick wall, or moated gate;
Not cities proud, with spires and turrets crowned,
   Not bays and broad-armed ports,
Where, laughing at the storm, proud navies ride;
   Not starred and spangled courts,
Where low-browed baseness wafts perfume to pride!
   No!—*men*,—high-minded MEN,—
   Men who their duties know,
But know their rights, and, knowing, dare maintain."

CHAPTER X.

WHEREIN IS GIVEN SOME ACCOUNT OF THE TIMES OF THE ELEVEN ROYAL GOVERNORS AND OF THE OLD PROVINCE HOUSE.

THESE were the days of Queen Anne and the Georges.

The democratic governors of the golden age of the charter were gone, — Winthrop, Sir Henry Vane, Dudley, Endicott, Haynes, Bellingham, Leverett,— and with them the republicanism of half a hundred years. A new period of growth and prosperity was at hand, but with it came a struggle against the encroachments of a foreign power, that lasted nearly a century before blood was spilt. It was a brilliant period of progress, education, thrifty industry, and religious development, — that of the eleven royal governors.

These governors were : —

SIR WILLIAM PHIPS,	JONATHAN BELCHER,
RICHARD, EARL OF BELLOMONT,	WILLIAM SHIRLEY,
JOSEPH DUDLEY,	THOMAS POWNALL,
SAMUEL SHUTE,	SIR FRANCIS BERNARD,
WILLIAM BARNET,	THOMAS HUTCHINSON,

GEN. THOMAS GAGE.

The period of growth under political repression, during which the colony was subject to the vice-regal power of these eleven governors, lasted from 1692 to the Revolution, or more than eighty years. It began under the reign of

William and Mary, and continued through the reigns of Queen Anne, George I., George II., and a part of that of George III.

The first of these governors had a very wonderful history.

THE STORY OF SIR WILLIAM PHIPS, AND HIS GREAT GOOD FORTUNE.

William Phips was a poor boy. He rose to eminence by energy of character, but was helped by a series of fortunate circumstances that make his life read like a romance in which some magic power leads an ambitious adventurer to caverns of gold.

The first statement to be made in his biography is different from any other we have ever seen. He was one of a family of *twenty-one sons*, and of twenty-six children born to the same mother. Families were very large in old colony times. His father was James Phips, a blacksmith, and an early settler in the woods of Maine. He little dreamed while working to support his large family in the wilderness of the Kennebec that one of his sons would become the first man in the country in wealth and position, and wear the star of knighthood.

William was born Feb. 2, 1651, and soon after his birth his father died. We know nothing about the other members of the family except their astonishing number. He tended sheep amid wolves and savages until he was eighteen years of age, and his education was confined to the stories of the foresters alone.

But he had in him that restless energy which, rightly directed, leads to success. He learned how to build coasters on the Kennebec, and he began to make voyages in them. It was a profitable business, and proved the beginning of the great shipbuilding industry of Maine.

QUEEN ANNE.

Young Phips now began to hear of the great world, and to have visions of wealth and greatness. He came to Boston at the age of twenty-two. Here he learned to read and to write his name. He married a widow who had once been in comfortable circumstances, but had lost her property.

"Never you mind," he said, "we will have a fair brick house in the Green Lane of North Boston some day."

The Green Lane was the Beacon Street of Boston then.

He went back to Maine and engaged in shipbuilding. Sailors told him exciting stories of sunken treasures in the Spanish Main. One of these stories of a sunken treasure-ship was known to be true.

Could she not be recovered?

Could he not recover her?

If so, wealth untold would be his!

Dreaming of gold he went to London and applied to the Admiralty for the use of an eighteen-gun ship, for the purpose of bringing up the lost treasure-ship. It was granted him. He went to Bahama. From an old Spaniard he learned the precise spot where the galleon had foundered nearly a half-century before. This was the only fruit of his first voyage.

He returned to England full of glittering visions and asked for a better outfit. The Duke of Albemarle provided him with vessels. In this voyage he beheld in reality the prize of the sea. He fished up its bullion from the rocks to the value of more than $1,500,000, in gold, silver, and precious stones. He returned to England in triumph, and was hailed as a hero. He was knighted. *Lady* Phips was presented with a gold cup worth $5,000.

He was made governor of the Colony of Massachusetts in 1692, and he and Lady Phips did indeed occupy a "fair brick house in the Green Lane."

In 1697 Richard Coote, Earl of Bellomont, an Irish peer, was appointed governor. He came to Boston at the close of the century, in 1699. New England contained a population of about seventy-five thousand at this time. He was a popular governor. He died in 1701.

He was succeeded by Joseph Dudley, son of Thomas Dudley of the times of Winthrop. He was an unpopular governor. He had difficulties with the Mather family, and came to be held in general ill esteem. Having been intimate with Andros and Randolph, he was believed to be too fully in sympathy with the English policy of denying the rights of the people to shape the government of their own affairs. He tried to compel the General Court to pay him a salary, which it refused to do. The Court had made the former governors " presents," and as they had been very accommodating, these presents had been liberal. To the Earl of Bellomont had been given £1,875. But the Court allowed Dudley but £600 a year. Governor Shute, who succeeded him, was even less appreciated, for he was allowed but £360.

The royal governors occupied the Province House, a stately mansion with a broad lawn filled with noble trees, which stood nearly opposite the Old South Church. The builder and first occupant of this house was Mr. Peter Sergeant, a wealthy London merchant, who came to Boston in 1667. It was built of brick, was three stories high, with a gambrel roof and conspicuous cupola.

In 1716 the authorities purchased this house for £2,300, and it was fitted up with great elegance. Here the governors held their vice-regal court. The royal arms, carved in deal and gilt, crowned the wide portico. Here, at the official receptions, ladies shone in silk and satin, and gentlemen in purple and scarlet embroidered with gold. Up the great staircase in military boots the new governor strode, and looked out from the high cupola over a most picturesque part

THE PROVINCE HOUSE.

of the pleasant province. In the great court below the military were from time to time reviewed. The royal arms that were placed above the door may still be seen in the rooms of the Massachusetts Historical Society, and the old vane, which was a gilded Indian, forms, or has formed, a part of the historical collection in the Old South Church. Hawthorne's "Stories of the Old Province House," giving views of the beautiful ladies, provincial warriors, and proud royalists who once attended its festivals, are masterpieces of fiction, and perhaps the most elegant ever written by a New England author.

After the evacuation of Boston by the British this house was used for the public business of the colony.

Governor Shute came to dwell here in 1716. Here came Governor Burnet, son of the celebrated Bishop Burnet the historian, escorted to the door by a cavalcade. Mather Byles composed a poem for the pompous reception, full of soaring metaphors. The festivities on the occasion cost the treasury £1,100.

The royal governors worshipped in King's Chapel, where was a state pew with canopy and drapery. The first King's Chapel was built of wood about the year 1689, at the time of Andros. As the colonists would not sell the unpopular governor land for the purpose of a church, he used one corner of the public burying-ground. The corner-stone of the present King's Chapel was laid by the brilliant Governor Shirley Aug. 11, 1749. Governor and Lady Shirley, who died at Dorchester, were entombed under the church.

The first newspaper in America was published in 1704. It was called the *Boston News-Letter*.

Benjamin Franklin, the most eminent American philosopher of the eighteenth century, was born in Boston, Jan. 17, 1706. His birthplace was on Milk Street, where the *Boston Post* building now stands. The tomb of the Franklin family is the most conspicuous in the Granary Burying-ground, near Park Street Church, and may be seen from the street. Benjamin was the fifteenth of seventeen children. "I remember," he says, "thirteen children sitting at one time at the table." He was baptized on the day of his birth in the Old South Church. At the age of twelve he was apprenticed

FRANKLIN.

to his brother, who was a printer. He had a great thirst for learning, and read constantly. Among the boy's books were Addison's "Spectator," then just published, Locke on the "Understanding," and Xenophon's "Memorabilia," which were quite unlike the boys' books of to-day. When he was fourteen years of age his brother established the *New Eng-*

KING'S CHAPEL, TREMONT STREET.

land Courant, the second newspaper in Boston, and fourth in America, and he himself carried it to the subscribers.

He wrote poetry, and was ambitious to contribute articles to the paper. As he feared that his brother did not appreciate his literary abilities, he tucked certain contributions under the door of his shop, which James Franklin thought so good that he printed them, not knowing from whom they came. James was much offended when he discovered their authorship. He never treated Benjamin well, and he used sometimes to beat him. Determined to be free from so arbitrary a master, Benjamin went to Philadelphia, where he ultimately established a printing press of his own. He had a hard experience in youth, but he once said in regard to such discipline, "A good kick out of doors is worth all the rich uncles in the world."

A STORY OF FRANKLIN'S EARLY STRUGGLE FOR SUCCESS.

When Benjamin Franklin opened his printing office in Philadelphia, he was obliged to struggle against many adverse circumstances.

He was young and poor; the country was new, and the public mind was unsettled, and two printing offices of established reputation were already doing a thriving business in the place. He knew that he must succeed, if he succeeded at all, by honorable dealing, energy, and perseverance.

There lived in Philadelphia, at this time, a gentleman of wealth and position by the name of Samuel Mickle. He was one of those morose persons who take a most dismal view of human affairs, and go about prophesying disaster and ruin. He looked upon the settlements in the New World as failures, and expected that Philadelphia would speedily decline and return to the primitive wilderness.

Having plenty of leisure, he made it a sort of missionary

work to disseminate these startling opinions and to warn those who were prospering in a business way, and those who were engaging in new enterprises, of the impending doom.

Hearing that young Franklin had opened a printing office, he concluded to make him a call, and accordingly appeared, one day, at the door of the new establishment. Franklin's experience in business had not been promising thus far, and his view of the future was anything but cheerful. His face brightened, however, as he saw the portly old gentleman at his door, and noticed his elegant and courtly bearing, thinking that he might have come with proposals for work.

"Are you the young man that has just opened a printing office?" asked Mr. Mickle.

Franklin answered in the affirmative.

"I am sorry, very sorry," said the old gentleman, looking very solemn, and speaking in a very impressive tone. "It must be an expensive undertaking, and your money will all be lost. Don't you know Philadelphia is already falling into decay? Most of its business men are obliged to call their creditors together. I know, as an undoubted fact," he continued, with great emphasis, "that all of the circumstances that might lead one to think otherwise, such as the erection of new buildings and the advanced prices for rent, are deceitful appearances, that will only make the ruin more sweeping and dreadful when it comes!"

He then proceeded to illustrate these statements by detailing the private affairs of a number of individuals into whose business he had been prying.

"He gave me," says Franklin, "so long a detail of misfortunes actually existing, or about to take place, that he left me almost in a state of despair."

Franklin, however, recovered his self-possession, and resolved to redouble his energy and to work as he never had worked before.

GEORGE I.

"The industry of this Franklin," said Dr. Bard, at a meeting of the Merchants' Club, not long after the occurrence of the incident we have related, "is superior to anything of the kind I have ever witnessed. I see him still at work when I return from the club at night, and he is at it again in the morning before his neighbors are out of bed."

The success of Franklin as a printer is well known, and we need only allude to it here. But poor Mr. Mickle?

"He continued," says Franklin, "to live in this place of decay, and to declaim in the same style, refusing for many years to buy a house, because all was going to wreck; and in the end I had the satisfaction to see him pay five times as much for one as it would have cost him had he purchased it when he first began his lamentations."

Almost every young man of enterprise encounters a Samuel Mickle. To such the example of Franklin affords a wholesome lesson.

FRANKLIN'S BIRTHPLACE.

"A FLEET with flags arrayed
　　Sailed from the port of Brest,
And the Admiral's ship displayed
　　The signal, 'Steer southwest.'
For this Admiral d' Anville
　　Had sworn by cross and crown
To ravage with fire and steel
　　Our helpless Boston Town."
　　　　　　　　　　LONGFELLOW.

CHAPTER XI.

THE TIMES OF THE ELEVEN ROYAL GOVERNORS AND OF THE OLD PROVINCE HOUSE, CONTINUED.

THE Old South Church was erected in 1729. As King's Chapel is associated with the royal governors, so this church gathers historic fame from all the great episodes of the struggle for liberty. It became the church of the people.

In 1744 began the war between England and France known as "King George's War." The colonies entered into it by preparing an expedition against Louisburg, Cape Breton, then occupied by the French. The contest on this side of the water was called "Governor Shirley's War."

The fleet of the expedition sailed from Boston. It carried away three thousand men. Louisburg was regarded by the French as the Gibraltar of America, and its fortifications cost some five million dollars. The fleet came in sight of Louisburg April 30, 1745, and on the 17th of June the besiegers compelled its surrender. Joy filled the colonies over this great victory.

The joy in Boston, however, was soon changed to anxiety by the news that Admiral d' Anville was preparing an expedition at Brest for the destruction of the town. In anticipation of the attack nearly seven thousand men were placed under arms on Boston Common.

It was September, — the Sabbath. In his lofty pulpit in the Old South Church Rev. Thomas Prince rose to pray for deliverance from the impending danger. While he was praying "a sudden gust of wind arose, the day having until now been clear and calm, so violent as to cause a loud clattering of the windows. The pastor paused in his prayer, and, looking around upon the congregation with a countenance full of hope, he again commenced, and with great devotional ardor supplicated the Almighty to cause *that* wind to frustrate the object of 'our enemies.' A tempest ensued, in which the greater part of the French fleet was wrecked on the coast of Nova Scotia. The Duke d' Anville committed suicide."

Longfellow has thus paraphrased Thomas Prince's prayer, perpetuating the story in song : —

" ' O Lord, we would not advise ;
But if in thy providence
A tempest should arise
To drive the French fleet hence,
And scatter it far and wide,
Or sink it in the sea,
We should be satisfied,
And thine the glory be.'

" ' This was the prayer I made,
For my soul was all on flame,
And even as I prayed
The answering tempest came ;
It came with a mighty power,
Shaking the windows and walls,
And tolling the bell in the tower
As it tolls at funerals." [1]

In 1734 a great religious awakening under the powerful preaching of Jonathan Edwards began in New England. As by one impulse people turned their attention to their spiritual concerns. In 1740, while Belcher was governor, George

[1] *Atlantic Monthly*, 1877.

FANEUIL HALL.

Whitefield came to Boston. He was welcomed by the governor's son, a "train of clergy, and principal inhabitants." No church would hold the throngs of people who came from all quarters to hear him, and he was obliged to preach on the Common. He once attempted to preach in the Old South Church, but such a crowd gathered that he himself was obliged to crawl into the house by the window. It was early autumn. The Common was beautiful with its bright tinted trees. Ten thousand people used to gather in their shade to hear the matchless eloquence of the English evangelist. He preached his farewell sermon there to twenty thousand people.

Notwithstanding the royal governors, this was a bright, happy period of history. The city was kept from hostile attacks, from disease, and every great calamity, and she grew in wealth, prosperity, and population, and in the determination that she would yet control her own liberties and be independent and free.

There were many elegant residences in Boston at this time. One of them belonged to the Faneuil family. It was on Tremont Street, opposite the King's Chapel Burying-ground.

THE OLD SOUTH CHURCH.

It had a "deep court-yard ornamented with flowers and shrubs, divided into an upper and lower platform by a high glacis, surmounted by a richly wrought iron railing, decorated with gilt balls. The hall and apartments were spacious and elegantly furnished. The terraces, which rose from the paved court behind the house, were supported by massy walls of hewn granite, and were ascended by flights of steps of the same material."

Andrew Faneuil was a French Protestant or Huguenot. He escaped to Holland after the revocation of the Edict of Nantes, which destroyed the religious privileges of the Protestants in France. He came to America about 1691. A church of French Protestants was gathered here, and Peter Daillé, whose headstone may still be seen in the Granary Burying-ground, was the pastor. Faneuil and Bowdoin were leading members.

Peter Faneuil was a nephew of the French pioneer, and he inherited his estate and wealth. He gave to the city the large building for a market that became known as Faneuil Hall. At the first town-meeting held in the hall over the market, his own eulogy was pronounced, he having died shortly after the gift (1742).

The funeral oration of Peter Faneuil was delivered by John Lovell, master of the Latin School. It was the first of a long series of orations delivered in Faneuil Hall on Boston's public men as the by-gone generation of patriots and benefactors one by one disappeared. It was printed on the town records. Near the close appears this striking, eloquent, and almost prophetic passage: —

"What now remains, but my ardent wishes that this hall may be ever sacred to the interests of truth, of justice, of loyalty, of honor, of liberty.

"May no private views or party broils ever enter within these walls, but may the same public spirit that glowed in the

REVOCATION OF THE EDICT OF NANTES.

breast of the generous founder influence all your debates, that society may reap the benefits of them.

"May Liberty always spread its joyful wings over this place! — Liberty, that opens men's hearts to beneficence, and gives the relish to those who enjoy the effects of it.

"And may Loyalty to the King, under whom we enjoy this liberty, ever remain our character."

This was the town hall, — the Hotel de Ville after the manner of European cities. The town showed its loyalty by adorning it with the picture of George II. In 1761 it was nearly destroyed by fire; it was rebuilt 1763-64. In the second hall Revolutionary meetings were held. A new hall was added to the building in 1805. This third hall Webster, Everett, Choate, Sumner, and Philipps have made famous by their eloquence.

For the following account of another colonial mansion, I am indebted to a lady who copied it from a verbal description by a very aged member of her own family: —

"Lord Frankland's Palace" has formed the theme of many writers, and his romantic history has been a fruitful subject. The novelist Cooper visited the house with a grandson of Governor Winthrop, that he might make it the scene of his "Lionel Lincoln." Although better known by the name of Frankland, the house was built by Hon. William Clark, a wealthy merchant, whose tomb may be seen in the old part of Copp's Hill Burying-ground. It was purchased from him by Sir Henry Frankland, who in 1741 was appointed Collector of the Port of Boston.

Hither it was that he brought Agnes Surriage, a poor girl of Marblehead. Her beauty attracted Lord Frankland in one of his visits to that town, as he saw her, barefooted and poorly clad, passing from the tavern door to the well for water. Upon his return to England he took her with him. His wealthy and aristocratic family refused to notice her.

They travelled extensively. At the time of the earthquake in Lisbon, in 1755, she was the means of saving his life. For this and her constancy he married her, and from henceforth she was recognized as Lady Frankland.

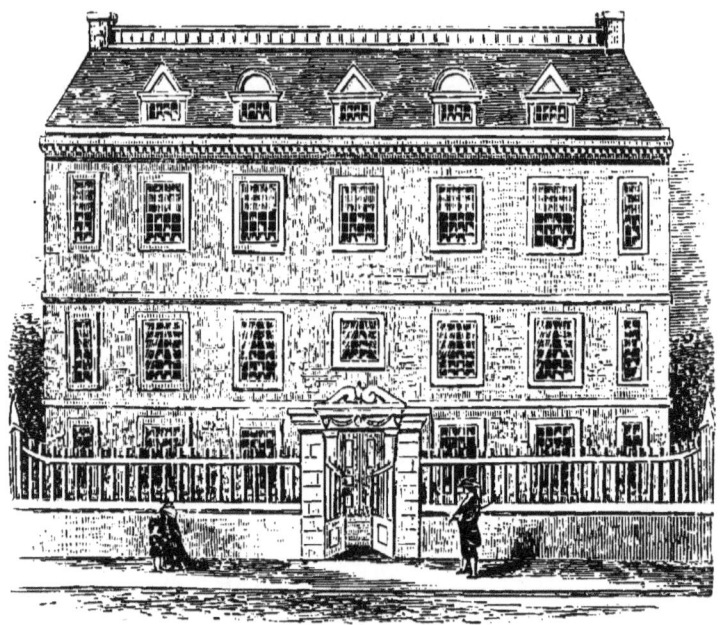

THE FRANKLAND HOUSE.

Upon one of the attic doors in the old house, written in a childish hand with something resembling chalk, and yet which no amount of scouring would efface, were the words: "Isaac Surriage is a naughty boy and deserves a horse-whipping."

Who was Isaac Surriage?

He was a brother of Agnes, some years younger. One day he was sent by the captain of the vessel on which he was cabin-boy, to the house of Lord Frankland with a message. Returning to the ship he said to a companion, —

"My sister lives there."

The next day they went to view the house; the front door being open they saw a lady pass through the entry.

"There is your sister, Isaac," said his companion.

The lady hearing the words turned and recognized her brother. He was welcomed to her home, and afterwards became the possessor of the elegant mansion.

The house was situated at the North End, for many years the fashionable part of the town and city. It was on Garden Court Street. There was a side gate on Bell Alley, now New Prince Street.

From the top could be obtained an extensive view of the harbor, forts, and islands. With spy-glass in hand one could discern the coming of homeward-bound vessels.

Although the outside of the house has been to some extent described by others, there are only a few left who can speak of the interior.

Passing up a flight of stone steps, one entered by the front door a large hall; midway of this was an arch, in the centre of which was suspended a large brass lantern. On either side of the door were very large parlors. In one the floor was inlaid with hundreds of pieces of wood of various forms. The centre of this floor has been made into a table. All the windows had low mahogany seats, broad enough for two or three to sit upon them.

Here in this room the Duke of Argyle, grandfather of the Marquis of Lorne, son-in-law of Queen Victoria, was married.

Under one of the flights of stairs was a dark closet, where, it is said, a refugee was hid during the Revolution.

Except in the parts my father had repaired, the house reminded one of those old castle-like structures described by story-writers. But all has been gone for many years, and a number of houses and stores now occupy the site of this old landmark.

E. C. W.

Oliver Wendell Holmes has told the story of Lady Agnes in one of his long poems. You may like to read it in this connection.

THE LIBERTY TREE.

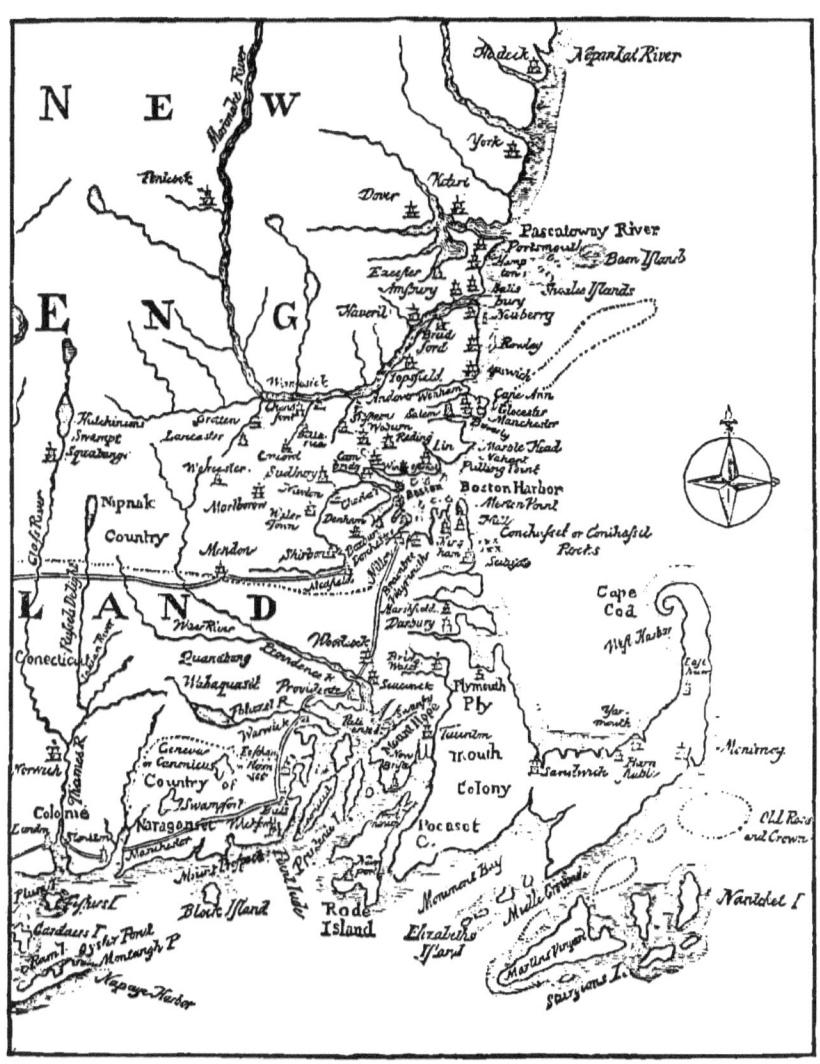

MAP OF NEW ENGLAND ABOUT 1700.

"They left the ploughshare in the mould,
  Their flocks and herds without a fold,
  The sickle in the unshorn grain,
  The corn, half-garnered, on the plain;
  And mustered, in their simple dress,
  For wrongs to seek a stern redress.
  To right those wrongs, come weal, come woe,
  To perish, or o'ercome their foe.

"And where are ye, O fearless men?
    And where are ye to-day?
  I call, — the hills reply again
    That ye have passed away;
  That on old Bunker's lonely height,
    In Trenton, and in Monmouth ground,
  The grass grows green, the harvest bright,
    Above each soldier's mound.

"The bugle's wild and warlike blast
    Shall muster them no more;
  An army now might thunder past
    And they not heed its roar.
  The starry flag, 'neath which they fought
    In many a bloody day,
  From their old graves shall rouse them not,
    For they have passed away."

CHAPTER XII.

THE EVE OF REVOLUTION.

A SHADOW fell on the golden age of the colonial period when the old charter was taken away; political clouds gathered again and again, and as often melted into sunshine during the long period of the royal governors, but now the tempest was gathering indeed.

The Stamp Act was passed in 1765. It decided the people. The colony needed leaders, and in this necessity, Otis, Hancock, Adams, and Warren appeared.

The Stamp Act laid a duty on every piece of paper on which anything of value could be written or printed. It was designed thus to raise a revenue for the Crown from the colonies. The people of the colonies said, "We are not represented in Parliament, and taxation without representation is tyranny."

James Otis, a man of powerful genius and ardent temper, of brilliant and impetuous eloquence, was one of the earliest advocates of the independence of the colonies in the management of their local affairs. He was born at West Barnstable in 1725. In 1764 he published a masterly pamphlet entitled "The Rights of the Colonies Vindicated." In 1765 he moved the calling of a congress of delegates of the several colonies, a plan which met with popular favor and was adopted. This was the first decisive step towards independence. He lost his reason in his last years. As if fulfilling a wish that he had often expressed, that he might die suddenly, he was killed by a stroke of lightning in May, 1783.

John Hancock was born at Quincy, 1737. He was the son of Rev. John Hancock of Braintree, and was educated by his uncle, Thomas Hancock, of Boston, a gentleman of wealth, whose fortune he received. He visited England in 1760, where he witnessed the coronation of George III. He was a member of the Provincial Congress, and so strongly opposed the measures of the British ministry that he was exempted from the general pardon offered by General Gage when the latter attempted to stay the tide of revolution by pacific measures.

Samuel Adams was born in Boston in 1722. He was a cousin of John Adams, afterwards President of the United States. He studied for the ministry. As early as 1743, when he received the degree of A. M., he proposed a discussion of the question, "Whether it be lawful to resist the supreme magistrate, if the commonwealth otherwise cannot be preserved." He strongly opposed the Stamp Act, and favored the Provincial Congress. He was also exempted from pardon in the proclamation of General Gage to which we have just referred.

General Joseph Warren was born in 1741, at Roxbury, Mass., where his place may still be seen. He was a physician. He became an ardent patriot, and, in advance of the public sentiment of the time when he first espoused the cause of liberty, he maintained that all taxation which could be imposed by Parliament on the colonies was tyranny.

Here were the four leaders, brave, strong, educated men. Their cause was liberty, and events were hurrying.

In October, 1760, George II. died suddenly in his palace at Kensington. The bells of Boston tolled; it was the last time they were ever tolled for a king. George III. was proclaimed, and his favorite minister, the Earl of Bute (Lord

BOSTONIANS READING THE STAMP ACT.

North), soon entered upon a policy hostile to the peace of the colony.

"What shall we do?"

Every patriot asked the question. Conventions were called in various places to answer this inquiry that rose to every lip.

It was the period of lawful and peaceable resistance to taxation, when the fiery spirit of the patriots was curbed by the bridle of English law. The Stamp Act, or a heavy tax on all kinds of paper, for the purpose of supporting the British government, had checked the growth of trade. Nothing could be done legally — newspapers could not be issued, the business of the courts could not proceed, no property could be transferred, no vessel could go to sea, no person could be married — without the use of the paper bearing upon it the odious stamp.

In the middle of May, 1766, the news of the repeal of the Stamp Act was received in Boston. The town then numbered some twenty thousand people. The fate of the bill for the repeal of the Stamp Act had been for weeks almost the only subject of discussion. Upon it the patriots felt rested the destiny of the colonies.

Men scanned the blue line of Boston harbor, to see the white sails rise from the sea, and rushed to the wharves to receive the first intelligence from London. At length, on May 16, a lovely day, a brigantine flying the English flag was seen beyond the green islands of the bay, and soon entered the inner harbor. She was met at the wharf by a crowd, restless and impatient with anxiety.

An hour later the bells of the town began to ring; the long idle ships in the harbor shot their ensigns into the warm May air; the booming of cannon startled the people of the neighboring towns, and, as evening came on, great bonfires on Beacon Hill blazed upon the sea. From lip to lip passed the single expression of joy and relief, — "The Stamp Act is repealed!"

A few days later witnessed a more remarkable scene, — a public holiday to give expression to the joy. At one o'clock in the morning the bell of Dr. Byles's church, standing near the Liberty Tree, where the Colonists used to meet, gave the signal for the beginning of the festival. It was followed by

THE HANCOCK HOUSE.

the melodious chimes of Christ Church, at the North End, and then by all the bells of the town.

The first shimmering light and rosy tinges of the May morning found steeples fluttering with gay banners, and the Liberty Tree on Essex Street displaying among its new leaves an unexampled glory of bunting and flags.

The festivities lasted until midnight. At night an obelisk which had been erected on the Common in honor of the

ADAMS OPPOSING THE STAMP ACT FROM THE OLD STATE HOUSE.

occasion was illuminated with two hundred and eighty lamps, and displayed upon its top a revolving wheel of fire, as the crowning pyrotechny. The Hancock House, which stood on Beacon Hill where the Brewer residence now stands, was a blaze of light, and Province House was in its vice-regal glory.

The Stamp Act was repealed, but the British government continued to tax the colonies, and the sudden sunshine of joy soon was overcast, and the storm gathered again.

The article upon which the Crown made the most persistent attempt to raise a revenue was *tea*. The tax was a small matter, of itself; but if the right to tax one article was admitted, it acknowledged the right to tax all articles.

As the excise officers of Great Britain held control of the ports, and in some cities were supported by soldiery, no tea could be obtained without paying the tax. The people therefore resolved that they would neither use, sell, nor buy an ounce of tea upon which this unjust tax had been paid.

In February, 1770, the mistresses of three hundred families in Boston signed their names to a league, by which they bound themselves not to drink any tea until the obnoxious revenue act was repealed.

Of course the young ladies were as ready to deny themselves the use of this fashionable beverage as were their mothers; and only a few days later, a great multitude of misses, pretty and patriotic, signed a document headed with these words : —

"We, the daughters of those patriots who have and do now appear for the public interest, and in that principally regard their posterity, — as such do with pleasure engage with them in denying ourselves the drinking of foreign tea, in hopes to frustrate the plan which tends to deprive a whole community of all that is valuable in life."

The spirit of liberty spread. Tumultuous meetings became common in the street. In 1768 the officers of customs seized a sloop, named Liberty, belonging to John Hancock, and placed her under the guns of a ship-of-war in the harbor. A mob collected, seized one of the collector's boats and burned it on the Common. In 1770 a boy was accidentally killed by a royalist whom the crowd were deriding by an effigy. The funeral of the boy was made the occasion of a great popular gathering.

The corpse was taken to the Liberty Tree on Essex Street, amid tolling bells, where the immense procession began. Fifty schoolboys led, and were followed by about two thousand citizens. The pall was supported by six boys; the coffin bore a Latin inscription, — " Innocence itself is not safe." Business was suspended. The whole population of the town was in the streets, and the bells of the neighboring towns were heard echoing the solemn funeral bells of Boston.

Such was the temper of the people. The royal governor was almost powerless, and troops were brought to Boston and stationed on the Common. Ships arrived bringing reinforcements; the Common became a camp, and difficulties between the citizens and foreign soldiers were frequently occurring. Every one seemed to feel that the storm of war was gathering.

. It was the 5th of March, 1770, a clear moonlight night, with a light snow upon the ground, soon to be tinged with blood. A mob had assembled in front of the Custom House in State Street, where the British guard were stationed. Citizens had been insulted by a British soldier, and the town was again electric with excitement. Bells were ringing, people were running through all the streets.

The crowd pressed upon the British soldiers and attacked them with snow and ice.

"Fire, fire, if you dare!" was cried on every hand.

There was heard the crack of a musket in the keen March air; another, and another. Three citizens fell dead.

"To arms! to arms!"

The cry ran through the town.

Drums beat, bells rang madly, the King's Council immediately assembled.

The citizens triumphed. The troops were removed to Castle William, on the island at the entrance to the harbor.

The funeral of the slain was attended by a great concourse of people, and another day of clanging bells and feverish excitement was added to those of the past.

The boys were fired with the spirit of their fathers. General Gage was the commander of the military forces of New England, and his head-quarters were at Boston. During the winter, when the Common was a camp, the British soldiers destroyed the boys' coasting grounds. The larger boys called a meeting and resolved to wait upon General Gage and report to him the conduct of the soldiers.

When they presented themselves before him he asked with surprise, —

"Why have you come to me?"

"We come, sir," said the leader, "to ask the punishment of those who wrong us."

"Why, my boys, have your fathers made rebels of you and sent you here to talk rebellion?"

"Nobody sent us, sir; we have never insulted your soldiers, but they have spoiled our skating ground, and trodden down our snow hills. We complained; they laughed at us: we told the captain; he sent us away. Yesterday our works were again destroyed. We can bear it no longer."

"Good heavens!" said General Gage to an officer at his side; "the very children draw in the love of freedom with the air they breathe!"

Turning to the boys, he said, —

"You may go; if any of my soldiers disturb you in the future they shall be punished."

The English East India Company obtained a license to export a large quantity of tea to America. The news reached Boston in October, 1773; meetings were called and resolutions were passed that no taxed tea should be landed.

The ships arrived. A great meeting was held in the Old South Church, at which at least two thousand men were present, who were addressed by the patriots.

In the evening strange-looking people began to mingle with the crowd. They were dressed like Indians. One of them at last shouted, —

"Who knows how tea will mingle with salt water?"

There was heard a wild cry, an Indian war-whoop. The strange-looking people disappeared, and the assembly dispersed.

In the morning it was found that the men disguised as Indians had boarded the ships and emptied two hundred and forty chests and a hundred half-chests into the dock.

The news of this transaction enraged England. Parliament passed an act closing the port of Boston. Business in the town now almost ceased.

All the summer of 1774 troops were arriving from England. At the close of the year there were eleven regiments of Red Coats, as the British soldiers were called, in Boston.

Governor and General Gage had arranged to assemble a General Court at Salem in October. But the excitement was so great that he deferred the call by proclamation. The representatives, however, appeared at the previously appointed place and time, and formed a Provincial Congress, and then adjourned to meet at Concord. This Congress called upon the people to arm. General Gage thus found himself ignored, his power as governor gone; and with it the

DESTRUCTION OF THE TEA.

rule of the royal governors came to an end, after a period of more than eighty years.

The Provincial Congress at Concord placed under arms the whole militia of the province. It took measures for the establishment of two magazines, one at Concord and the other at Worcester. General Gage, who was in command at Boston, was soon informed of what the assembly had done. He was watchful of the patriots; they were also watchful of him. The slightest movement of the loyalists was suspected. The whole population was prepared to rise in arms to resist the oppressor.

PAUL REVERE'S RIDE.

A day or two before the eventful 19th of April, 1775, General Gage began preparations for an expedition to destroy the military stores that the patriots had collected. Boats from a ship-of-war were launched to carry the troops across the Charles River. The movement was observed by the patriots. Companies of soldiers were massed on Boston Common, under pretence of learning a new military exercise.

Dr. — afterwards General — Warren, who fell at Bunker Hill, at once sent Paul Revere to arouse the country. He was to notify Hancock and Adams, who were at Lexington, that a plot was on foot to arrest them, and to warn the people of Concord that the troops were coming to destroy the military stores collected there.

"As soon as the British troops begin to move," said Revere to a patriot, "hang out two lanterns in the steeple of the North Meeting-house."

From this position the people of Charlestown would see the signals at once. The officers at the Province House would not discover them.

Revere rowed across the river with muffled oars. He reached Charlestown, and not a moment too soon.

April 18th, — ten o'clock. The British troops are in motion. Two lights flash into the darkness from the old North steeple.

"The British troops have marched, but will miss their aim," said a patriot in the hearing of Lord Percy, one of the British commanders.

"What aim?"

"The cannon at Concord."

Percy hastened back to the Province House and told Gage what he had heard.

"I am betrayed," said Gage; "let no one leave the town."

But Revere was in Charlestown already.

He flew on horseback over the country roads alarming every household, warning Hancock and Adams at Lexington, and despatching a friend with the news to Concord.

The British troops embarked at the foot of Boston Common, for the tide then came nearly up to the side of the hill where the Soldiers' Monument now stands. They landed at Cambridge, and after a night's march reached Lexington early in the morning. They found there sixty or seventy armed farmers waiting to defend their liberties.

In the chilly spring morning, just before sunrise, Major Pitcairn rode upon Lexington Common.

"Disperse, you rebels," he cried to the armed patriots, accompanying the order with an oath.

He himself fired upon the patriots, at the same time calling upon the troops to fire.

The British fired. Eleven patriots fell dead, and nine were wounded. The patriots retreated.

The sun rose over the gray hills.

"Oh what a glorious morning this is!" said Samuel Adams, when he heard that the contest for liberty had indeed begun.

The British hurried on to Concord, a distance of six miles. They found the country rising in arms, and that the military stores they sought to destroy had been removed. Companies of militia were hastening to Concord from the neighboring towns. Minute-men were gathering there from every road.

PROVINCIALS RALLYING AT CONCORD.

Two parties of British troops went in search of concealed supplies, one over the south bridge and the other over the north bridge. They were watched by the Provincials, who presently saw houses bursting into flame, and resolved to march to the defence of their homes. They advanced towards the north bridge, but the order was that not a shot should be fired unless the regulars attacked them.

At last the British fired. Two patriots fell.

"Fire! for God's sake, fire!" shouted Major Buttrick of Concord, leaping into the air, and turning round to his men.

The patriots fired.

The American Revolution had begun.

The British had found themselves surrounded by enemies on every hand. They knew they must retreat, and at once.

Back to Boston all the warm April day they marched, fired at by the minute-men who lay in ambush on every side. Finding the dangers increasing they began to run. At two o'clock in the afternoon they reached a point about a mile from the place where they had murdered the people of Lexington in the morning. Here they were met by the flower of the British army, that had been sent for their succor from Boston.

These troops were under Lord Percy, and were twelve hundred strong, with two field-pieces. They were not a moment too soon. Lord Percy formed a hollow square to receive the fugitives, who, as a British writer of the time said, lay down to rest, "their tongues hanging out of their mouths like those of a dog after a chase."

Even when the regulars were thus reinforced their position was very perilous. Their enemies were increasing in numbers every moment. In a short time the troops would certainly be cut off and overwhelmed unless they moved at once.

The march was resumed and the fighting began again. More men came up to help the patriots, who had become weary with their long, irregular march and hard work. It was seven o'clock in the evening when the British force reached Charlestown. Protected by the guns of the ship-of-war in the harbor, they took to their boats and were ferried across to Boston.

The losses of the British were seventy-three killed, one hundred and seventy-two wounded, and twenty-six missing; while the Americans lost forty-nine killed, thirty-six wounded, and five missing.

CONFLICT AT THE NORTH BRIDGE.

We will close this chapter with some stories of these days of patriotism and some account of the memorials of that noble and heroic period.

THE STORY OF DOROTHY QUINCY'S WEDDING.

In a Connecticut newspaper, printed one hundred and six years ago, appears this brief, business-like announcement: —

"September, 1775, on the 28th ult., was married at the seat of Thaddeus Burr, Esq., in Fairfield, by the Rev. Andrew Eliot, John Hancock, Esq., Prest. of the Continental Congress, to Miss Dorothy Quincy, daughter of Edmund Quincy, Esq., of Boston."

Dorothy Quincy was the youngest of nine children, and in 1775 was living with her father in a pretty wooden dwelling on Summer Street, not far from the stately Hancock mansion, which fronted on the Common. She was fully the equal of Governor Hancock in social position if not in wealth, and had the advantage of him in age, he being some years her senior. She was the petted belle of Boston society at this time. The marriage was arranged, so the gossips said, by Madam Hancock, aunt of the governor, and widow of Thomas Hancock, the great Boston merchant, from whom Governor Hancock derived the bulk of his fortune. Miss Dolly being motherless, the madam chaperoned her about, and conceiving a deep affection for the beautiful girl busied herself in promoting a union between her two protégés with such good effect that in the winter of 1775 their engagement was announced.

On the eve of the eventful 19th of April, 1775, Madam Hancock and Miss Dolly were visiting in Lexington at the house of a relative of the former, — a Rev. Mr. Clark. This had been the home of Governor Hancock that winter during the sitting of the Provincial Congress at Concord, and as it happened both he and Samuel Adams were present on this occasion.

At midnight Paul Revere startled this company by riding up with a message from Dr. Warren advising them to save themselves and alarm the country, as General Gage had ordered a force to march that night to destroy the stores at Concord. There was great excitement in the little village; the church-bell was rung, and the patriots came pouring in from all sides. Hancock and Adams remained on the green organizing and encouraging the militia until daybreak, when, learning that their capture was one of the objects of the expedition, they retired to Woburn, and found shelter at the house of the Rev. Mr. Jones. The ladies remained in Lexington and witnessed the fight, Madam Hancock from the open door and Miss Dolly from the chamber window, until they were called away to attend to the wounded who were brought in.

After the British had passed on to Concord a message from Mr. Hancock arrived telling them where he and Mr. Adams were, and asking them to drive over in the carriage and bring the fine salmon they had ordered for dinner. The ladies did so; the salmon was cooked, and the party was just sitting down to it when a man rushed in with the news that the British were coming, and the persecuted patriots were again obliged to flee, this time to a friendly swamp, where they remained until the alarm was proven a false one.

Next day Miss Dolly informed Mr. Hancock that she should return to her father in Boston.

"No, madam," he replied, "you shall not return as long as there is a British bayonet in Boston."

"Recollect, Mr. Hancock," she replied, "I am not under your control yet. I shall go in to my father to-morrow."

She did not go, however; Madam Hancock would not hear of it, and it was nearly three years before she saw her

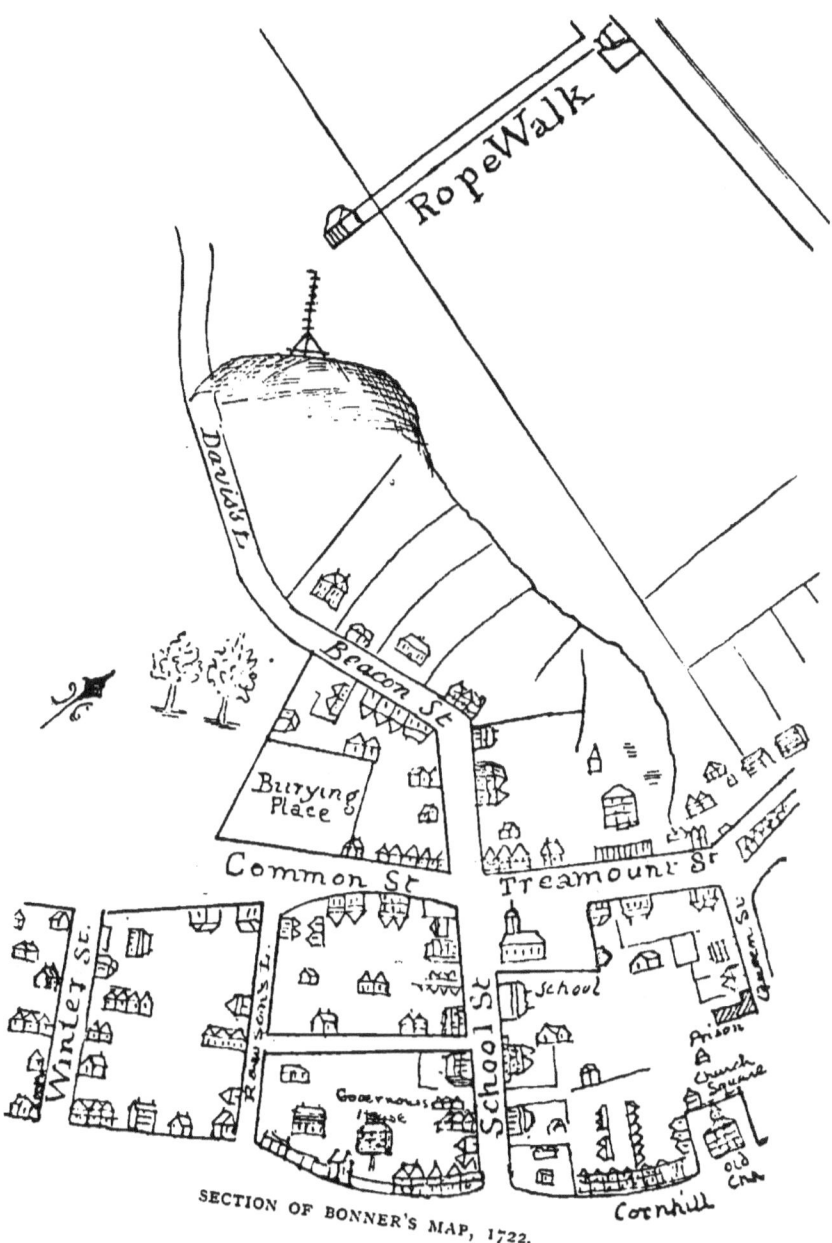

SECTION OF BONNER'S MAP, 1722.

native town again. Madam Hancock, poor lady, never returned.

After the battle Hancock and Adams found themselves proscribed men, and as the neighborhood of Boston was unsafe, they passed down through the interior counties of Massachusetts and Connecticut to Fairfield and the hospitable mansion of their mutual friend, Thaddeus Burr.

Madam Hancock and Miss Dolly accompanied them. Mr. Burr was a gentleman of good family and ample estate, and received his guests with the utmost cordiality. At his hospitable mansion the two refugees remained for several weeks and then went on to the Second Continental Congress, which met at Philadelphia, and of which Mr. Hancock was President. Miss Dorothy and the madam, however, remained at Fairfield all through this eventful summer.

In August Governor Hancock returned from Congress, and on the 28th they were married at Mr. Burr's house by the Rev. Andrew Eliot, pastor of the Fairfield church. It could not have been a very merry gathering, I think, for the groom was a proscribed man, and his house and property, as well as that of his bride, were in the hands of the enemy. Quite a number of guests were present, however, political friends of the Governor, and young lady companions of Miss Dorothy's whom the war had driven into exile. After the blessing had been pronounced the newly wedded pair entered their carriage and were driven by slow stages to Philadelphia, where Mr. Hancock resumed his duties as President of the Congress.

Perhaps the reader is curious to know how this bride of high degree spent the hours of her honeymoon? Chiefly, she tells us, in packing up commissions to be sent to the officers of the volunteer army recently created by Congress.

After the evacuation of Boston Mr. Hancock became governor, and he and his wife took up their residence at the Hancock House.

DOROTHY QUINCY'S RECEPTION.

Dorothy Quincy, afterwards wife of John Hancock, was the leader of Boston society at the beginning of the Revolution. She lived in a stately residence on Summer Street. Her grandfather, Edmund Quincy, was Judge of the Supreme Court of Massachusetts and the colony's agent at the Court of St. James. We have told you the story of her romantic marriage with John Hancock.

The fine old Hancock House stood on Beacon Hill; Hancock Street descends almost directly from the place. After Dorothy Quincy became Madam Hancock and returned to Boston with her husband after the evacuation of the town, she still led society, and the Hancock House was at times the scene of elegant receptions.

In 1778 a French fleet under Count d'Estaing came sailing into Boston harbor.

"We must give a reception to the officers," said Governor Hancock to the stately Dorothy.

The grand lady thought a breakfast to the officers would be the courteous thing, and so it was arranged that the French Count and thirty officers should be invited to breakfast at the Hancock House.

The Count cordially accepted the invitation, but instead of inviting only thirty officers to accompany him he asked all the officers of the fleet, including the midshipmen.

When John Hancock saw the great crowd of Frenchmen coming he sent word to his wife, —

"Get breakfast for *one hundred and twenty more!*"

Here was a situation requiring good management indeed.

JOHN HANCOCK.

We can imagine the stately Dorothy at the Hancock House enjoying the fine appearance of her tables with the ample food for thirty plates. She looks out over the Common to see the French party in gold lace make its appearance. There comes a messenger in great haste.

"Get breakfast for one hundred and twenty more."

John Hancock was always equal to an emergency, and so was Dorothy. In this trying situation she did not rush into her room, lock the door, and sit down to cry, nor did she abuse her husband and call him a brute.

How did the energetic Dorothy meet the difficulty? She sent word to the guard to milk all the cows on the Common and bring the pails of milk to her, then she despatched her servants who could be spared to borrow cake and other good things of the first families of the town for a breakfast table.

When the great crowd of Frenchmen came she was mistress of the situation and prepared to receive them with dignity.

"The Frenchmen," said Dorothy, "ate voraciously, and one of them drank *seventeen* cups of tea."

Some of the midshipmen destroyed the fruit in the garden. The Count seemed to feel that he had encroached on the rule of hospitality, and to make amends he invited Madam Hancock and *her friends* to visit his fleet.

Dorothy accepted the invitation and determined to invite all of her friends to accompany her.

She invited *five hundred*.

The Count received the party graciously, and provided an elegant entertainment.

The Count with a polite gesture handed Madam Hancock a string and desired her to pull it. She did so, causing the firing of a cannon. This was a signal for a *feu de joie* to the fleet. Reports of cannon came from all the ships, and the party was enveloped in smoke and almost deafened at the sound.

Good Boston ladies are, we hope, always pleasant and beaming when their husbands introduce more company than was expected, — following the example of Dorothy Hancock.

STORY OF A VISIT TO CHRIST CHURCH.

We recently spent a Sabbath at Christ Church, whose steeple is associated with the historic signal lights that gave warning to Paul Revere. It was a late autumn day in which something of summer mildness yet lingered, though the flowers were gone and the trees were bare. We had often seen the sharp spire of Christ Church rising above the havened shipping at the docks and wharves near Charlestown Navy Yard, and had recalled the historic lanterns that once shone as a signal in its high window, and inspired the intrepid rider. The old chimes were ringing as we passed up Salem Street, filling the mellow air with the sweet music of "Antioch."

A great change has passed over this part of the city of Boston since those same chimes rung out in colonial days. Excepting Christ Church and Copp's Hill Burying-ground, little remains to remind the visitor that this was once the place of residence of the best English families. Salem Street is full of tenement-houses, and the streets that intersect this once fine thoroughfare swarm with the children of a foreign population, representing half a dozen nationalities. The air, though cleared on Sunday, is usually smoky from mechanical workshops, and hardly a house remains that would indicate any association of the locality with the best days of the New England colonies.

The church is a plain structure. Except in the music of

its chimes, which is particularly joyous on Sabbath mornings and on Christmas Day and at Easter, there is nothing about it to arrest the step of the stranger. But the interior is quaint and remarkable. One seems to pass in a moment from the busy scenes of one generation to the stately and quiet habitudes of another as he puts behind him the door.

CHRIST CHURCH.

A choir of children, composed of about an equal number of boys and girls, was singing in the orchestra, accompanied by the organ, as we entered. In front of the orchestra, to which our eye was first directed, stand four wooden angels with trumpets, carved after some antique pattern, and highly painted. They were taken by a privateer from a captured vessel bound for Spain, and so found their way to a Protestant church, instead of a Catholic cathedral. The odd chandeliers, to which our eye was next turned, have a similar history.

The pews are straight, stately, and old, and the old pulpit is furnished with a Bible and Prayer-Book, the gift of George II. The communion service was the gift of the same king, as that of King's Chapel was the endowment of William and Mary.

The chancel looks more like a faded picture than anything in American decorative art, though the old-time chancel window has been closed. Near it stands the first monument and bust of Washington ever made in this country.

The church has its memorial inscriptions, and, like most churches of colonial date, its tombs. The remains of Major Pitcairn were interred under this church, and are still supposed to be there by certain antiquaries, notwithstanding the record on the monument in Westminster Abbey. It is said that the body of Lieutenant Shea, who was also interred under this church, was forwarded to England as that of Pitcairn, by mistake, the sexton at the time of the removal not being able to identify the remains. It was afterward remembered that Shea had worn a plaster on his head, which was the case of the body sent over the sea.

The steeple of Christ Church bears the date of 1723. It is the oldest church in Boston standing on its original ground, and was erected six years before the Old South. Except King's Chapel, it is the only house of worship that remains for the most part unaltered since colonial days. Brattle Street Church has been taken down, and the congregations accustomed to worship there erected a new and costly church on the Back Bay, which has lately been sold. King's Chapel has lost much of its old-time expression in the retouches of decorative art. But the removal of business and wealth to the southern portion of the city has proved the protection of this venerable Episcopal edifice, on the same principle that cathedrals and abbeys best preserve their ancient features in ruinous and decaying towns.

At the close of the service, which was after the most simple Episcopal form, we ascended the old tower to the steeple. The church stands on rising ground overlooking the harbor,

and the tower and steeple, which are one hundred and seventy-five feet high, command an extensive view of the city and adjoining towns. It was from this steeple that General Gage witnessed the battle of Bunker Hill and the burning of Charlestown.

The view from the steeple is rich with subjects for historical study. Immediately below and only a few steps from the church is Copp's Hill Burying-ground, where lie the remains of Cotton, Increase, and Samuel Mather, of ecclesiastical fame. The willow that bends over their tomb was cut from a tree which shaded the grave of Napoleon at St. Helena. Here also repose the relics of some of the most respectable colonial families: the Huguenot Sigourneys, Edmund Hatt, the builder of the Constitution, the Mountfort family, claiming descent from the Norman conquest. It was from Copp's Hill that Burgoyne and Clinton directed the fire of the battery which set fire to Charlestown at the battle of Bunker Hill.

The harbor lies below with the navy-yard spired with ships. Beyond flows the Mystic through wooded hills and past steepled towns. Across the long bridge is Bunker Hill Monument. On one hand stretches the city as far as the eye can see; on the other the inlets to the bay with the continuous dotting of fortifications and islands.

The bells themselves have an historical interest. They were cast in England, and were hung in 1744. They have an aggregate weight of seven thousand two hundred and twenty-two pounds. All of them have inscriptions. On the first two is some account of the church's early history. On the third is the following : —

"We are the first ring of bells cast for the British Empire in North America, A. R. 1744."

On the fourth : —

"God preserve the Church of England."

On the seventh this quiet humor: —

"Since generosity has opened our mouths, our tongues shall ring aloud its praise."

These chimes have pealed in sunshine and storm for more than one hundred and thirty years.

> "Low at times and loud at times,
> And changing like a poet's rhymes,
> Rung the beautiful wild chimes."

They were at first an unwelcome sound in the colonies, for the chimes of motherland had small charms for the practical Puritan ear. They rang through the palmy days of the English Georges: they were revolutionary tones, and they have rung through all the republic's years of prosperity and peace. Boston has stretched her limits far beyond their sound. But no new chime rings out so melodiously, and it is well worth a stranger's walk from the Common on a Christmas morning to hear the full, joyous, inspiring tones of Christ Church bells.

We have spoken of the First Church, the Old South Church, and the Old North Church, all of which are associated with interesting historic events. We should add to the list Arlington Street Church, which is the successor of the first Presbyterian Church gathered in Boston. It was founded in 1727, and was called Federal Street Church after the Revolution. It was in the second house of worship, erected in 1744, that the convention met that ratified the Constitution of the United States. It became a Unitarian church and changed its location to Arlington Street. It is one of the most beautiful churches of the city.

"HAIL to the morn, when first they stood
    On Bunker's height,
And, fearless, stemmed the invading flood,
And wrote our dearest rights in blood,
And mowed in ranks the hireling brood,
    In desperate fight!
Oh, 'twas a proud, exulting day,
For even our fallen fortunes lay
    In light."

                      PERCIVAL.

CHAPTER XIII.

BUNKER HILL.

THERE was to be war.

After the shattered British regiments came running back from Concord the whole country became aware that war was at hand; that the thirteen colonies must unite in it, and that the issue was doubtful.

The British army in Boston was soon reinforced. Howe, Clinton, and Burgoyne were the commanders. The farmer-soldiers were on the alert, building rude fortifications at places more or less remote from the town, which was gradually being placed in the condition of siege. On the 15th of June the Committee of Public Safety voted to fortify Bunker Hill.

The work was begun at once, — on the evening of the following day. Fourteen hundred infantry troops and a company of artillery were ordered to parade on Cambridge Common at six o'clock on the evening of the 16th; twelve hundred met at the time appointed; they listened to a fervent prayer from the President of Harvard College, and then marched to Charlestown, under General Prescott.

They carried, besides arms, shovels and dark-lanterns.

They marched in silence.

They were ordered to erect earthworks first on Breed's Hill. About midnight the work began under the dim light of the stars.

The workmen were so near the enemy, and the night was so still, that they could hear the sentinel's cry, "All's well," in the sleeping town across the river. By early morning they had raised intrenchments six feet high.

And now the light slowly brightened in the east, and the soldiers began to bestir themselves in the town.

There was a man-of-war lying in the stream, named the Lively.

When the captain of the Lively came upon deck and scanned the pleasant green shore he was greatly astonished at the sight which met his eyes.

"What are the Yankees doing on the hill?" he must have asked excitedly.

"They *have* built a breastwork," some one undoubtedly answered.

When he was certain that this was the case he did not wait for orders as to what to do.

He at once gave the command, —

"Fire!"

The sound of the guns from the man-of-war threw the town into great alarm. The British hurried to the shore and saw a fortification menacing them across the narrow stream.

The red-coats were at once put in motion. Firing on the new earthworks began from Copp's Hill.

The British held a council of war immediately. It was decided that an attack must be made on the new earthworks as soon as the troops could be set across the stream.

It was a hot morning, but the tired Americans continued their work with the shovels, and at noon, as they saw the preparations of the enemy to cross the stream, they knew that more dangerous implements must shortly be used. They were reinforced, about two o'clock, from the main army which was at Cambridge.

At three o'clock General Howe, at the head of three thousand men, was ready for the attack. His troops came gayly marching up the hill.

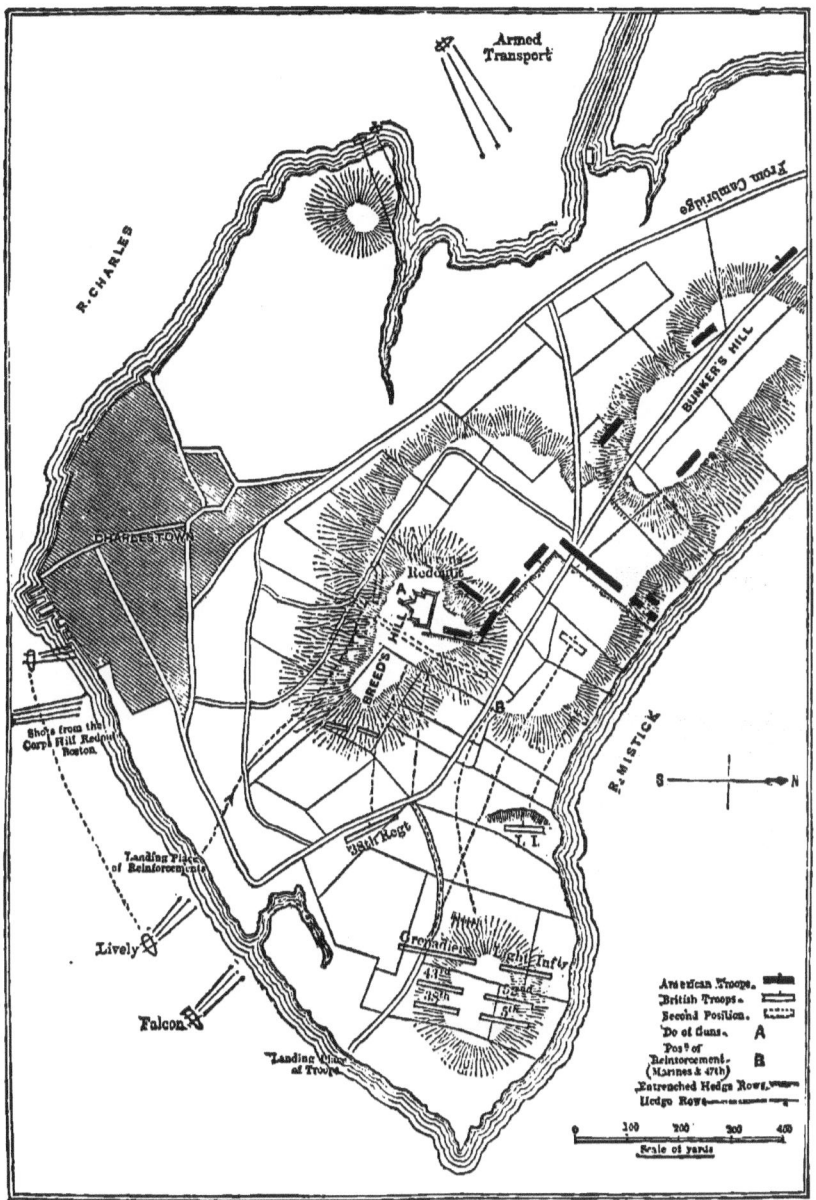

PLAN OF THE BATTLE OF BUNKER HILL.

The colonial troops were short of ammunition. They were, however, well officered. General Putnam was there; General Warren; the brave General Stark.

"Aim low," was the order given, "and do not fire until you see the whites of the enemies' eyes."

The required distance was at last reached by the enemy. The provincials fired with awful effect. The red-coats reeled back in confusion.

The provincials shouted, and thought the battle already won.

General Howe rallied his forces, and again the men faced the levelled muskets.

The scene now became fearful indeed. Charlestown had been set on fire in two places, and whole streets were in flames. The cannon on Copp's Hill in Boston were throwing their heavy iron balls across the river, and the guns of the ships-of-war were as active in the stream.

Amid the roar and smoke the British army advanced, with less confidence than before. Again came a raking fire from the provincials; nothing could stand before it, every bullet seemed to meet its mark. The enemy reeled back again, filled with terror, leaving on the hillside the bodies of the slain.

The British officers swore. They even pricked their men with their swords. They knew not what to do.

General Clinton crossed over from Boston, bringing reinforcements. General Howe resolved to change his plan of attack.

Now there was terror in the provincial ranks, not on account of any lack of bravery, but because the ammunition was nearly spent.

"Do not fire a musket until the British are within twenty yards," said General Prescott.

At that distance the provincials poured a deadly volley

into the ranks of the enemy; the latter wavered, but only for a moment. The Red-coats came rushing forward again; the ammunition of the Provincials was gone; the battle was lost.

The Provincials retreated under the enemy's fire; at this point the brave Warren fell. The survivors returned to Cambridge, and the British held the hill.

Night came, and the shadows fell on homes filled with anxiety, on the wounded in their sufferings, and on the dead whom the green earth was soon to cover. There was small joy in the Province House that night, for victory had cost the British too great a flow of blood. There was despondency and distress in Cambridge. The Provincials, after the work of the day, there slept their troubled sleep. Merciful night! It was the saddest that Boston ever had known, or has ever unto this time seen, — that night of the 17th of June.

The Americans had one hundred and fifteen killed and three hundred wounded. The British more than two hundred killed, and more than eight hundred wounded. Such was the British *victory* at Bunker Hill.

THE BATTLE OF BUNKER HILL.

"Though ages long have passed
    Since our fathers left their home,
  Their pilot in the blast,
    O'er untravelled seas to roam, —
Yet lives the blood of England in our veins!
  And shall we not proclaim
  That blood of honest fame,
  Which no tyranny can tame
    By its chains?

"While the language, free and bold,
    Which the bard of Avon sung,
  In which our Milton told
    How the vault of heaven rung,
When Satan, blasted, fell with his host;
  While this, with reverence meet,
  Ten thousand echoes greet,
  From rock to rock repeat,
    Round our coast;

"While the manners, while the arts,
    That mould a nation's soul,
  Still cling around our hearts,
    Between let ocean roll,
Our joint communion breaking with the sun:
  Yet, still, from either beach,
  The voice of blood shall reach,
  More audible than speech, —
    'We are One!'"

                    WASHINGTON ALLSTON.

CHAPTER XIV.

THE SIEGE OF BOSTON.

THE whole country was now alarmed.

A congress of the colonies was held at Philadelphia; it resolved to raise an army of twenty thousand men, and George Washington was appointed commander-in-chief.

On the 2d of June Washington arrived at Watertown, and was welcomed by the Committee of Public Safety. On the following morning he rode in a phaeton drawn by two horses to Cambridge.

His arrival at Cambridge is thus described in a private letter written at the time: —

"Just before the chief came into town," says the writer, "the soldiers stationed here in Cambridge were drawn up in a straight line on the Common. It was a very quaint sight to behold some seven or eight thousand militia vieing with each other in the want of waistcoats and of shoes and stockings. As you must imagine, there is a chance here for tailors and cobblers.

"The line extended from the elm-tree opposite Deacon Moore's house" [the present site of the Shepard Church], "which you must not have forgotten, on account of the crow's nest, directly eastward. . . . Since the fight in Charlestown, the men look more timid than formerly, and some, indeed, are quite out of courage. The officers exercise small control over the soldiery, and the want of discipline is very plain to perceive. . . .

"Towards mid-day the chief, riding in a carriage pulled by two horses, and escorted by some of the Safety Committee, came in sight. The road was crowded with bystanders, and the ovation which Washington received must have been gratifying to him.

"As he rode along, he never so much as looked to the

THE WASHINGTON ELM.

right or to the left, but kept his head erect, his eyes forward, with a demeanor somewhat grave and lofty. In no whit did he manifest a familiar air, which conduct some people mistook for haughtiness, which I do not admit.

"Having advanced near by, the chief mounted a horse, received his sword, — it may have been his own, — and rode up and down the line, followed by the under officers. There

Bunker Hill.　Charlestown.　Breed's Hill.

VIEW FROM BEACON HILL, BOSTON.

was the greatest eagerness to see him and to hear the reading of the commission. Washington, by his looks, appeared to esteem the army."

Washington took command of the army under the Old Elm on Cambridge Green. It was a king among trees then, full of foliage in the glowing midsummer weather. It stands on crutches by the wayside to-day, a monarch discrowned, but beautiful in age. No one knows how many winters have whitened it, and how many summers have clothed it with green. Beneath its propped-up boughs is a granite tablet that reads, —

UNDER THIS TREE
WASHINGTON
FIRST TOOK COMMAND
OF THE
AMERICAN ARMY,
JULY 3, 1775.

Washington's headquarters were at first in the old buff-colored, gambrel-roofed house which may still be seen just east of the Common. In this house Oliver Wendell Holmes was born, and here he wrote "Old Ironsides." Washington's permanent headquarters was the house now occupied by Henry W. Longfellow, a short distance from Harvard Square.

After the battle of Bunker Hill, General Putnam fortified Prospect Hill, and covered the town of Cambridge from an advance by the enemy. Works had been thrown up on Winter Hill; these were strengthened. All the roads leading out of Boston were seized and guarded. The British took possession of Dorchester Heights, and strengthened their position on Bunker Hill.

Quiet reigned in the hostile camps. But Boston was invested by the Provincials.

July passed with little action in the field by either army.

In August a reinforcement of fourteen hundred riflemen, chiefly backwoodsmen of the Shenandoah Valley, arrived in the American camp. In September Washington received about three tons of gunpowder from Rhode Island.

Winter came, a severe one to the Provincials, a terrible one to the British in the invested city. Food there became

THE HOLMES HOUSE.

scarce and dear; luxuries there were none; complaining was everywhere heard. To make the supplies last as long as possible General Howe sent seven hundred of the poorest inhabitants out of the town. To provide fuel he caused houses to be demolished.

Washington, knowing the distress within the town, now began to plan an assault upon it. It was decided at a council

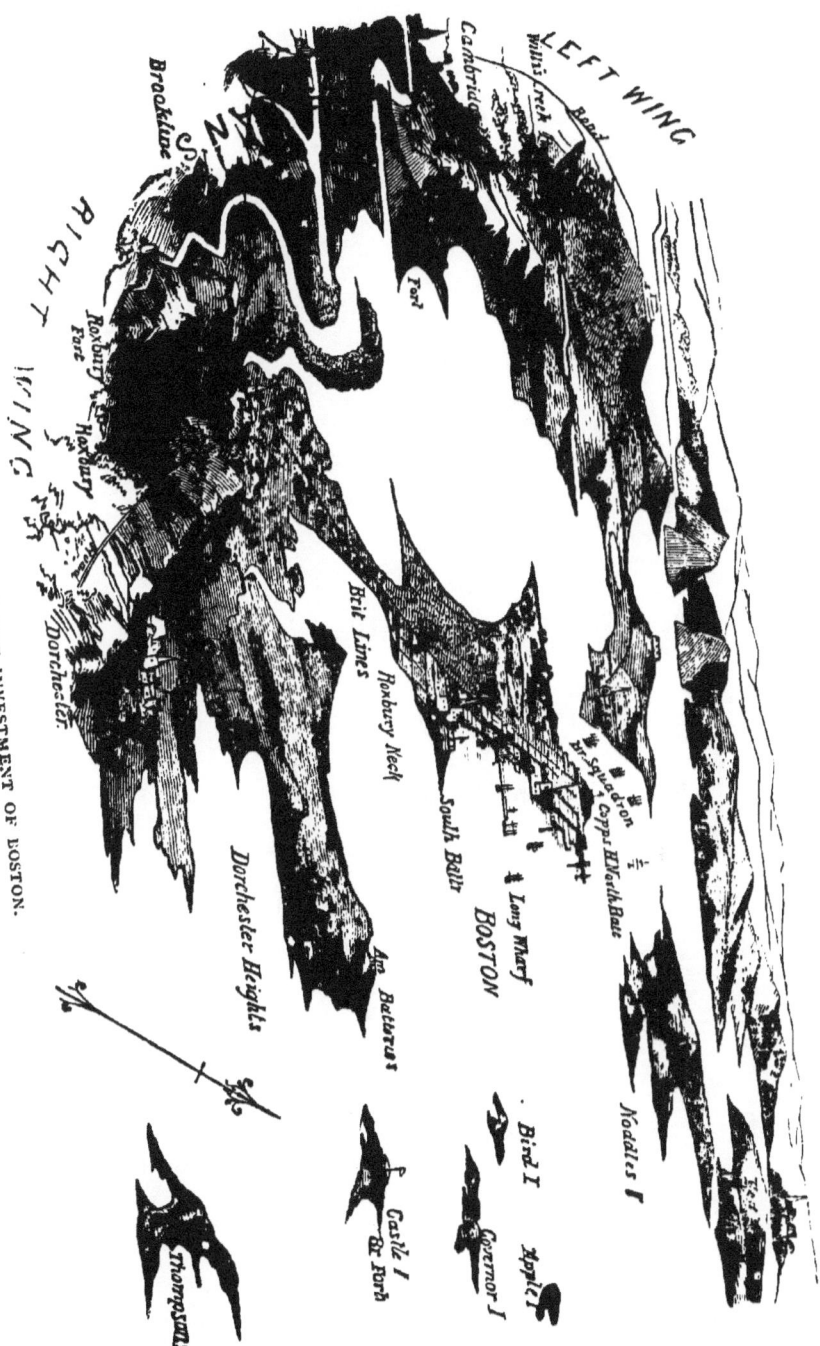

PLAN OF THE INVESTMENT OF BOSTON.

of war to make an attempt to seize Dorchester Heights, and thus to bring the enemy directly under the American guns.

The first thing to be done was to deceive the British in regard to the point it was intended to attack. With this object, Washington ordered his troops to bombard the town from various hills on the west. This attack began on March 2. It continued for three nights, and the British were completely deceived by it, and the Heights were left unprotected.

While they were watching the bombardment in the west, preparations were rapidly made in the south to advance upon the Heights.

On the night of the 4th of March, a strong detachment, under General Thomas, set out from Roxbury. It was a hazy but not very cold winter's night. There was little or no snow on the ground, which was, however, frozen hard.

First went eight hundred picked patriots, who acted as a covering party. Following these were carts with intrenching tools, such as pickaxes and spades; then came twelve hundred men, as a working party, to throw up breastworks; then rumbled along two hundred carts, with fascines (fagots for building ramparts) and bundles of hay.

They moved very silently and cautiously; meanwhile they could hear the roar of the cannon in the west, where the bombardment to distract the attention of the British was going forward. At last they ascended the Heights, creeping up its sides. The carts were arranged in convenient spots, and the working party took their tools, while the others kept guard at various points on the hill. Then a scene similar to that on Bunker Hill took place. The task was yet more difficult, for it was winter, and the ground was hard.

The men worked diligently, plying their tools, and piling up the hay and fagots, until a long, broad breastwork gradually rose on the crest of the Heights.

With the early dawn of morning, the British in Boston saw, with amazement and dismay, what had been done in the night. There was a sort of fog, which made the breastworks seem even greater and more formidable than they really were.

All the hills around were soon covered with spectators. General Howe at once saw the great advantage which the possession of Dorchester Heights gave to the patriots. From them, Washington's guns and mortars commanded the town, and might besiege it with far better prospects of success.

The British General decided to lose no time in trying to re-take the Heights. He chose two thousand of his best troops, and embarked them on vessels, with the object of landing them below the fortified eminence.

No sooner had they got on board, however, than a great tempest of wind and furious rain arose. The ships were driven into port again, amid much danger of being lost. Thus the patriot cause was served by the elements, just as it was years after at Yorktown, where another storm prevented the escape of Cornwallis and his army.

There was now but one thing for the British to do, and that was to abandon Boston. General Howe was afraid that an assault would be made before he could get his troops away; so he sent a message to Washington, threatening to

PINE-TREE FLAG.

WASHINGTON'S TREASURE-CHEST.

burn the town if such an assault was made. Meanwhile the patriots went on strengthening and extending their works on and around Dorchester Heights; and on the morning of March 17, Howe was more than ever alarmed to see that breastworks had been raised over night on Nook's Hill, a place completely commanding the Neck and the southern end of Boston.

He at once called a council of war, in which it was resolved to evacuate Boston without delay. The British soldiers set to plundering the linen and woollen shops. They hastily spiked their cannons and mortars, which they could not carry away with them, and demolished Castle William.

The ships in the port were made ready for departure. All through the night of the 17th the good people of Boston saw strange movements going on. Troops were marching silently through the streets toward the wharves. On the wharves all was hurry and bustle.

Besides the soldiers, very many citizens and their families were busily preparing to embark. These were the "Tories," — those who took the part of the British in the war, and who feared to remain behind among the indignant patriots.

It was still dark — not quite four o'clock in the morning — when the signal was given for the ships to move away from the docks; and slowly and mournfully this fleet, laden with Red-coats, rode out of Boston harbor, to enter it no more.

When the morning light came the citizens who crowded the streets, with joyful faces, found their beloved town freed from the soldiers of King George.

Already Washington had learned what was going forward, and the rear-guard of Howe had scarcely set foot on board ship before the patriot advance-guard, with the general-in-chief at its head, marched into the town, amid shouts and cheers of eager welcome.

The capture of Boston was hailed throughout the colonies with much rejoicing. Congress thanked Washington, and ordered a medal to be struck in honor of the event. The Massachusetts Legislature passed an address to the commander, in which it was said, " May you still go on, approved by Heaven, revered by all good men, and dreaded by those tyrants who claim their fellow-men as their property."

THE SAD KING.

We are accustomed to find the name of George III. associated with the word " tyrant" in the early history of our country. When the writer was a boy he was taught that King George was a very bad man, and he looked upon him as a Henry VIII. or James II.

The king made many stupid political mistakes, or left his ministry to make them; but in his private life George III., a name in the days of our fathers always spoken with hate, was one of the purest, kindest, and the best of English kings.

His was a sad life, with all of its power and splendor.

Let me tell you some stories of it, and you will regret that so good and so sorely afflicted a king should have been led to treat his American colonies with injustice.

The discipline of insanity has refined many rough natures and quickened many cold hearts that otherwise might have passed as misanthropes in the world. Among these may fairly be classed George III. " Few princes," says Lord Brougham, " have been more exemplary in their domestic habits or in the offices of private friendship. But the instant his prerogative was concerned, or his bigotry interfered with, or his will thwarted, the most bitter animosity, the most calculating coldness of heart, took possession of his breast and swayed it by turns." This disposition made him unpopular at times, and but for a correcting providence — the chastisement of his constantly threatening affliction — might have lost him his throne. His frequent mental distresses made him humble, and kept his heart open to the unfortunate and the poor. Like Lear, he could look upon the meanest of his subjects and say, —

"Expose thyself to feel what wretches feel."

The king was first attacked by insanity in 1765, when he was twenty-seven years old. It was in the spring-time. As is usual with the first manifestations of disease of this kind, when constitutional, he soon recovered.

In the latter part of the autumn of 1788 the king appeared to be nervous and restless, unsettled in mind and apprehensive. He had often been low-spirited in recent years, which had been attributed to the loss of his American colonies. Returning from a long ride one bright October day, he hurried by, entered his apartment with an anxious, distressed look upon his face, and, flinging himself into a chair, burst into tears, exclaiming, " I am going to be mad, and I wish to God I might die ! "

The sufferings of the king during the first apprehensive days of his malady were painful to witness, and his conduct was most humiliating for the monarch of a realm whose empire followed the sun. " He awoke," says one of Sheridan's correspondents on one occasion, " with all the gestures and ravings of a confirmed maniac, and a new noise in imitation of the howling of a dog." He seemed tempted with suicidal thoughts, and required constant watchfulness and restraint. " This morning," says one, " he made an attempt to jump out of the window, and is now very turbulent and incoherent."

The king grew worse during the last days of fall. On the 29th of November he was removed to Kew, where he was to experience almost unspeakable horrors. Here he grew worse, his disease became settled, and the sad particulars of his conduct during the dreary months of December and January have, perhaps with commendable prudence, been withheld from the public eye.

Distressing indeed must have been the spectacle presented by the English monarch at this period of his incapacity; how distressing a single anecdote will show. During his convalescence some friends of the royal household were passing through the palace accompanied by an equerry, when they observed a strait-jacket lying in a chair. The equerry averted his look as a mark of respect for the king. The latter, who had joined the company present, observed the movement and said, —

"You need not be afraid to look at it. Perhaps it is the best friend I ever had in my life."

The recovery of the king from his second attack thrilled the nation with joy and awakened a spirit of loyalty from sea to sea. London, on the night following the day on which the king resumed his functions, was a blaze of light from the palaces of the West End to the humblest huts in the suburbs. But the great illumination was a rising splendor, which only had its beginning here; it flashed like a spontaneous joy over all the cities of the realm. Gala days followed gala days, the nights were festive; the release of the king from his mental bondage seemed to lighten all hearts. On the 23d of April the royal family went to the old cathedral of St. Paul's in solemn state to return thanks to God. It was an imposing procession. The bells rung out, the boom of the cannon echoed through the mellowing air, and light strains of music rose on every hand. As the king entered the cathedral between the bishops of London and Lincoln, the voices of five thousand children burst forth in grand chorus, "God save the king!"

GEORGE III.

At the sound of the jubilant strain, the king's emotions overcame him. He covered his face and wept.

"I do now feel that I have been ill," he said to the Bishop of London, as soon as he could restrain his tears.

The joy of the nation was sincere. As delightful to the king must have been the days that followed, when he set forth with the queen and a part of the royal family for a long tour to the west of England. The roads were lined with people and spanned with arches of flowers; girls crowned with wreaths strewed flowers in the streets of the villages through which he passed; bells were rung, the bands were out, all was festivity from London to Weymouth. Wide must have been the contrast between this new freedom and good Dr. Willis's strait-jacket.

Weymouth at this time possessed rare charms for the king. Unvexed by ministerial disputes and the cares of state, free from the last shadow of the clouds that had darkened his mind, with a humble heart, feeling that he was after all but a dependent man among weak and dependent men, he joined the peasants in their sports, he caressed their children, he gave pious advice to old women and wholesome counsel to ambitious lads and buxom lassies; he wandered through the hay-fields with the mowers, and was rocked by the common sailors on the foamy waters of Portland Roads. His intercourse with the peasantry at this period gave him a popularity that he never outlived.

The familiarity of notable monarchs with their poorer and meaner subjects has ever been an engaging theme with the historian and the poet. Thus we have the child-charming stories of Henry VIII. and the miller of Dee; of King John and the abbot; of Edward IV. and the tanner; of Philip of Burgundy and the tinker, which, with some shifting of scenes, is told in the Induction to Shakespeare's Taming of the Shrew. About few monarchs have so many pleasing anecbotes of this kind been related as about George III. This humility was a result of his great afflictions, and a most fortunate one for his popularity, since in the eyes of the people his charity covered a multitude of political errors.

After the first beating of the storm of affliction upon his own head, he had a sensitiveness that would never allow him to witness a scene of suffering without emotion, however humble might be the condition of the sufferer. A volume of anecdotes might be collected to illustrate this gentleness of character when want or woe was presented directly before him. He was walking one day, during the hard winter of 1785, unbending his mind from the cares of state, when he chanced to meet two little boys, who, not knowing whom they were addressing, fell upon their knees in the snow, and, wringing their hands, said, —

"Help us! We are hungry; we have nothing to eat."

Their pinched faces were wet with tears.

"Get up," said the king. "Where do you live?"

"Our mother is dead, and our father lies sick, and we have no money, food, or fire."

"Go home," said the king, "and I will follow you."

They at last reached a wretched hovel, where the king found the mother dead, having perished for the want of the necessities of life, and the wretched father ready to perish, but still encircling with his bony arm the deceased partner of his woes. The king's eye moistened, and he hurried back to the Queen's Lodge and related to the queen what he had seen. He not only immediately relieved the present necessities of the family, but gave orders that the boys should be supported and educated from the royal bounty.

George III. was fond of children. All crazy people are, in their better moods. Walking one day near Windsor, he met a stable-boy, and asked, —

"Well, boy, what do you do, and what do they pay you?"

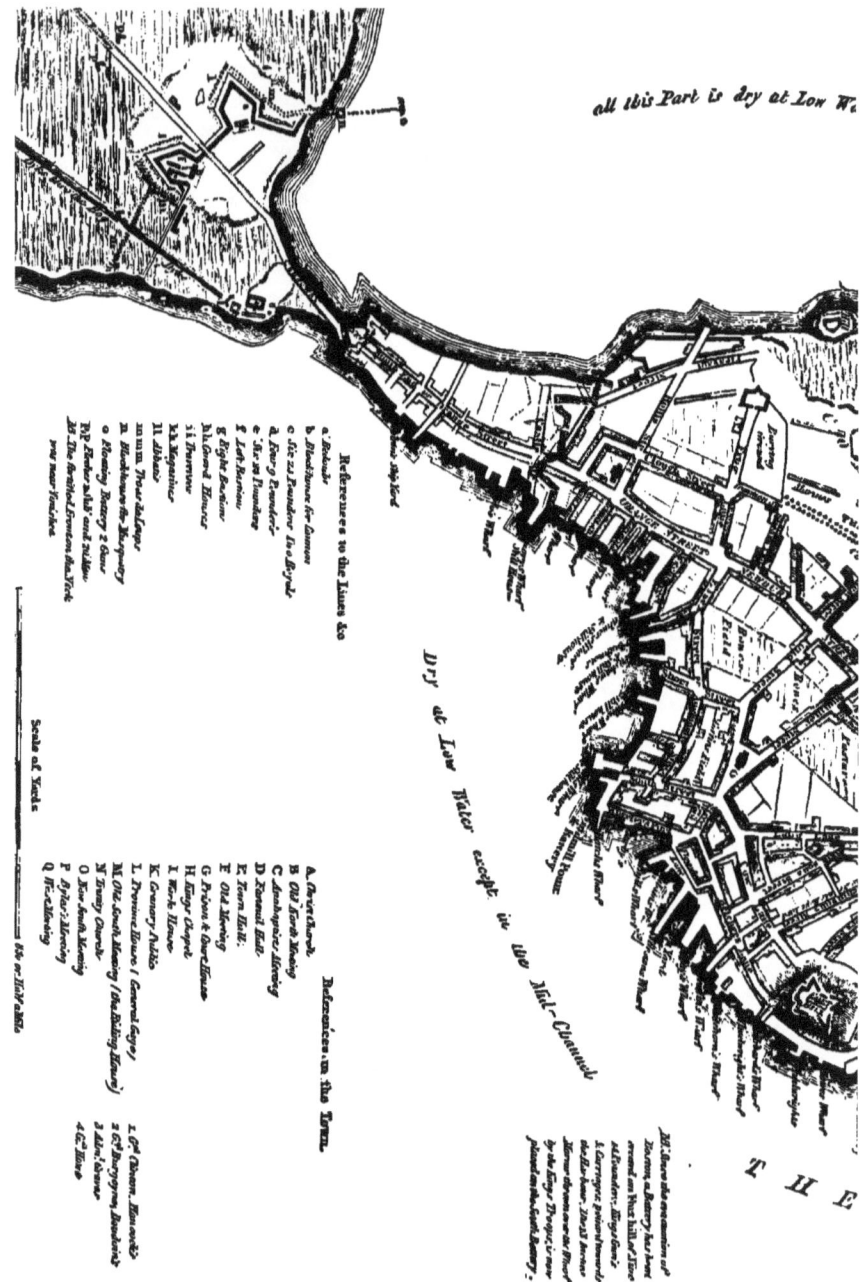

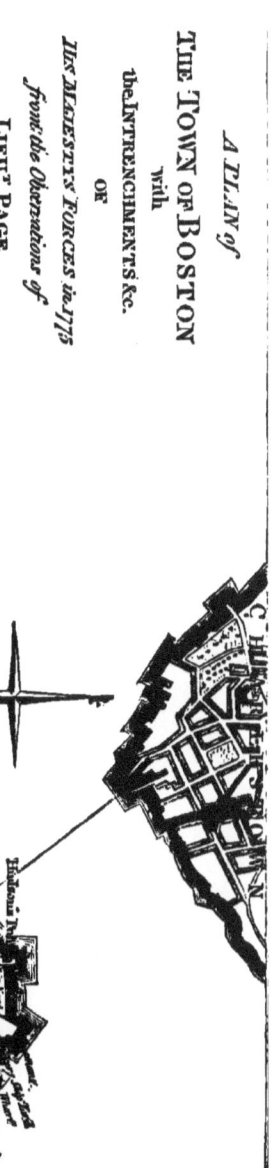

A PLAN of THE TOWN of BOSTON with the INTRENCHMENTS &c.
OF
HIS MAJESTY'S FORCES in 1775
from the Observations of
LIEU.T PAGE
of His MAJESTY'S Corps of Engineers;
and from the Plans of other GENTLEMEN.

Engraved & Printed for W.m FADEN, Charing Cross, as the Residence of Oct.r 1777.

"I help in the stable, sir; but they only give me my victuals and clothes."

"Be content," said the king, in a philosophical mood: "*I* can have nothing more."

He was accustomed to refer to "the loss of *my* American colonies" with sadness, but we do not know that he ever condemned the policy of his advisers, Lord Bute, the Earl of Granville, and Lord North.

The king surpassed all other monarchs in the whimsical play of "good Haroun Alraschid." He loved nothing better than to meet his poorer and meaner subjects incognito, and learn their good opinion of him. He once played the part of Saxon Alfred as well as that of the Persian caliph, and turned a piece of meat in a cottage. When the old woman returned, what was her delight at finding a royal note, with an inclosure. It ran, "Five guineas to buy a jack."

Among the statesmen of his reign favorable to the American cause were Fox, Pitt, and Burke. The Earl of Chatham was a friend to America until France espoused the cause of the colonies. He fell dead while speaking on the American question.

Age as well as trouble at last battered the strong form of the king, and his life became more Lear-like as the twilight shadows began to fall. His sympathies seemed to take a wider range, and his charity to gather new sweetness, as the evening of age came on. In 1786 a poor insane woman, named Margaret Nicholson, attempted to assassinate him as he was in the act of stepping from his carriage. The king, on finding that she was insane, remembered his own frailty, spoke of her with great pity, and tried to disarm the popular prejudice against her. In 1790 John Frith, an insane man, attempted the king's life, and another lunatic shot at him in 1800, for each of whom the king was moved to extreme pity when he understood the nature of their malady.

George III. had fifteen children. His favorite was the Princess Amelia. In her early days she was a gay, light-hearted girl; but as she grew older she became affectionate and reflective, yielding to the deeper sentiments of her emotional nature, and making herself the companion of the king in his decline. She once told her experience in life in two fair stanzas, that have been preserved: —

> "Unthinking, idle, wild, and young,
> I laughed and danced and talked and sung,
> And, proud of health, of freedom vain,
> Dreamed not of sorrow, care, or pain,
> Concluding, in those hours of glee,
> That all the world was made for me.

> "But when the hour of trial came,
> When sickness shook this trembling frame,
> When folly's gay pursuits were o'er,
> And I could sing and dance no more,
> It then occurred how sad 't would be
> Were *this* world only made for me."

In 1810 she was attacked with a lingering and fatal illness. Her sufferings at times were heart-rending to witness, but her sublime confidence in God kept her mind serene, and brought the sweetest anticipations of another and a better world.

The old king lingered by her bedside, her affectionate watcher and nurse. They talked together daily of Christ, of redemption, and of the joys of heaven. "The only hope of the sinner is in the blood and righteousness of Jesus Christ. Do you feel this hope, my daughter? Does it sustain you?"

"Nothing," says an English clergyman who witnessed these interviews, "can be more striking than the sight of the king, aged and nearly blind, bending over the couch on which the princess lies, and speaking to her of salvation through Christ as a matter far more interesting than the most magnificent pomps of royalty."

As she grew weaker, he caused the physicians to make a statement of her condition every hour. When he found her sinking, the old dejection and gloom began to overcast his mind again. He felt, like Lear, that he had one true heart to love him for himself alone. This love was more precious to him than crowns and thrones. The world offered nothing to him so sweet as her affection. She was his Cordelia. One gloomy day a messenger came to the king's room to announce that Amelia had breathed her last. It was too much for the king: reason began to waver and soon took its flight. "This was caused by poor Amelia," he was heard saying, as the shadows deepened and the dreary winter of age came stealing on.

"Thou 'lt come no more,
Never, never, never, never, never!"

This was in 1810. The remaining ten years of his life were passed, with the exception of few brief intervals, in the long night of mindlessness, and the last eight years were still more deeply shadowed by the loss of sight. In May, 1811, he appeared once outside of the castle of Windsor, and henceforth the people saw him no more. Thackeray represents him as withdrawn from all eyes but those that watched his necessities, in silence and in darkness, crownless, throneless, sceptreless; there was for him neither sun, moon, nor stars, empire, wife, nor child. The seasons came and went, — the springtime lighted up the hills and autumn withered the leaves, the summer sunshine dreamed in the flowers and the snows of winter fell; battles were fought; Waterloo changed the front of the political world; Napoleon fell; the nation was filled with festive rejoicings over the battles of Vittoria, the Pyrenees, and Toulouse, but he was oblivious of all. His sister died, his beloved queen died, his son, the Duke of Kent, died, — but he knew it not. He was often confined in a padded room; his beard grew long; he seemed like a full personification of the character of Lear. Once he was heard repeating to himself the sad lines of Samson Agonistes, —

> "Oh, dark, dark, dark! Amid the blaze of noon,
>   Irrecoverably dark! Total eclipse,
>   Without all hope of day!"

Some incidents of this period are very touching. One day, while his attendants were leading him along one of the passages of the castle, he heard some one draw quickly aside. "Who is there?" asked the king.

He was answered in a well-known voice.

"I am now blind," said the king.

"I am very sorry, please your Majesty."

"But," continued the king, "I am quite resigned; for what have we to do in this world but to suffer as well as to perform the will of the Almighty?"

Music seemed to collect his thoughts and soothe his feelings, and the piano and harpsichord were his favorite instruments. In 1811 he, for the last time, made the selection of pieces for a grand sacred concert. It comprised Handel's famous passages descriptive of madness and blindness, the lamentation of Jephthah on the loss of his daughter, and the list ended with "God save the King." The performance of the last moistened all eyes, after what had gone before.

Thus passed the last ten years of the monarch's life, in a gradual decline, amid an obscurity lighted by occasional gleams of reason and always full of the keenest pathos; until, in 1820, the great bell of St. Paul's announced his final release.

The popularity of George III. in England was largely due

to his humble piety, and to his familiarity with his poorer and meaner subjects. Each of these characteristics was the result, in a measure, of his mental misfortunes. It was because the king never dared to forget that he was a man, that the people always loved to remember that he was a king.

"The torch of freedom God has lit
Burns upward for the Infinite,
And through all hindrances it will
And must and shall burn upward still;
And all whose hands would hold the torch
Inverted, must to ashes scorch;
And they who stay its heavenward aim
Shall shrivel, like the fly, in flame!"

GERALD MASSEY.

CHAPTER XV.

THE STORY OF HOLLIS STREET MEETING-HOUSE AND CURIOUS OLD MATHER BYLES, THE ROYALIST.

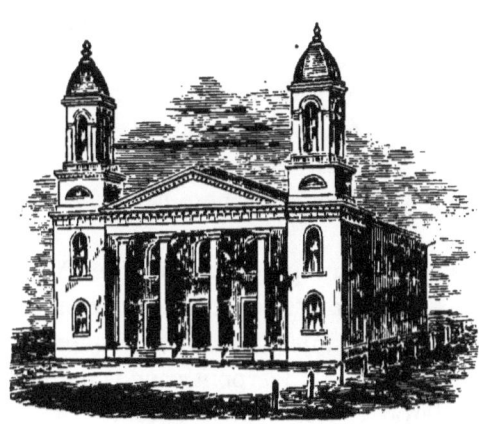

THE OLD HOLLIS STREET CHURCH.

You may see the tall spire of the new Hollis Street Church from almost any point of the city. The Stars and Stripes used to wave from it in the days of the war.

This church is as a monument to several men in Boston's history. Here John Pierpont fought his grand battle for temperance against the wealthy members of his society who stored their wine-casks even in the church's cellar. Here Starr King poured forth his fiery eloquence, — a man who had the heart of hearts, and whom Whittier in his sonnet to him well says was beloved as few men ever were, and for whom Mt. Starr King is an eternal memorial.

Most people are familiar with one or more of Pierpont's poems, and have seen them, if nowhere else, in that wonderful patron of poetic fame, — the reading-book. We seldom see Hollis Street Church spire without recalling a poem of this writer, which seems to have come to him like an inspiration. He became pastor of the church in 1819. Our own country was just entering upon an era of peace and prosperity, and all eyes were turned to the political events of Europe, where the throne of Napoleon had lately fallen. The military pageant of France was being withdrawn from the eyes of the world, and the nations were fast undoing all Napoleon had done. The Emperor himself died, and was buried at St. Helena amid the solitudes of the sea, where he had passed his last unquiet years.

Pierpont's heart was in human progress, and the fall of Napoleon seemed to him an impressive commentary on the instability of military glory. Many poets were inspired to take a text from Napoleon's fall, but Pierpont caught the true spirit of the event, as Byron did of Waterloo, and there is hardly anything in the language more fine than his lines entitled —

NAPOLEON AT REST.

His falchion flashed along the Nile;
　His hosts he led through Alpine snows;
O'er Moscow's towers, that blazed the while,
　His eagle flag unrolled, — and froze.

Here sleeps he now, alone! Not one
　Of all the kings whose crowns he gave
Bends o'er his dust; — nor wife nor son
　Has ever seen or sought his grave.

Behind this sea-girt rock, the star
　That led him on from crown to crown
Has sunk; and nations from afar
　Gazed as it faded and went down.

High is his couch; the ocean flood,
　Far, far below, by storms is curled;
As round him heaved, while high he stood,
　A stormy and unstable world.

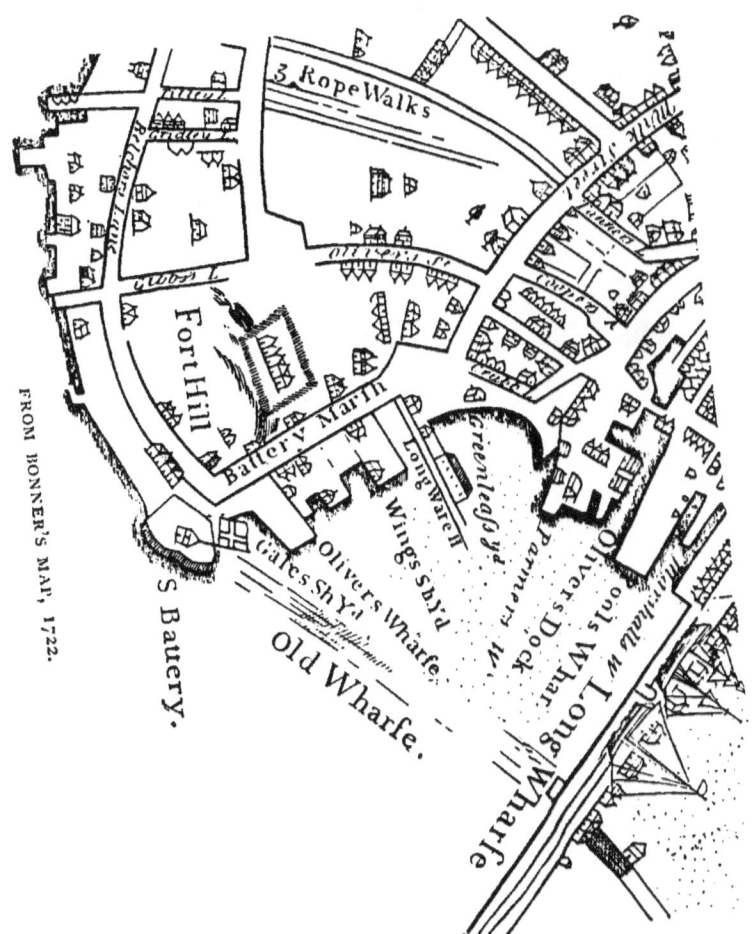

> Alone he sleeps ! The mountain cloud,
>   That night hangs round him, and the breath
> Of morning scatters, is the shroud
>   That wraps the conqueror's clay in death.
>
> Pause here ! The far-off world, at last,
>   Breathes free ; the hand that shook its thrones,
> And to the earth its mitres cast,
>   Lies powerless now beneath these stones.
>
> Hark ! comes there, from the pyramids,
>   And from Siberian wastes of snow,
> And Europe's hills, a voice that bids
>   The world he awed to mourn him ? — No:
>
> The only, the perpetual dirge
>   That 's heard there is the sea-birds' cry,
> The mournful murmur of the surge,
>   The cloud's deep voice, the wind's low sigh.

The first pastor of Hollis Street Church was a poet, curious old Mather Byles, who assumed his clerical duties in 1733. He was a very popular minister before the Revolution, and he had an English as well as European reputation as a poet, and numbered among his correspondents Lansdown, Dr. Watts, and Pope, the latter of whom sent him one of the first copies of his translation of the Odyssey.

Byles declared himself a Tory at the beginning of the Revolution, and his reputation immediately vanished. In 1777 he was denounced in Boston town-meeting, and was ordered to be confined in his own house, which stood at the corner of Nassau and Tremont Streets, and a guard was stationed over his door. The guard was accustomed to pace backward and forward in a pompous way, as though performing a duty of very great responsibility.

One day Byles came to the door and asked him to go on an errand for him.

"I will stand guard while you are gone," said he, taking the sentinel's gun, and pacing back and forth in front of his own house in the same important way the guard had done. The sentinel did the errand, and in the meantime Byles excited the laughter of every one on the street by the way in which he stood guard over himself and his house.

Mather Byles

Another guard was appointed who could not be persuaded to change places with the man he was guarding, and at last, the thing becoming quite ridiculous, the guard was removed entirely. When Byles saw this he said, —

"I have been guarded, reguarded, and now I am disregarded," and disregarded he lived to the end of his life.

Old-time Boston was full of anecdotes of this witty parson, and an early Boston poet has left the following photograph of him in two rather acrimonious stanzas : —

> "Here's punning Byles provokes our smiles,
> A man of stately parts,
> He visits folks to crack his jokes,
> Which never mend their hearts.

> "With strutting gait and wig so great
> He walks along the streets,
> And throws out wit, or what's like it,
> To every one he meets."

In 1780 the famous Dark Day occurred, and a frightened lady sent her son to Parson Byles to inquire the cause of the appalling obscurity.

"I don't know," said Byles, whose habit of joking was too chronic to be set aside even at the prospect of the near approach of the judgment day. "Go home and tell your mother I am just as much in the *dark* as she is."

When the great religious awakening in England, under the preaching of the Wesleys and Whitefield, began to excite the attention of the colonies, the Methodists were known in this country as "New Lights," and Methodist revivals were called the New Light stir. One day a ship arrived in Boston harbor with three hundred street-lamps, and on the same day a gossiping lady called on Dr. Byles, whose visit he wished to cut short by some startling intelligence.

"Have you heard the news?" he asked of his visitor.

"What news?" asked the lady.

"Three hundred *new lights* have just arrived in a ship from London, and the selectmen have ordered them to be put in irons," which astonishing bit of news, we suppose, the good woman spread through the town.

He once courted a lady who refused his hand and married a man by the name of Quincy. He met her after her marriage and greeted her blandly : —

"So it seems, madam, that you prefer the Quincy to Byles."

"Yes," said the lady, "for if there had been any affliction worse than Byles, God would have sent it upon Job."

He remarked, on seeing the lower tier of windows in King's Chapel, which were in his day the same as now, "I have often heard of the *canons* of the church, but I never heard of the *port-holes* before."

But though he was so witty in conversation, his poetry has much of dignity and strength. For example, take his New England Hymn : —

> "To Thee the tuneful anthem soars,
> To Thee, our fathers' God and ours,
>   This wilderness we chose our seat;
> To rights secured by equal laws
> From persecution's iron claws,
>   We here have sought our calm retreat.
>
> "See! how the flocks of Jesus rise,
> See! how the face of Paradise
>   Blooms through the thickets of the wild.
> Here Liberty erects her throne;
> Here Plenty pours her treasures down;
>   Peace smiles, as heavenly cherubs mild.
>
> "Lord, guard thy favors; Lord, extend
> Where further western suns descend;
>   Nor southern seas the blessings bound;
> Till Freedom lift her cheerful head,
> Till pure Religion, onward spread,
>   And beaming, wrap the world around."

Near Hollis Street Church, in the house where Byles lived, his two eccentric daughters continued to live until 1835. These ladies remained Royalists until the day of their death. They used to go to church in the dresses of the last century, they blew their fire with the old-time colonial bellows, and ate from the table from which Franklin had used to take his tea. In 1835 the city ordered a part of the house to be taken down, in order to widen the street, which caused one of these ancient ladies so much grief that she is said to have died in consequence.

"O, is not this a holy spot?
   'T is the high place of Freedom's birth!
God of our fathers, is it not
   The holiest spot of all the earth?

"Quenched is thy flame on Horeb's side;
   The robber roams o'er Sinai now;
And those old men, thy seers, abide
   No more on Zion's mournful brow.

"But on *this* hill thou, Lord, hast dwelt
   Since round its head the war-cloud curled,
And wrapped our fathers, where they knelt
   In prayer and battle for a world.

"Here sleeps their dust: 't is holy ground,
   And we, the children of the brave,
From the four winds are gathered round,
   To lay our offering on their grave.

"Free as the winds around us blow,
   Free as the waves below us spread,
We rear a pile that long shall throw
   Its shadow on their sacred bed.

"But on their deeds no shade shall fall
   While o'er their couch thy sun shall flame,
Thine ear was bowed to hear their call,
   And thy right hand shall guard their fame."

On laying the Corner-Stone of the Bunker Hill Monument. — PIERPONT.

CHAPTER XVI.

FREEDOM AND PROSPERITY.

The evacuation of Boston was the end of the Revolutionary War on the soil of that city. The colonies declared their independence in 1776, and the contest for liberty went on with varying fortunes until the surrender of Lord Cornwallis at Yorktown, but Massachusetts blood was shed elsewhere and not here.

The government of the colony now returned to its primitive form, — the election of a Legislature, or General Court, by the people, to manage all public affairs. In 1780 Massachusetts adopted a constitution, and under it John Hancock was elected governor.

Peace between England and America was declared in 1782. In 1787 the United States Constitution was framed, and under it George Washington was elected President in 1789.

The same year Washington, shortly after his election, visited Boston, and was received with great rejoicing.

In 1822 Boston became a city.

Lafayette, the friend of Washington, whose coming to America during the Revolution gave hope to the colonies in the darkest period of the contest, and who rendered America great service both in councils of war and on the battle-field, visited Boston in 1825, and in his presence the corner-stone of Bunker Hill Monument was laid, on the 17th June.

The scene on that day was not forgotten by the generation

that witnessed it. Mr. Frothingham, in his History of the Siege of Boston, vividly describes the day and a part of the ceremony: —

"This celebration was unequalled in magnificence by anything of the kind that had been seen in New England. The morning proved propitious. The air was cool, the sky was clear, and timely showers the previous day had brightened the vesture of Nature into its loveliest hue.

"Delighted thousands flocked into Boston to bear a part in the proceedings, or to witness the spectacle. At about ten o'clock a procession moved from the State House towards Bunker Hill. The military, in their fine uniforms, formed the van. About two hundred veterans of the Revolution, of whom forty were survivors of the battle, rode in barouches next to the escort. These venerable men, the relics of a past generation, with emaciated frames, tottering limbs, and trembling voices, constituted a touching spectacle. Some wore, as honorable decorations, their old fighting equipments, and some bore the scars of still more honorable wounds. Glistening eyes constituted their answer to the enthusiastic cheers of the grateful multitudes who lined their pathway and cheered their progress.

"To this patriot band succeeded the Bunker Hill Monument Association; then the Masonic Fraternity, in their splendid regalia, thousands in number; then Lafayette, continually welcomed by tokens of love and gratitude, and the invited guests; then a long array of societies, with their various badges and banners. It was a splendid procession, and of such length that the front nearly reached Charlestown Bridge ere the rear had left Boston Common. It proceeded to Breed's Hill, where the Grand Master of the Freemasons, the President of the Monument Association, and General Lafayette performed the ceremony of laying the corner-stone in the presence of a vast concourse of people."

Daniel Webster, then at the beginning of his great fame, delivered the oration. It was one of the finest products of American eloquence. In closing, he said, —

"We come, as Americans, to mark the spot which must forever be dear to us and our posterity. We wish that whosoever, in all coming time, shall turn his eye hither, may behold that the place is not undistinguished where the first great battle of the Revolution was fought. We wish that this structure may proclaim the magnitude and importance of that event to every class and every age. We wish that infancy may learn the purpose of its erection from maternal lips, and that wearied and withered age may behold it, and be solaced by the recollections which it suggests. We wish that labor may look up here and be proud in the midst of its toil. We wish that in those days of disaster, which, as they come on all nations, must be expected to come on us also, desponding patriotism may turn its eyes hitherward and be assured that the foundations of our national power still stand strong.

"We wish that this column, rising toward heaven among the pointed spires of so many temples dedicated to God, may contribute also to produce in all minds a pious feeling of dependence and gratitude. We wish, finally, that the last object on the sight of him who leaves his native shore, and the first to gladden his who revisits it, may be something which shall remind him of the liberty and the glory of his country. Let it rise till it meet the sun in his coming; let the earliest light of the morning gild it, and parting day linger and play on its summit!"

Rev. Ray Palmer, then a youth, was present, and he has kindly allowed us to republish his recollections of the event.

MEMORIES OF BUNKER HILL. — JUNE 17, 1825.

Of those who were present when the corner-stone of the Bunker Hill Monument was laid, more than half a century ago, but few, comparatively, now survive.

Lafayette, the hero of two worlds, died in a good old age not many years after. Daniel Webster, the illustrious orator and statesman, worn out with public labors, was many years since laid in his sepulchre.

All the then surviving participators in the scenes of the Revolution have passed away. A limited number only, it is probable, even of those who constituted the younger part of the vast assembly gathered there, still live and keep in memory the details of what was done.

It has been suggested to the writer, who was himself present, and retains the freshest recollection of persons and things, that a brief account of the occurrences of that interesting day would be a valuable piece of history. Such a sketch — of course it must be little more than an outline — he will accordingly attempt to give.

First of all, we may bring back in our thought the Boston and the Charlestown of that date.

Boston had only some three years before been made a city, with a population of not far from fifty thousand. Its business area was comparatively small. Immediately in the rear of the State House, and forming the top of Beacon Hill, there was a large field or common, since graded away, but then flat, and serving as a play-ground for the lovers of base-ball.

The street at the east end of the State House was in the condition of a country road, strewed with boulders and loose stones, with a rough bank on either side.

Between the city and the village of Roxbury there was quite a piece of country road called the Neck, with here and there a house, and the water of the South Cove and the West

LAFAYETTE.

Bay visible at a short distance on either hand. But one bridge — the old wooden Charlestown Bridge — connected Boston with Charlestown, which was not then a city.

Both the heights of the latter town, the one on which the battle was fought, and the higher one to the northward, were almost entirely naked fields. At the southwest part of the battle-hill the houses pressed close around the base; but the whole battle-ground and all the eastern and northeastern slope were as bare as when the shots from the British fleet in the Mystic River swept over them on the eventful day whose deeds are enshrined in history. It is only by recalling the surroundings as they were that one can get a clear conception of the scene presented on the 17th of June, 1825, and feel the contrast between that time and the present.

The whole country anticipated the occasion with the most lively interest, and many came from great distances to attend the celebration.

I was at that time a student in Phillips Academy, Andover. With two or three classmates I obtained leave of absence, and retiring immediately after tea for a few hours sleep, we set out at about twelve o'clock and walked to Boston, reaching the city by seven in the morning. The historic memories of the great battle, the fame of the already renowned orator, the presence of Lafayette, the companion and trusted friend of Washington, — these were enough to set youthful hearts aglow, and to awaken an almost romantic enthusiasm. We were destined to no disappointment.

The procession moved over from the summit to the northeastern side of the hill. A platform had been erected far down the slope and covered with a tent open on the side towards the ascent.

There the different sections of the long array were seated in order, rank rising above rank, and covering the hillside so as to form a vast amphitheatre. It was, indeed, as Webster said in his first sentence, an "uncounted multitude" on which the orator looked when he ascended to his position.

He himself was then only in his forty-fourth year, and in the perfection of that nobleness of person and dignity of bearing for which he was so renowned. With Lafayette by his side, and surrounded by so many of the survivors of the desperate struggle on the spot where now they stood, and of other battle-fields of the Revolution, and by a multitude of the most illustrious men of the state and country, there was nothing wanting which could lend impressiveness to the occasion. Altogether it was a scene which no one who witnessed was likely ever to forget.

DANIEL WEBSTER.

It was my good fortune, in the seating of the procession, to push my way in boyish fashion to a seat on the grass among the highest order of Masons, directly in front of Mr. Webster, and not more than sixty or seventy feet from him.

I was in a position to see perfectly his great glowing eyes and every play of thought and emotion on his face, and to hear every syllable from first to last. When he rose to speak there was absolute silence, notwithstanding the multitude.

A considerable space was left him on the front of the platform; a small table was set ten feet or more from the place where he chiefly stood to speak, and on this he laid his manuscript unopened. The entire address was committed to memory; but now and then when he had finished some grand passage, while waiting for the resounding applauses to subside, he would walk slowly to the table and turn his leaves to the point which he had reached in his discourse.

The impression made by his general manner was that of perfect self-command. Not a nervously hurried look or motion disturbed the reposeful bearing. His voice at that period of his life was exactly one's ideal, — deep, clear, full, flexible, capable of great power without losing its natural quality, and sympathetically responsive to his emotions. He began on a natural key, but spoke so deliberately and with such distinctness of articulation that he seemed to be heard to the outmost lines of the assembly.

His speaking, in the variety of its intonations, was like a *magnificent talk* from first to last; rising often into the noblest elocution, but never passing into that declamatory and monotonous vociferation into which so many public speakers fall. Making every allowance for youthful susceptibility, I cannot but believe that few orators, in any age, have furnished a finer specimen of discursive eloquence than this.

It seems to me some evidence of this that after almost fifty-four years many passages of that oration, with the exact tone and emphasis and gesture with which they were pronounced, remain as fresh in my memory as though I had heard them only yesterday.

The clear and silvery ring of the voice, when he cried, " Let it rise ! — let it rise, till it meet the sun in his coming; let the earliest light of the morning gild it, and parting day linger and play on its summit ! " still echoes in my ear.

I still seem to hear him say to the veteran survivors of the battle, as they stood, warworn and infirm, before him, — " Venerable men ! . . . the same heavens are indeed over your heads; the same ocean rolls at your feet; but all else, how changed ! "

I still feel the inimitable tenderness of the minor key in which he uttered the pathetic apostrophe to Warren : "But ah ! him ! the first great martyr in this great cause ! Him ! the premature victim of his own self-devoting heart ! . . . Our poor work may perish, but thine shall endure ! this monument may moulder away, the solid ground it rests upon may sink down to a level with the sea ; but thy memory shall not fail ! "

I still feel the thrill stirred by the majestic power of voice and action with which, in allusion to Greece, then in her revolutionary struggle, he said, " If the true spark of religious and civil liberty be kindled, it will burn. Human agency cannot extinguish it. Like the earth's central fire, it may be smothered for a time ; the ocean may overwhelm it ; mountains may press it down ; but its inherent and unconquerable force will heave both the ocean and the land, and at some time or other, in some place or other, the volcano will break out and flame up to heaven."

Such are some of the recollections of the scenes connected with the laying of the corner-stone of the monument on Bunker Hill. No intelligent young man or woman, it would seem, can recall them, and read Mr. Webster's grand oration, without a deeper sense of the value of our free, civil and religious institutions, and the price they cost our venerated ancestors.

MONUMENT GROUNDS.

The beautiful grounds on which Bunker Hill Monument stands retain not a vestige of the fortifications of 1775. A flat granite stone marks the place of the breastworks, and another, nearly at the foot of the grounds, the spot where Warren fell. The base of the monument stands on the spot of Prescott's famous ditch, which was dug on the starry night in June, just before the battle. The fosse and breastworks were quite prominent at the time the foundation of the monument was laid by Lafayette, in 1825, but the building of so stupendous a structure of granite on the spot caused them to be levelled and obliterated.

A few incidental facts about the monument may be of interest to the stranger. The foundation is composed of six courses of stone, and extends twelve feet below the surface of the ground. There are in the whole pile ninety courses of granite blocks. The base of the obelisk is thirty feet square, and fifteen feet at the spring of the apex. The number of steps in the spiral stone stairway is two hundred and ninety-five. The cap-piece of the apex, which crowns the whole at an elevation of two hundred and twenty-one feet, consists of a single stone, weighing two and a half tons.

The historical relics in the monument consist of a beautiful model of Warren's statue, which was erected over the spot where the General fell, and two cannon in the chamber of the obelisk, which were used during the war, and on which is inscribed their own history.

The remains of Warren were interred at the place where he fell. Here a monument was erected in 1794, of which the model is seen in the monument on the inside at the base. After the evacuation of Boston the patriot's body was disinterred, and removed with impressive ceremonies to King's Chapel. The body was again removed to St. Paul's Church on Tremont Street, and now rests at Forest Hills.

CAMBRIDGE CHURCHYARD.

The monument to the patriots who fell in 1775 is in Cambridge Churchyard.

It is a lovely spot, full of historic associations, and we will speak of it here.

The Vassal family sleep here, who built two stately mansions in Cambridge, one of which is known as the Vassal House, now the residence of Professor Longfellow. The tomb of the Vassal family, which is celebrated in Holmes's poetry, is marked by a freestone tablet supported by five pillars, on which are the sculptured reliefs of a vase and the sun, — *Vas*, in the Latin, meaning a vase, and *Sol*, the sun, and Vas Sol representing the ancient emblems of the family. Here is the resting-place of the poet-artist, Washington Allston, in the old Dana tomb, where he was interred by torch-light one quiet midsummer eve in 1843.

Allston entered upon his life-work with a religious enthusiasm that ennobled his personal character. It is said that

WASHINGTON IRVING.

when he first went to England to study painting he on one occasion sold a certain picture to a nobleman to meet his pressing necessities. After he parted with the picture, the thought came to him that the moral influence of it on a person with a perverted taste and prurient imagination might not be good; the thought haunted him and so wrought upon his sensitive conscience that he went to the nobleman and repurchased the picture.

Washington Irving was an intimate friend of Allston in his youth; they were in Italy at the same time; they visited the studios of Rome together, and made arm-and-arm walks to those relics of antiquity that recall the Rome of the Cæsars. Irving has left a most beautifully written account of his old friend, in which he describes his affectionate, enthusiastic disposition, and the awe and reverence with which he beheld the pictures of the old masters, or walked about the stupendous pile of St. Peter's where art looked down on every hand. "His eyes would dilate," said Irving, "his pale countenance would flush; he would breathe quick, and almost gasp, in expressing his feelings when excited by almost any object of grandeur and sublimity."

The old house stands in Cambridgeport where he lived; and the magnificent picture of Belshazzar's Feast, on which he spent the last week and the last day of his life, may be seen at the Art Museum.

The old-time presidents of Harvard College rest here in crumbling tombs. One of Dr. Holmes's most beautiful poems describes this churchyard.

> "Go where the ancient pathway guides,
>   See where our sires laid down
> Their smiling babes, their cherished brides,
>   The patriarchs of the town.
> Hast thou a tear for buried love?
>   A sigh for transient power?
> All that a century left above,
>   Go, read it in an hour."

"High walls and huge the BODY may confine,
    And iron gates obstruct the prisoner's gaze,
And massive bolts may baffle his design,
    And vigilant keepers watch his devious ways;
Yet scorns th' immortal MIND this base control!
    No chains can bind it, and no cell enclose;
Swifter than light, it flies from pole to pole,
    And in a flash from earth to heaven it goes!
It leaps from mount to mount, from vale to vale
    It wanders, plucking honeyed fruits and flowers;
It visits home to hear the fireside tale,
    Or in sweet converse pass the joyous hours.
'T is up before the sun, roaming afar,
And in its watches wearies every star!"

                    WILLIAM LLOYD GARRISON.

CHAPTER XVII.

THE ANTISLAVERY STRUGGLE.

ABOUT half a century ago a young New England journalist accepted a position in Baltimore.

The state of society which he beheld in that city surprised and shocked him.

Baltimore then was one of the marts of the domestic slave trade.

Slave-pens flaunted their signs upon the principal streets, and vessels loaded with slaves who had been bred and raised like cattle for the market, were constantly departing for Mobile, Savannah, and New Orleans. Coffles of slaves, chained together, moved through the streets. The traffic in human flesh was one great business of the day.

Yet the people engaged in raising slaves for the market moved in the best society, and were members of the leading Christian churches.

The young man publicly protested against this great wrong.

He was imprisoned for making this protest.

On the walls of his cell he thus wrote with a pencil: —

> "A martyr's crown is richer than a king's.
> Think it an honor with thy Lord to bleed,
> And glory 'midst intensest sufferings;
> Though beat, imprisoned, put to open shame,
> Time shall embalm and magnify thy name."

That prophecy was to be fulfilled.

But not until after many years.

This young man returned to New England and was the leading mind of the first Antislavery Society in America, which was formed on "Nigger Hill," Boston, in a school-room under the African Baptist Church, Jan. 6, 1832.

There seem to have been some men "of property and standing" in Boston at this time whom history will not love to remember by their names, but will be glad to mention them merely as people that have been.

Some of these nameless people, in October, 1835, attacked a female antislavery meeting. While one of the ladies, Miss Mary S. Parker, was engaged in prayer, we are told that the company was assailed by "hisses, yells, and curses," sounds not often heard in Boston to-day on any occasion, and never from men "of property and position." What great men they must have been!

They next threw the Testaments and Prayer-Books out of the window. They then seized a young man who was editing an antislavery paper in the city, and coiled a rope around his body, intending to drag him through the streets.

A cry was raised, —

"He sha'n't be hurt: he is an American!"

At this he was beset by the mob, and the clothes were torn from his body.

He was at last taken in charge by the city officers, and was placed in jail for his personal safety.

This young man was the same who was imprisoned in Baltimore, — William Lloyd Garrison, — at the time of this last arrest, the editor of *The Liberator*.

The antislavery society he had formed proved the beginning of many such societies, and the principles to which the young agitator devoted his life, and for which he lived many years in poverty, spread by persecution. This uncompromising young man became a moral power in the land.

MR. GARRISON IN THE HANDS OF THE MOB.

In no single city did the principles for which he contended gain a firmer or wider influence than in Boston, where he had been mobbed.

In the autumn of 1842 George Latimer, a native of Virginia, was arrested in Boston without a warrant, on the claim that he was a fugitive slave. The case was brought before the courts. Chief Justice Shaw ruled that "the statute of the United States authorized the owner of the fugitive to arrest him in any State to which he might have fled."

Latimer was held as a prisoner to await further action.

The old spirit of the Revolution was revived again. The city was full of indignation at such an infringement on the rights of personal liberty.

In October, on the last Sabbath evening in the month, a great audience met in Faneuil Hall. Speeches were made and the citizens recorded themselves as protesting: —

"By all the glorious memories of the Revolutionary struggle,

"In the names of justice, liberty, and right,

"In the awful name of God,

"*Against* the deliverance of George Latimer into the hands of his pursuers."

Letters in sympathy with the spirit of the meeting were read from John Quincy Adams, George Bancroft, and others.

Latimer was set free, a philanthropist paying to his owner the price of his freedom.

The event caused the question of the moral right of slaveholding to be everywhere discussed, and the result was a growing sense of the wrong of the institution of slavery. Some of the most brilliant men of Boston became eloquent advocates of the antislavery cause. Among these were Wendell Phillips, Theodore Parker, and Dr. Samuel G. Howe. John G. Whittier became the poet of the cause, and young Charles Sumner began to bring to it the weight of his scholarship and convincing eloquence.

The antislavery societies prepared the way for the Free Soil party, and this party was in turn the beginning of the great political movement against slavery.

On the 3d of October, 1850, there was another exciting antislavery meeting in Faneuil Hall, at which words of electric and impassioned eloquence were spoken. Millard Fillmore had signed the Fugitive Slave Law. The Free Soil party, hitherto small, under the influence of the popular indignation awakened by this law became strongly reinforced. It held its convention on the date and at the place we have named, and was addressed by Charles Sumner, who was just entering upon his public career.

Mr. Sumner's condemnation of the Fugitive Slave Law was unsparing in the extreme. He said, —

"Other presidents may be forgotten, but the name signed to the Fugitive Slave Bill can never be forgotten. There are depths of infamy as there are heights of fame. I regret to say what I must, but truth compels me: better for him had he never been born."

THEODORE PARKER.

A more exciting scene was witnessed in Faneuil Hall in 1854. Anthony Burns had been arrested under the Fugitive Slave Act and lodged in jail. The antislavery men called a meeting.

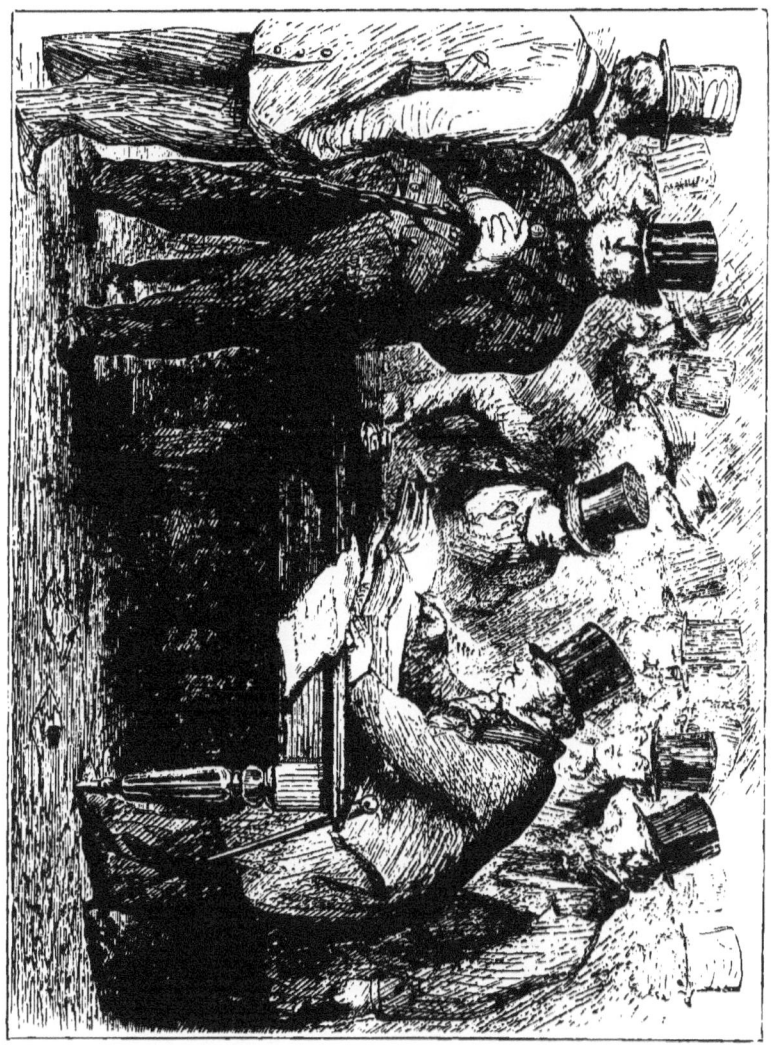

FIRST SUBSCRIPTIONS FOR SOLDIERS' FAMILIES.

Theodore Parker was present; Phillips, Stowell, and Dr. Howe. Such an influence went from this meeting that the militia had to be called out to guard the Court House.

Burns was surrendered to his master on the 2d of June. He was to be taken from his cell to the ship. The city became feverish with excitement. He was conducted from Court Street to the wharf in the centre of a hollow square of armed men, protected by the militia and by cannon. The streets were draped in black, the bells tolled, the expression of public disapproval was so emphatic as to be awe-inspiring and terrible.

The contest between freedom and slavery ended in war. Fort Sumter fell in the spring of 1861. The whole North burned to retrieve the nation's honor.

Washington was threatened. On the 15th of April Governor Andrew received a telegram from Washington, asking him to send fifteen hundred men for the protection of the city. The answer of the governor to the president was immediate, and the response of the militia to the governor's call as prompt.

FORT SUMTER.

On the morning of the 16th volunteers began to arrive. The State soon became a camp. The wealthy men of Boston pledged their money for the support of the soldiers' families. The Boston banks offered to loan the State $3,600,000 without security, to meet any emergency that might arise. On the 19th of April — the Lexington and Concord Day — the 6th Massachusetts regiment was attacked in Baltimore and four of the men were killed.

Boston now gave her resources to the struggle. At the close of the year 1862 Massachusetts had in active service fifty-three regiments of infantry, twelve companies of light artillery, three of heavy artillery, and one regiment and several companies of cavalry.

In 1864 Governor Andrew said to the Legislature, "Our volunteers have represented Massachusetts during the year

MASSACHUSETTS SIXTH IN BALTIMORE.

just ended on almost every field and in every department of the army where our flag has been unfurled, — at Chancellorsville, Gettysburg, Vicksburg, Port Hudson, and Fort Wagner; at Chickamauga, Knoxville, and Chattanooga; under Hooker, Meade, Banks, Gilmore, Rosecrans, Burnside, and Grant. In every scene of danger and duty, — along the Atlantic and the

Gulf, on the Tennessee, the Cumberland, the Mississippi, and the Rio Grande; under Dupont, Dahlgren, Foote, Farragut, and Porter, — the sons of Massachusetts have borne their part, and paid the debt of patriotism and valor."

Massachusetts sent 159,165 of her sons to the war.

On the high ground of the Common the tall shaft of the Soldiers' and Sailors' Monument shines through the trees; and in the public square from which Columbus Avenue stretches away amid streets and blocks of wealth and taste, stands the Emancipation Monument, and all good people look upon them both with patriotic pride as they recall the war record of Boston and Massachusetts.

> "Truth crushed to earth shall rise again,
> The eternal years of God are hers."

"O, MANY a time it hath been told,
 The story of those men of old:
 For this fair Poetry hath wreathed
  Her sweetest, purest flower;
 For this proud Eloquence hath breathed
  His strain of loftiest power;
 Devotion, too, hath lingered round
 Each spot of consecrated ground,
  And hill and valley blessed;
 There where our banished fathers strayed,
 There where they loved and wept and prayed,
  There where their ashes rest.

"And never may they rest unsung,
 While Liberty can find a tongue.
 Twine, Gratitude, a wreath for them,
 More deathless than the diadem,
 Who to life's noblest end
  Gave up life's noblest powers,
 And bade the legacy descend
  Down, down to us and ours."
                    CHARLES SPRAGUE.

CHAPTER XVIII.

THE BOSTON OF TO-DAY.

SUCH was Boston in the past; such were its founders; such were the foundations that these great and good men laid.

How wonderful in contrast is the scene to-day!

In colonial times Boston embraced a peninsula of six hundred and ninety acres. The peninsula has vanished; 1700 acres were acquired by the city when South Boston and East Boston were added to its area; 10,100 when Roxbury and West Roxbury were annexed; 4800 when the gardens of beautiful Dorchester were received. To-day the area of Boston is more than 20,000 acres. Bridges span its rivers on every hand. Its suburbs are among the most lovely in the world.

In 1790 Boston had a population of something more than 18,000; in 1800, of 24,000; in 1820, of 43,000; in 1840, of 93,000; in 1850, of 136,000; in 1860, of 177,000; and in 1870, after the annexation of Roxbury in 1867, and of Dorchester in 1869, of 250,000. The annexation of Charlestown, West Roxbury, and Brighton added greatly to the population, and to-day (1881) Boston contains about 370,000 souls.

We said the peninsula had vanished. The neck of it has been broadened into a wide and populous area, and where the high tides once washed the sands the finest private residences now stand. Over the old flats or Charles River marshes

Commonwealth Avenue now stretches more than a mile in length and two hundred and forty feet wide. The old salt meadows are grand squares; the very hills have been lowered to push away the embouchures of the Charles.

The city has nearly thirty thousand buildings. Over it shines the gilded dome of the State House on Beacon Hill. This building was commenced in "Governor Hancock's pasture" in 1789. From the dome, which is open to the public, the harbor with its fifty islands, the Blue Hills of Milton, and an immense extent of country full of elegant houses, with clustering spires and towers, may be seen. In the Doric Hall, or rotunda, are many historic relics and beautiful busts and statues.

The valuation of Boston in 1800 was a little more than $15,000,000; in 1870 it was nearly $600,000,000. In 1840 the average amount of property to each inhabitant was less than $900; to-day it is nearly $2,500. Boston is one of the richest cities in the world.

It was a town of churches at the beginning. It has now one hundred and fifty regular churches and some two hundred religious societies.

The Puritans esteemed education next to religion, and provided the best schools for their children. The schools in Boston number nearly four hundred; they are the best in the country, and the free public school buildings are the finest ever erected. Harvard University is the leading college of America. The music schools of Boston are the best in the country, and one of them is the largest in the world.

In 1852 Joshua Bates, whose bust may be seen in Bates Hall, offered the city $50,000 for the purchase of books, if a suitable library were provided. The offer was accepted, and thus began the Boston Public Library on Boylston Street. The library now contains nearly four hundred thousand vol-

STATE HOUSE.

umes, and is, next to the library of Congress, the largest in the country, and in point of value one of the best in America.

When the Puritans came to Boston it was because of the healthful springs of water on the peninsula. The fountains that welled up from the earth where is now Louisburg Square, with its odd figures of Columbus and Aristides, have disappeared, long ago drawn away by the over-demand on their hidden sources. The spring near Governor Winthrop's old residence, where now is dark Spring Lane (beyond the Old South Church), around whose pump the women used to gossip in Anne Hutchinson's time, is also gone. But Boston is a place of pure water, now as of old. In 1848, while Josiah Quincy, Jr., was mayor, water was successfully introduced into the city from Lake Cochituate, twenty miles distant. The lake covers six hundred and fifty acres. It was arranged that this water should be brought in a brick conduit eleven miles long to a grand reservoir in Brookline, and thence to distributing reservoirs in Boston, East Boston, South Boston, and the Highlands. The principal reservoir in Brookline covers twenty-three acres. In 1869 a stand-pipe was erected in Roxbury by means of which pure water is supplied to the highest levels of the city houses.

In 1869, after the settlement of the issues of the war, a great musical festival, called the "Peace Jubilee," was held in Boston in a coliseum, built to accommodate fifty thousand people. One hundred and eight musical societies united in forming a chorus of some ten thousand voices, and these, to the accompaniment of nearly one thousand instruments, a battery of artillery, and anvils and bells, sang the favorite hymns and songs of America and the great patriotic chorals of the world. It was June; the city was filled with beautiful flowers; the singers of all the towns of New England gathered here, and the Common wore the appearance of a great fair. No one who attended can ever forget Boston in those serene,

328   *Young Folks' History of Boston.*

fragrant, and bright June days. Another jubilee, at which the singers numbered nearly twenty thousand and the instruments nearly two thousand, was held in 1872.

On the evening of the 9th of November, 1872, a fire was discovered in a dry-goods building on the corner of Kings-

CORNER OF WASHINGTON AND MILK STREETS, BEFORE THE GREAT FIRE.

ton and Summer Streets. A cold wind was rising, and about nine o'clock the people were greatly excited to behold Summer Street a wall of flame. In the night the wind blew heavily, the flames spread in all directions, and the great granite warehouses seemed to melt before them like lead. It

"SUMMER STREET A WALL OF FLAME."

was Saturday night. The fire raged until Sunday noon. Sixty-five acres, the centre of the wholesale trade of the city, were covered with blackened heaps of ruin. Eight hundred buildings were destroyed. The loss was estimated at $80,000,000.

The fire was arrested at a point near the Old South Church. This historic building was saved by the heroic efforts of the firemen.

"THE OLD SOUTH STANDS."

Loud, through the still November air,
    The clang and clash of fire-bells broke ;
From street to street, from square to square,
    Rolled sheets of flame and clouds of smoke.
The marble structures reeled and fell,
    The iron pillars bowed like lead ;
But one lone spire rang on its bell
    Above the flames. Men passed, and said,
        " The Old South stands ! "

The gold moon, 'gainst a copper sky,
    Hung like a portent in the air ;
The midnight came, the wind rose high,
    And men stood speechless in despair.
But, as the marble columns broke,
    And wider grew the chasm red, —
A seething gulf of flame and smoke, —
    The firemen marked the spire and said,
        " The Old South stands ! "

Beyond the harbor, calm and fair,
    The sun came up through bars of gold,
Then faded in a wannish glare,
    As flame and smoke still upward rolled.
The princely structures, crowned with art,
    Where Commerce laid her treasures bare ;
The haunts of trade, the common mart,
    All vanished in the withering air, —
        " The Old South stands ! "

> "The Old South must be levelled soon
>   To check the flames and save the street;
> Bring fuse and powder." But at noon
>   The ancient fane still stood complete.
> The mitred flame had lipped the spire,
>   The smoke its blackness o'er it cast;
> Then, hero-like, men fought the fire,
>   And from each lip the watchword passed, —
>   "The Old South stands!"
>
> All night the red sea round it rolled,
>   And o'er it fell the fiery rain;
> And, as each hour the old clock told,
>   Men said, "'T will never strike again!"
> But still the dial-plate at morn
>   Was crimsoned in the rising light.
> Long may it redden with the dawn,
>   And mark the shading hours of night!
>   Long may it stand!
>
> Long may it stand! where God was sought
>   In weak and dark and doubtful days;
> Where freedom's lessons first were taught,
>   And prayers of faith were turned to praise;
> Where burned the first Shekinah's flame
>   In God's new temples of the free;
> Long may it stand, in God's great name,
>   Like Israel's pillar by the sea!
>   Long may it stand!

On the 17th of June, 1875, occurred the Centennial Celebration of the Battle of Bunker Hill. It was one of the most imposing peace pageants ever seen in America. It also happily proved the occasion of a formal exchange of expressions of good-will and renewed friendship between the representatives of the North and South.

Boston is a lovely city in mid-June, with its old historic streets, fine avenues, and grand trees; but the day of the celebration was one of the most delightful of the season. An immense concourse of people, estimated at a quarter

"THE OLD SOUTH STANDS."

of a million, witnessed the march of the Centennial procession through streets roofed with banners that gayly toyed and played with the mellow sunlight. The procession itself was nearly ten miles long.

In the procession were a Baltimore regiment and parts of a Virginia and South Carolina regiment. The splendid New York Seventh Regiment, with its glittering uniforms; the Pennsylvania regiments, with Governor Hartranft; the Providence Light Infantry, with General Burnside; General Sherman, Vice-President Wilson, and a large number of men associated with recent history, — all received a hearty recognition.

HENRY WILSON.

The march of the Southern regiments was a complete ovation through all the route.

The celebration was full of incidents calculated to inspire harmony of feeling between the late hostile States. A palmetto-tree was planted at the foot of Bunker Hill Monument, and so Massachusetts and South Carolina were made by their traditional emblems to stand side by side. The great organ was surrounded by palmettos and palms, and it pealed forth a fortissimo welcome when the troops from Charleston came filing into the Music Hall. Yet nowhere have been heard stronger or more stirring words, presenting Northern views of the late war, than on that same platform of Boston Music Hall.

On the Soldiers' Monument in Charlestown — an imposing granite structure which especially honors Massachusetts soldiers who fell in the streets of Baltimore — the Maryland regiment placed an immense shield of flowers, bordered with trailing smilax, which was itself inwoven with flowers.

General Fitz Hugh Lee spoke in Music Hall on the occasion of the Governor's reception to invited guests. When he closed his address the orchestra burst forth with "Auld Lang Syne." The flag of Eutaw, which had just been unfurled in honor of the South Carolina soldiers, was

SOLDIERS' AND SAILORS' MONUMENT.

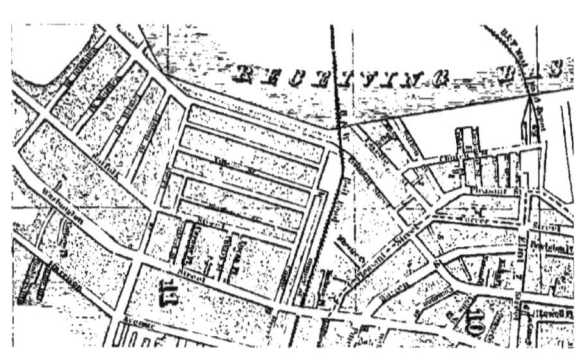

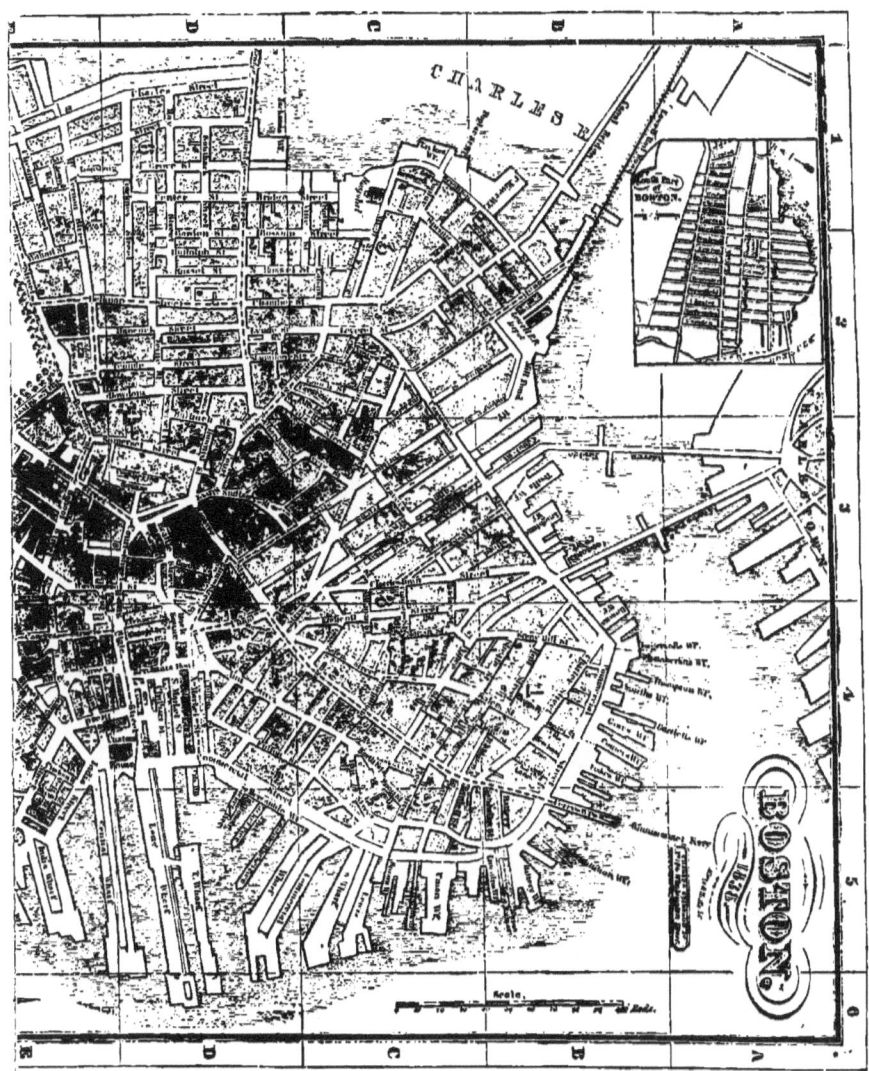

waving before the great organ, among the palmettos, and the audience was deeply stirred by old memories and new hopes.

On Sept. 17, 1877, there was another great military and civic procession on the occasion of the dedication of the Soldiers' and Sailors' Monument. The entire military force of the State paraded, and was reviewed by President Hayes. From the top of this lofty monument the statue of America overlooks the city.

Our young readers have nearly all seen this beautiful work of art, but not all who have seen it may know the meaning of the four large bronze reliefs.

The one in front represents the departure for the war. A regiment is seen marching by the State House steps. The figures are —

Colonel Lowell,
Colonel Shaw,
Colonel Cass, } Mounted officers from left to right.
General Butler,
General Reed.

On the steps of the State House are —

Rev. Turner Sargent,   Governor Andrew,
Rev. A. H. Vinton,   Wendell Phillips,
Rev. Phillips Brooks, H. W. Longfellow,
Archbishop Williams,   and others.

The second relief represents the work of the Sanitary Commission. The principal figures are —

Rev. E. E. Hale,
E. R. Mudge,
A. H. Rice,
James Russell Lowell,
Rev. Dr. Gannett,   } From left to right.
George Ticknor,
W. W. Clapp,
Marshall P. Wilder,

The third relief gives a view of the return from the war. It contains forty figures. Among them are —

General Bartlett,	Governor Claflin,
General Underwood,	Charles Sumner,
General Banks,	C. W. Slack,
General Devens,	James Redpath,
Senator Wilson,	J. B. Smith.

The fourth relief is a naval scene.

The most interesting locality in Boston, after the Common, is, perhaps, Art Square. Fronting it, or very near it, are the Art Museum, Trinity Church, the new Old South Church, Second Church, the Institute of Technology, and the Museum of Natural History. The boulevard of Commonwealth Avenue is near, and the boulevard of Huntington Avenue stretches away from the square for more than a mile.

Trinity Church, a French Romanesque structure, such as might have been seen in Aquitaine in the Middle Ages, is one of the most beautiful buildings in America. It was consecrated in 1877, when a procession of more than one hundred clergymen entered the main portal. Its famous frescos are by John La Farge. In the great tower these frescos represent Moses and David, Peter and Paul, Isaiah and Jeremiah.

The Museum of Fine Arts is both a school and an exhibition. In the entrance hall are works by great sculptors, pottery by the mound-builders, Gobelin tapestry, and antiques from the Alhambra. The Greek rooms are rich in casts and statues, including the Sumner Collection. The Egyptian room contains the Way Collection of Egyptian antiquities. The picture galleries have works by nearly all the great masters of art of recent times, and many specimens of the old masters.

In the hall, just over the staircase, are two remarkable pictures. One of these is the Madness of King Lear, by Benjamin West; the other is Belshazzar's Feast, by Washington Allston, — a work that occupied the painter's attention for forty years, and on which he spent the last days of his life.

A STORY OF WASHINGTON ALLSTON.

Allston was one of the purest of men from youth to age.

He taught his pupils that character was the first essential to success in any art.

We once met a pupil of Allston, now one of the most famous landscape painters in the country. He related many beautiful anecdotes of the great painter, and described his sudden death, and the scene in Cambridge churchyard when the moon broke through the summer clouds as the coffin was opened for the last time.

"There is one thing that Allston used to say to me that I shall never forget," he said with feeling: "it was a lesson that every young man should learn.

"'Young man,' he would say, 'be pure. No one ever can become a truly great artist without purity of character. Nature never reveals her beauties to a mind clouded with any grossness of character.'

"He seemed to try to impress upon me the fact that he who deviated in the least from strict morality became something less of a man than he might have been."

The lesson which Allston taught his pupils, and sublimely illustrated in his own life, is one that every young man who has an aspiration for success in any æsthetic calling should learn. "Nature never reveals her beauties to a mind clouded with any grossness of character." Men of weak moral character do often make a reputation in literature and art, but they are always "something less than they might have been."

Near West's picture is Scheffer's Eberhard Mourning over the Body of his Son.

EBERHARD.

The clarions rung, the bugles played,
    The fight was hot and hard ;
Before the town of Göttingen
Fast fell the ranks of Swabian men,
    Led on by Eberhard.

Count Ulric was a valiant youth,
    The son of Eberhard ;
The bugles played, the clarions rung,
His spearmen on the foe he flung,
    And pressed the foemen hard.

"Ulric is slain !" the nobles cried.
    The bugles ceased to blow.
But soon the monarch's order ran,
" My son is as another man,
    Press boldly on the foe."

And fiercer now the fight began,
    And harder fell each blow ;
But still the monarch's order ran,
" My son is as another man,
    Press boldly on the foe."

O, many fell at Göttingen,
    Before the day was done ;
But victory blessed the Swabian men,
And the happy bugles played again
    At the setting of the sun.

We have ended many of these chapters with a story. We will here close with some account of

A GIGANTIC RELIC.

The rarest collections of scientific relics are often the most unvisited, and it is a somewhat singular fact that the choicest and most instructive curiosities in many of our larger cities are not to be found in the popular museums. Thousands of people living in the city of Boston, who are familiar with the stuffed animals and astonishing wax figures in the old Boston Museum, and are accustomed to air their fancy among the respectable fossils and gorgeous tropical birds in the Museum of Natural History, have perhaps never so much as heard of the wonder-exciting collection of anatomical curiosities known as the Warren Museum.

The building stands in a quiet, tenantless part of Chestnut Street, between Charles Street and the Charles River, but a few steps from Beacon Street and the Public Garden. It is made of brick, with heavy iron doors and shutters, and of all places would be the least likely to attract the eye of the stranger, but for the inscription over the door, —

"ERECTED BY

DR. JOHN COLLINS WARREN."

Dr. John Collins Warren was the son of Dr. John Warren, a most skilful surgeon in the American army during the Revolutionary War, and the founder of the Medical School in Harvard College. He was educated in the best medical schools of London and Paris, and on the death of his father, in 1815, was elected Professor of Anatomy and Surgery at Harvard College, and in 1820 was placed at the head of the surgical department of the Massachusetts General Hospital, a position that he held for thirty-three years. During the latter period he made the most extensive collection of anatomical specimens to be found in the country. A part of these are still at the Massachusetts General Hospital, a part at the Boston Museum of Natural History, and a part, comprising the rarest and most valuable, constitute the Warren Museum.

The museum belongs to Dr. Warren's heirs. For a considerable period after his decease they used to open it on certain days to the public, but it ceased to excite curiosity, and it is now only opened by special permission on application to members of the family. Every courtesy is extended to those who wish to visit the place for scientific purposes, although no provision was made in Dr. Warren's will for the preservation of the relics or care of the building.

The Warren Museum consists of two fire-proof rooms, one of which contains gigantic fossils, and the other, relics which the great anatomist wished to preserve with more than ordinary care. Among these are the skull, brain, and heart of Spurzheim, the phrenologist and anatomist, who died in Boston in 1832, and whose monument graces one of the principal avenues of Mount Auburn.

Spurzheim was a martyr to science, and those who were familiar with his self-forgetful life and the vicissitudes of his career could hardly view these relics with unmoistened eyes. The heart is preserved in a glass jar of alcohol, and the brain in a glass box filled with liquid. The Prussian philosopher died only two months after his arrival in Boston, during the delivery of his first course of lectures. He gave his body to science, to which from boyhood he had devoted all the energies of his soul.

The most remarkable object in the Warren Museum is the largest skeleton of the *Mastodon giganteus* ever discovered on the continent. By its side, in way of contrast, is the frame of the elephant Pizarro, the largest ever brought to this country. The skeleton of the *Mastodon giganteus* will not fail to cause the visitor to start back in awe, and he will be hardly able to suppress that adjective of fools, "Impossible!" It is twelve feet high, and thirty-four feet in length, from the tips of the tusks to the extremity of its tail. Its trunk is seventeen

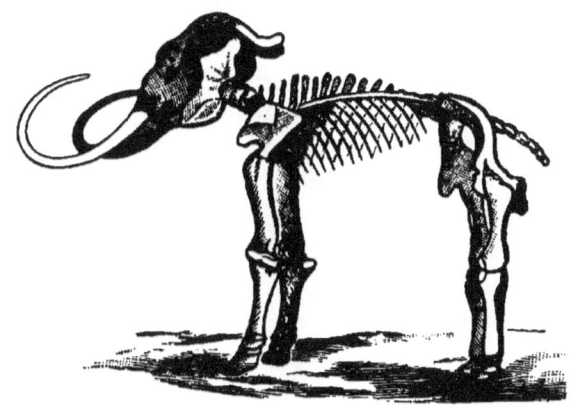

SKELETON OF MAMMOTH.

feet in length. The animal must have weighed more than 20,000 pounds!

Dr. Warren, in his magnificent and very costly work on the *Mastodon giganteus*, copies of which are only to be found in the rarest libraries, has given us an account of all that is known of this animal, and a very interesting description of the finding of this particular specimen, of which we make an abridgment: —

At a very early period after the settlement of this country, relics of the mastodon were found in the vicinity of the Hudson River. Among these were a tooth, which is described by Dr. Cotton Mather of Boston as weighing more than four pounds, and a thigh-bone, said to have been more than seventeen feet long.

As the country became settled, mastodon bones, in greater or less numbers, were found scattered over a large part of the territory of the United States, but chiefly near the Hudson, in the salt-licks of Kentucky, in the Carolinas, in Mississippi, and Arkansas. They have recently been found in California and Oregon.

The Hudson River country, between New York and Albany, seems to have been a favorite resort of the mastodon race. The lands here were fertile, undulating, and well wooded, and the valleys contained lacustrine deposits favorable to the growth of such trees and shrubs as would be likely to afford this animal subsistence.

In the year 1845 there was found, at Newburgh, on the Hudson, the largest perfect skeleton of a mastodon which has yet been exhumed on this continent. The summer had been exceedingly hot and dry. Many small lacustrine deposits had been exposed by the drought, and the farmers had industriously seized upon the opportunity to remove these rich beds of fertility to their tillage-lands and fields.

The drought at last laid bare one of these deposits in a bog on the farm of Mr. N. Brewster, a spot that had never been known to become dry before. Mr. Brewster at once summoned his men to remove the deposit, as rapidly as possible, to his fields and farm-yards. One day, toward evening, in the latter part of summer, these laborers struck a hard substance. Some said it was a "rock;" others, a "log;" others, jestingly, a "mammoth."

Early the next morning Mr. Brewster went with his laborers to the field, and found the supposed rock or log to be an immense bone. The men began digging, full of eager curiosity, and exposed to view the massive skull and long white tusks of a mastodon. These tusks were of such immense size and length as to cause the most wonderful reports to go flying about the neighborhood, and to draw the good people of Newburgh in crowds to the place. It was soon discovered that the perfect skeleton of a mastodon was imbedded in the peat. Sheer-poles and tackles were obtained, and, amid excitement, cheering, and many cautions, the bones of the monster were raised from the bed where they had lain no one can tell how many thousand years.

Two days were occupied in these interesting labors. The relics drew to them an immense number of people from the surrounding country. Beneath the pelvic bones of this mastodon were found five or six bushels of broken twigs, which evidently had constituted the animal's last meal. He had undoubtedly been mired while attempting to cross this bog, and in this manner perished. These twigs were from one-quarter to three-eighths of an inch in diameter, and a little more than an inch in length. They were supposed to belong to willow, linden, and maple trees.

It is vain to conjecture how many years ago this creature may have lived. What marvellous scenes must have passed before its eyes in its wanderings, what gigantic forests, what noble watercourses, what luxuriant vegetation! What strange animals may have been its companions, — species that passed away long before civilization brought its destructive weapons to the Western shores!

"O COUNTRY fair! how have thy green hills altered
    Since those dim, distant days
When, lost in beauty, olden voyagers faltered
    On bright New England bays;

"Since on thy tides the weary Northmen drifted,
    Safe havened from the seas,
And knighted sea-kings in thy calm capes lifted
    Their banners to the breeze;

"Since knelt the Pilgrim, by dark foes surrounded,
    In forests newly trod,
And in each place a templed city founded,
    Where he bent down to God.

    .   .   .   .

"'T is ours to tell no mythic hero's glory,
    Nor twine the victor's bays;
'T is ours to tell of praying men the story,
    And follow prayer with praise.

"'T is ours to mark upon a lengthened dial
    The finger of our God,
As we recount the paths of self-denial
    Through which our fathers trod.

" The rural homes among the oaks' broad shadows
    Upon the river's arms;
The fragrant orchards and the waving meadows,
    Of harvest-happy farms;

" The clustering steeples by the busy river,
    The towns on harbors fair,
Are but God's answers to their brave endeavor
    And self-forgetful prayer.

    .   .   .   .

" They prayed alone to know the path of duty,
    And duty's hardships bear;
And God for them has diademed with beauty
    Thy hills, O country fair!"

CHAPTER XIX.

THE PLEASURE RESORTS AND THE BEAUTIFUL SUBURBS OF BOSTON.

PEOPLE who have travelled extensively pronounce the suburbs of Boston among the most lovely of the cities of the world. It is a quiet loveliness of hill, glen, and river; fine public buildings and homes of taste. From all the hills, ocean views with white sails and green islands appear. The roads are wide and shaded. Broad lawns, flower-gardens, arbors, and decorations in marble and bronze are to be seen continuously for miles. The neighboring towns are as delightful. Few English landscapes are more beautiful than those at the Newtons, at Arlington, and Brookline. An excursion on the Charles River from Waltham in the little summer steamer takes one through a region of rural beauty that seems formed for a fairy land. Few schools in the world have a more pleasing situation than Wellesley College, with its extensive grounds, dotted with noble trees, its lake, its groves, its views of the winding Charles. The estates in Wellesley known as Hunnewell's Gardens and Ridge Hill Farms are among the most beautiful specimens of floral decoration and landscape gardening in the country.

The Blue Hills at Milton, Corey Hill in Brookline, Arlington Heights, Winter Hill, Somerville, and the hills of Malden, all present charming landscapes to the eye of the excursionist. He has not seen the beauties of Boston who has not visited the suburbs and the neighboring towns, in which a large proportion of those who do business in the city live and spend their wealth on homes of comfort and taste.

Many of the lovely places near Boston can be reached by the horse-cars. A ten-cent ride in the open cars will afford almost as much pleasure as a ride in one's own carriage. Among the many places that may thus be visited are

Dorchester, affording a view of the harbor and of Milton Hills.

Grove Hall, passing the residence of General Warren, and stopping near Dr. Cullis's well-known charitable institution, the Consumptives' Home.

Milton Lower Mills, a distance of six miles, with views of South Boston, the Harbor, the villas of Savin Hill, and Neponset River. A short walk from the Mills will take one to the highlands of Milton, whence very picturesque and extended scenes appear; another walk over a road lined with villas will bring one to Webster Garden, near which the Dorchester horse-cars may be taken for a return trip to Boston. This excursion, with its walks, would take some three or four hours. This is a very charming afternoon trip in June or September.

Forest Hills is a beautiful part of the suburbs. The distance by horse-cars is about five miles, into an open country full of rich landscapes, airy villas, and broad, beautiful lawns.

Jamaica Plain opens another horse-car ride through avenues of great beauty. The car track is about five miles in length. At the end of it, near the Soldiers' Monument, a carriage in summer will be found waiting to take excursionists to Allandale Mineral Spring, over a road of continuous villas, and in view of noble country-seats and quaint Queen Anne houses. The woods around Allandale Spring are full of walks, and a summer afternoon may be spent there as quietly as in a forest.

STATUE OF EDWARD EVERETT.

A visit to *Mount Auburn,* passing the colleges at Cambridge, and the residences of Longfellow and James Russell Lowell, may be made by the horse-cars. In this one gets fine views of the Charles. It is well to take a whole day for this excursion, and to stop in Cambridge and visit the Agassiz Museum and Harvard Memorial Hall. The excursion may be made, however, on a summer or early autumn afternoon. Arlington is reached by horse-cars which pass through Cambridge, and the horse-car route is one of the longest out of Boston. Before making excursions in this direction it would be well for the tourist to read Drake's " Historic Fields and Mansions of Middlesex."

A horse-car excursion to *Lynn* through Charlestown affords a view of Bunker Hill Monument, and of the Chelsea and Revere Beaches. A pleasant short excursion may be made by crossing to Chelsea on the ferry-boat and returning by the horse-cars to the city.

Among the places of especial interest only a few miles from Boston, but a little beyond the horse-car tracks, we may mention : —

    Middlesex Fells . . . . Medford.
    Old Powder House . . . . . . Somerville.
    " Merry Mount " . . . . Wollaston.
    Cradock House . . . . Medford.
    Waverly Oaks . . . . Belmont.
    Royall House . . . . Medford.
    Ten Hills . . . . Somerville.
    Adams Homestead . . . . Quincy.

These and many other places are interesting alike to the Bostonian and the traveller spending a few weeks in Boston. Many Boston people who have visited Europe are not well acquainted with the historic places of their own State. Others, as was the case with Charles Sumner, have taken new views of the beauties of Boston, after a residence abroad. "In all England," said Sir Charles Dilke, "there is no city which has suburbs so gray and venerable as the elm-shaded towns around Boston, — Dorchester, Chelsea, Nahant, and Salem." "It is a good thing for a Bostonian to go abroad," said a traveller, "it gives him such a satisfaction with his own city on his return."

As beautiful as are the suburbs and the inland towns near Boston, are the shores and green islands of the harbor and bay. Boston Bay has been compared to the Bay of Dublin and even to the Bay of Naples. The latter comparison is of course overdrawn; the bay has no Vesuvius, is canopied by no entrancing colors of sky, and terminated by no city of a history of thousands of years. But it is full of beauty, and the summer sunsets viewed from it are often magnificent, — crimson, violet, and pearl, with darkening clouds near the horizon that resemble mountain peaks, and complete an enchanting scene.

A fleet of steamers and excursion boats in summer gives the sheltered waters an animated appearance. Some of these go as far as Cape Ann, the Isle of Shoals, and the coast of Maine, but most of them to the Nantasket or Lynn Beaches. They all pass in sight of the terraced heights of Governor's Island and Fort Independence. Governor's Island was once known as Governor's Garden, it having been granted to Governor Winthrop for a garden, on the condition of his paying two bushels of apples a year to the colonial treasury.

Fort Independence is built upon Castle Island, so called because here was Castle William in colonial times. This island was fortified in 1633–34, and is the oldest military post in the eastern part of the country. It took the name of Castle William on the accession of William III., at which time it was repaired by Colonel Romer, and mounted with 100 guns. The castle was demolished by the British on the evacuation of Boston.

A new fortress was built and named Fort Independence by President John Adams.

Among the beautiful and interesting places on the bay and Atlantic coast to which excursions may be made by steamers or railroads, or both, we may name —

Point Shirley . . . . . . Narrow Gauge R. R.
Deer Island . . . Government Boat, by permission.
Revere Beach . . . . . Boat, steam or horse cars.
Nahant . Boat, or by rail to Lynn and barge to Nahant.

Nahant is famous for its "spouting rock" and fine villas. It has been the summer resort of many eminent people, among them Longfellow, Motley, Agassiz, and Prescott.

Swampscott,
Marblehead, } Railroad.
Newburyport,

Marblehead is one of the most quaint of American towns. It is full of old houses. It was the birthplace of Elbridge Gerry, Joseph Story, and Commodore Tucker. General Glover, whose statue may be seen in Commonwealth Avenue, lived here. Marblehead Neck is famous for its sea views, and its coolness in summer. The tomb of Whitefield is shown at Newburyport, in the Whitefield Church.

Salem . . . . Railroad.

The Marine Museum, the House of Seven Gables, Gallows Hill, and the court-house relics, such as the "witch pins," are here usually sought for by the historic tourist, and the associations of Hawthorne's books by the friends of the novelist.

Beverly,
Manchester, } Railroad.

Beverly Farms are famous in history. Beverly is the home of Lucy Larcom, and Manchester was the summer residence of the late James T. Fields.

Gloucester, Magnolia, Pigeon Cove, } Boat.

Scituate, Marshfield, } Railroad.

Plymouth, Provincetown, } Excursion Boat.

Chelsea Beach and Nantasket Beach are the principal resorts of those who have but a few hours at a time to devote to excursions. Downer Landing is also a favorite place.

Nantasket Beach is connected with Cohasset by the famous Jerusalem road. Nantasket is supposed to have been the first land on the bay ever visited by white men. If the antiquaries are right, this event took place hundreds of years before Columbus was born.

We had planned to end most of the chapters of this volume with a story. Let us here tell you the story of

LEIF.

Not long since, we heard a fairly well educated gentleman ask, "Who was Leif, of whom a statue is to be erected in Boston?"[1]

If most of my readers are similarly ignorant, it is not surprising, neither is it to their discredit. For those works especially treating of the race to which Leif belonged are inaccessible to the masses. The best cyclopædias consider the

---

[1] We are largely indebted to F. F. Foster, Weare, New Hampshire, for most of this narrative.

THE FRENCH KING TROUBLED AT THE APPROACH OF THE NORTHMEN.

subject — as they must, perforce, all subjects — very briefly; and of many histories by us carefully examined, no one devotes more than two pages thereto, which is insufficient to convey any adequate information concerning that with which, in our opinion, every American scholar should be somewhat familiar.

Before reading further in this chapter, find the map of North America, and keep it before the eye. You will thus be able to follow the course of the ships of Leif and Thorvald of which we are about to speak, and your eye will travel over all the wild coast from Greenland to Boston Harbor.

The Northmen — by this term are to be understood the inhabitants of ancient Norway and Sweden — were at one time navigators of wide reputation throughout the world, though their expeditions were, for the greater part, of a piratical nature. Scarcely was there a known coast which their squadrons did not touch; and, by their bravery and activity, these bold seamen gained and maintained the mastery over other nations.

They established one of their princes, Canute, on the British throne, despite the mighty resistance of their adversaries. About the same time they subjected to their power one of the fairest sections of France, to which they gave the name Normandy. Moreover, for a season, they ruled the Mediterranean regions, and held the supremacy in Constantinople and Jerusalem; everywhere exhibiting an unsurpassed energy and courage.

To both victors and vanquished these conquests were beneficial. The Southrons became more hardy, seeking to secure to themselves the physical vigor of their conquerors, which they could not but admire, so great was the contrast between it and their own weakness; the roughness of the northern invaders was toned down by association with the refinement of southern civilization.

In the year 875 Ingolf and Leif established in Iceland a colony of Northmen who were unwilling longer to submit to the tyranny of their king, Harold; and in 986, under the leadership of Eric, surnamed the Red, a colony of the same people settled in Greenland. Eric fixed his residence at a place to which he gave the name Brattalid; the inlet, at the head of which he settled, he called Eric's *fjord* or ford. He named the country Green-land.

Bjarne, son of Heriulf, — one of those who accompanied Eric to Greenland, and who gave his name to its southernmost cape, known to us as "Farewell," — was interested in maritime commerce, which he carried on with success.

One summer, on returning from a foreign voyage to his Norwegian home, he learned that his father had gone to Greenland, and immediately resolved to follow him to the new country, though entirely ignorant as to the necessary course, nautically speaking.

Finding his crew favorable to the project, he set sail for the land to which Heriulf had emigrated. For nearly two weeks, owing to a dense fog, he drifted at random; but when the fog lifted he discovered land. As it was low, sandy, and covered with wood, — quite unlike what they supposed Greenland was, — they passed it and continued towards the north.

The next day he again "made land." The physical characteristics of the coast were the same as those of the land previously seen; so they left it and put out to sea.

A few days later he for the third time discovered land, which, on exploration, proved to be an island. Leaving it, and sailing in a northerly direction, within three days they reached Heriulf's residence, Cape Farewell.

In the year 1000 Leif, his curiosity aroused by what he had heard of Bjarne's discoveries, determined to visit the unexplored regions; and, having purchased and equipped

Bjarne's ship, he set sail towards the south. The first land he reached was that last left by Bjarne, which Leif found a barren coast, gradually rising into mountains. On account of its extreme rockiness, he called the country Hella-land; *hella*, in the Icelandic vernacular, signifying "a broad rock."

This land Danish antiquaries regard as identical with Labrador. Owing to the fact that it was insular, we incline to believe Hella-land the modern Newfoundland.

Resuming his voyage, Leif a second time made land, like in appearance to that first land that greeted Bjarne's eyes; according to the aforementioned antiquaries, Nova Scotia.

Putting to sea, in two days he for the third time saw land. Near the coast and to the south of it was an island which he visited. Sailing westward from the island, through a strait separating it from the mainland, he ere long reached a locality where a river flowed into the sea.

This Leif deemed a suitable place for the establishment of a colony, and hither he brought the ship's stores. At first only rude huts were built; but when it had been decided to make the place a permanent residence, houses of a respectable size were erected, and the settlement was called *Leif's Booths*.

Among Leif's followers was a German who for many years had been a member of Eric's household. Possessing an investigating disposition, he was almost always sent with those detailed to explore the interior of the country. On one occasion he did not return with the rest of his party, and Leif, anxious in regard to his safety, took a squad of men and set out in quest of him. He was soon found.

Leif said to him, —

"Why art thou so late, my foster father? Why didst thou leave thy comrades?"

"I did not go much further than they, but I found something new, — vines and grapes."

"Is that true?"

"Yes, I was born in the land of grapes."

"We will gather grapes," said Leif.

The Northmen had never before heard of this fruit, but the German was thoroughly conversant with its properties and uses, and speedily acquainted his companions with it.

They filled the stern of one of their boats with clusters of grapes, and bore them away with them towards their own barren coast.

Leif named it *Wineland* because of the abundance of the grapes in this region. For various reasons, which it is not necessary to state, Wineland is supposed to be the present Massachusetts and Rhode Island. On this supposition, the island on which Leif landed is Nantucket; the mainland, north from it, Cape Cod. The *Booths*, probably, were near the site of the Bristol of to-day. After passing a few months in Wineland, Leif sailed for Greenland, which he reached in safety. From the success of his voyage he was thenceforth known as Leif, *the Lucky*.

So great an interest was aroused among the Greenlanders by Leif's discoveries that, in the autumn of 1001, his brother Thorvald set out upon an expedition to these newly found regions. He made the *Booths* his winter quarters.

In the spring of 1002 he sailed towards the east and was wrecked upon a cape to which, from its resemblance to the keel of a ship, he gave the name *Kialarness* — Keel Cape; the Cape Cod of to-day.

Having repaired his ship, he took a westerly course, and soon reached a most beautiful promontory. So attractive in its appearance was it, he determined to make it the place of his permanent abode.

Here the Scandinavians came upon three canoes, each containing three persons whom they designated *Skraellingar* — Esquimaux. There was an encounter between the two

NORTHMEN ON AN EXPEDITION.

parties, which resulted in the death of eight of the natives and the flight of the ninth. The fugitive shortly returned with new forces and resumed the combat, which quickly terminated in the discomfiture of the aggressors.

Thorvald, however, was mortally wounded in the engagement; and, calling his followers around him, he advised their immediate return to Greenland.

"But," said he, "first bury me on the beautiful promontory. Put a cross at my head and another at my feet, and let the name of the place be *Krossanes*" — Cape Cross. This is, supposably, some point near Plymouth, or at the extremity of Nantasket Beach.

A beautiful story is told about the gentle conduct of Thorvald in meeting his enemies, a story worthy of the pen of a poet.

He saw the boats of the savages approaching and noted the warlike attitude of the natives.

"Put up the war screens," he said, "and defend yourselves as well as you can, *but do not let us* use our weapons against them."

When the battle was over he said, —

"Is any one wounded?"

"No," was the answer.

"*I*," said the gentle navigator, "have received a wound. It is under my arm. It will be my death wound."

What a truly heroic soul Thorvald must have had! He deserves a monument as much as Leif.

"SOCIETY needs the well-trained, enlarged, and cultivated intellect of the scholar, in its midst; needs it, and welcomes it, and gives it a place, or, by its own capacity, it will take a place of honor, influence, and power. The youthful scholar has no occasion to deplore the fate that is soon to tear him from his studies, and cast him into the swelling tide of life and action. None of his disciplinary and enriching culture will be lost, or useless, even there. Every hour of study, every truth he has reached, and the toilsome process by which he reached it; the heightened grace or vigor of thought or speech he has acquired, —all shall tell fully, nobly, if he will give heed to the conditions. And one condition, the prime one, is, that he be a true man, and recognize the obligation of a man, and go forth with heart, and will, and every gift and acquirement dedicated lovingly and resolutely to the true and the right. These are the terms; and apart from these there is no success, no influence to be had, which an ingenuous mind can desire, or which a sound and far-seeing mind would dare to seek."

GEORGE PUTNAM.

CHAPTER XX.

THE OLD BOSTON SCHOOLS.

WE recently called upon that hale but venerable Bostonian, General H. K. Oliver, well known as an educator, an honored State officer during the late war, and the writer of " Federal St." and other musical compositions, for the purpose of asking information concerning the old Boston schools. The General for an hour or more related to us amusing anecdotes of his old school-days, and gave us one of his published addresses, entitled " How I was Educated," which presents a clear view of a schoolboy's life in Boston nearly seventy years ago.

"A short distance above Milk Street and a less distance above the old Province House, on Marlborough Street, now called Washington," says General Oliver in this address, "stood my father's house, to and from the barn of which I daily drove my father's cow from Boston Common through Bromfield's Lane.

"In 1805 I was placed under the educational influence of one Mr. Hayslop, who kept school on the corner of Franklin and Washington Streets. Well do I recall the look of the building, the old time-stained walls of wood, its *old* door, its *old* stairway, up which our little feet bore us to the *old* school-room, on the second floor, where ruled and feruled the good *old* master."

General Oliver describes the pedagogue's dress as unique in the extreme, from foot to head, "with its square-toed shoes and ponderous buckles, gray stockings, tabby-velvet breeches, and knee-buckles, vest of exaggerated length, ruffled shirt, seedy coat, with pockets vast and deep, ironed stock, and powdered wig." The General, speaking of his primary training, says it took him six weeks to learn the alphabet, though he found out correctly the names of all the scholars and his master's family in less than a week, — a good testimony certainly to the happy influence of object teaching.

THE OLD PEDAGOGUE.

We should judge from the following anecdote that boys then as now sought to improve *all* their opportunities.

"I well recall," says General Oliver, "one instance of severity at my first teacher's hands; like many other calamities it proved a blessing in disguise. For some roguery of mine, the good man shut me up in a closet ' black as Erebus and deepest night : ' —

"' No sun, no moon; all dark, amid the blaze of noon.'

Quivering with fright, I tried to penetrate the murky gloom. Blessed with keen nasal powers, I thought, as I became more calm, that I smelt some odorous savors sweet, and I soon found, greatly to my relief and comfort, that I was incarcerated in a store-closet wherein were boxes of sugar and toothsome things in general. I turned my attention to these sources of relief. When the door was opened, I made a straight line for home, considerably worse for gorging, and forgiving Master Hayslop in my heart.

"From this school," says the General, "I was removed to Madam Tileston's in Hanover Street. I was a restless lad, and Madam Tileston's customary punishment was sundry smart taps on my head, with the middle finger of her right hand, which was armed with a rough steel thimble. She once pinned me fast to a cushion of her chair, and following her example I also pinned her, when she was not looking, to the same seat. Shortly after, she arose to perform some duty. It was a triplicate transit, when the threefold firm of Tileston, Cushion, and Oliver changed base."

EAR PINCERS.

From Mrs. Diaz, who has published some popular articles on the subject in the *Youth's Companion*, we also collect some comical pictures of old-time primary schools.

"One of my teachers," says Mrs. Diaz, "was Marm Leonard. She used to wear a ruffled vandyke and a necklace of large blue beads, and a row of reddish false curls on each side of her forehead.

"Marm Leonard had a faculty for contriving punishments suitable to the nature of the offence. For example, when little Sethy Cushing tied his comforter around a kitten, and hung it on the clothes-line, she tied the comforter around little Sethy Cushing, and hung him on the crane in her great kitchen fireplace. Of course, the fireplace was not at that time in use.

"Scholars who told lies had mustard put on their tongues. When a little girl stole a vial of boxberry cordial from one of the other children, Marm Leonard held that little girl's fingers over the redhot coals.

"She had also other ways of persuading us to avoid the evil and take to the good. She kept a thin, oval-shaped silver locket, marked 'Best Scholar,' for the best scholar to wear. She also had ribbon bows of blue, pink, light-green, and black. All the good scholars went home with bright bows pinned on their shoulders. The marm had but one black bow, and that was reserved to be pinned on the one who was unusually bad.

"I must not forget to mention the Catechism, — or 'Catechise,' as it was usually called, — for in that Marm Leonard drilled us well. At the summons, 'All stand up and say your *Catechise!*' we all stood up in a straight line on a crack of the floor. She put out the questions in a high-pitched tone of voice, speaking very fast, and we answered with equal rapidity, running the words together and scampering along without stopping to breathe. In fact, we answered in one long word.

"The 'Catechise' contained one hundred and seven questions, their answers, the Lord's Prayer, the 'Ten Commandments,' and the Creed. Some of the scholars knew the book through, and the 'Primer' besides.

"The Primer was a thin book, about five inches long and four wide, with blue covers and leather binding. It had a woodcut of John Hancock, and a number of very small woodcuts, one for every letter of the alphabet. These were placed up and down the pages, six in a page, at the left-hand side, each with its couplet at the right. Thus, for 'A' there was the couplet,—

"'In Adam's Fall
We sinned all.'

"In the picture there were two droll-looking human images, whose bond of union seemed to be an apple, which both of them were holding. They stood close to a tree. It looked like a cedar or a hemlock tree, but we knew it to be an apple-tree, because there were apples on it. We were sure they were apples, for we had heard the story again and again. Around the trunk was coiled a serpent of the size — so it seemed to us — of a small anaconda, for with only two coils it reached from the ground to the branches.

"For 'O' there were three human images, two of them with crowns and sceptres, and the triplet, —

"'Young Obadias,
David, Josias,
All were pious.'

"Beside the pictures and rhymes, the Primer contained the alphabet, the 'abs,' a few pages of 'spelling words,' a variety of 'Lessons and Maxims for Children,' several prayers, the whole of the Catechism, the Golden Rule, and a number of verses, texts, and so forth."

Mrs. Diaz in the same admirable papers thus gives a picture of an old-time school committee and one of their visits to the town school : —

"It was always a marked event when the 'committee' visited the school. If the President and all his Cabinet were to walk into the room where I am writing, they would not seem half so stately and grand to me as did those four gentlemen who used to visit the school once or twice during the winter. They came up from town on horseback; a wheeled vehicle was rarely seen in those days. Their arrival was usually announced by some scholar who had peeped through a crack, or who had stood up and looked out of the window.

"'Committee's come!' was the whisper which ran through the room.

"Its effect was magical. The schoolmaster, startled by the sudden silence, would throw a hurried glance at the window, and then try to put on a serene and lamb-like expression. We would listen as still as mice till we heard voices outside; then came steps in the entry; then a rap at the door. At the moment of their entrance the stillness was such that we hardly breathed.

"Oh, how majestic they looked with their nice broadcloth (our folks wore homespun), their ruffled shirts, their heavy watch-seals, and their gold-headed canes! Walking along the alley-way, they fairly lighted up that dingy, low-walled little building. With what an air they looked down upon us! How could anything we might do seem good in their sight?

"They usually heard the classes read, looked at the writing-books, and gave out 'spellings.' Mr. Bixby was the most pompous member of the committee. He felt himself the grandest. I remember his hanging cheeks, and his quick, puffy way of talking. I also recall what he once said when the other gentlemen were in favor of our taking up a new study.

"'Oh, it's of no consequence — no consequence at all! They are not intended to grace a *drawing-room*.'

"The 'committee' heard us all read and spell, turned over the leaves of the writing-books, talked in undertones with the schoolmaster and with each other, said 'a few words' to the scholars, — then they walked out, hats and canes in hand, and the whole school standing as they passed down the alley. When, at last, the closing door shut them out, it seemed as if the school-room had met with an eclipse.

"We listened in silence while they trotted away, and then, as if just awakened from a dream, scholars resumed their mischief-making, the schoolmaster his natural expression of countenance, and flogging, hair-pulling, and ear-pulling went on as usual, accompanied by the whizzing of rulers."

THE BOSTON LATIN SCHOOL.

The Boston Public Latin School is older than Harvard College, and was the first educational institution of the country. "Its first masters," says Henry F. Jenks in an article in the *Harvard Register*, "might have seen Shakspeare act in his own plays; its second master preceded John Milton and John Harvard at Cambridge, England, by nearly a quarter of a century."

It was doubtless founded by John Cotton, "who brought to this country a knowledge of the High School which was founded by Philip and Mary in Boston, Lincolnshire, in 1554, in which Latin and Greek were taught." The Boston Latin School, we are informed, was established "on the 13th of the 2d moneth, 1635." No single school has prepared for the larger duties of life so many distinguished Americans. The names of its eminent graduates would fill pages. We give a few of them here : —

Patriots.

Benjamin Franklin.	Samuel Adams.
John Hancock.	R. T. Paine.

Governors and Lieutenant-Governors.

Bowdoin.	Cushing.
Eustis.	Winthrop.

Presidents of Harvard College.

Leverett.	Everett.
Langdon.	Eliot.

Clergymen.

Cotton Mather.	Henry Ward Beecher.
Joseph Tuckerman.	John F. W. Ware.
N. L. Frothingham.	Edward E. Hale.
James Freeman Clarke.	Phillips Brooks.
William Henry Channing.	

Mayors.

Harrison G. Otis.	Frederic O. Prince.
Samuel A. Elliot.	

Statesmen.

Robert C. Winthrop.	Charles Sumner.
Charles Francis Adams.	William M. Evarts.
George S. Hillard.	Charles Devens.

Literary Men.

R. W. Emerson.	Francis Parkman.
J. Lothrop Motley.	Alexander Young.
N. P. Willis.	

We condense from an article in *Education* prepared by a Boston school officer, a brief history of this remarkable school: —

Among other proceedings of "a generall meeting upon publique notice," held "13th of ye 2d moneth [April], 1635," we find the following duly recorded: "Likewise it is gen'rally agreed vpon y't o'r brother Philemon Pormort" (sometimes spelled Portmorte) "shal be intreated to become schulemaster for the teaching and nourtering of children w'th us." For his support, a tract of land of thirty acres at "Muddy River" (supposed to be a part of Brookline) was allotted. Other grants of land were subsequently made for the maintenance of a "Free Schoole for the Towne." An income also was derived from the letting of "Deare Island" of £7 per annum, for three years, 1644-47, which was appropriated to the support of the school. On the expiration of the lease in 1647, it was renewed for seven years at £14 per annum, and the next year was extended to twenty years at the same rent. It appears, moreover, that before the expiration of the twenty years — *i. e.*, in the year 1662 — the island was leased to Sir Thomas Temple, Knight and "Barronnight," for thirty-one years at a rent of £14 a year, "for the use of the 'Free Schoole.'"

The immediate successors of Mr. Pormort were Daniel Maude, John Woodbridge, Robert Woodmansey, Benjamin Thompson, and Nathaniel Williams.

One of the ushers of the school, for some time previous to the resignation of Mr. Williams, was John Lovell. "Master Lovell" may be said to have been one of the "institutions" of Boston. For four years he was the assistant master, and for forty-two years the head-master of the Latin School. A part of this period was a time of the most exciting character, embracing as it did the years which immediately preceded the Revolutionary War. Not a few of the men who were prominent in those times had been the pupils of "Master Lovell," and had been subjected to his rigid discipline as an instructor. In this discipline he is said to have been rough and severe. His portrait may be seen in the Harvard Memorial Hall, "drawn," says Judge Cranch, as quoted by Mr. Jenks, in his sketch of the Boston Latin School, "by his pupil Smibert, while the terrific impressions of the pedagogue were yet vibrating on his nerves.

JOHN LOVELL.

I found it so perfect a likeness of my old neighbor that I did not wonder when my young friend told me, 'A sudden, undesigned glance at it made me shudder.'" Lovell was a bitter Tory, and did not hesitate to give expression to his sentiments in his school. It is not unlikely that views advanced by a teacher not especially beloved by his pupils may have been looked upon with disdain because they were enforced by lips which too often indulged in words of censure and fault-finding. An antidote, however, to the Royalist poison was found in the teachings and influence of his assistant and son James, who was as strong a Whig as his father was Tory. We are told that "the two masters occupied desks at the opposite ends of the room;" and a pupil of a later day pictures them as "pouring into infant minds as they could, from the classics of the empire or the historians of the republic, the lessons of absolutism or of liberalism." That one of these pupils caught his inspiration from the so-called "rebel" James is plain from the following incident, which is related of Harrison Gray Otis : " Coming to school April 19, 1775, he found his way stopped by Percy's brigade drawn up across the head of School Street, in preparation for their march to Lexington. He had to pass down Court Street and come up School, and just entered the room to hear Master Lovell dismiss the boys : 'War's begun and school's done : *Deponite libros.*'" Upon the evacuation of Boston by the British, "Master Lovell" went to Halifax, where he died.

The books used at this period were : *First year*, Cheever's "Accidence," "Nomenclatura Brevis," Corderius's "Colloquies." *Second year*, Æsop's "Fables," "Eutropius," Ward's Lilly's Grammar. *Third and fourth years*, Clark's Introduction, Cæsar's Commentaries, Tully's Orations, the Æneid, Xenophon, and Homer.

"The methods of Mr. Benjamin Apthorp Gould (at the time of his election a member of the Senior class of Harvard College) were, in many respects, just the opposite of his immediate predecessors. He sought to break down the barriers which hitherto had existed between teacher and pupil, and make his scholars feel that he was their personal friend. Like that prince of instructors, Dr. Thomas Arnold, he appealed to the manly and generous side of the nature of his scholars, inspiring their confidence and winning their affection, while he commanded their respect in the enforcement of salutary rules, the justice and propriety of which they could not themselves help acknowledging. Mr. Gould held his position some fifteen years, 1813-28, when he resigned.

"The successor of Mr. Gould was his assistant, Frederic P. Leverett. He is best known as the author of the Latin lexicon which was so extensively used in our advanced schools forty or fifty years since. He remained in office three years, 1828-31, when he resigned to take charge of a private school. For four years previous to the year of Mr. Leverett's resignation, Mr. Charles K. Dillaway, a graduate of Harvard College in the class of 1825, had been the submaster. He was now chosen master of the school, and was in office five years, 1831-36, when he resigned, and Mr. Leverett was reappointed and accepted, but before the time had arrived for commencing his duties he died.

CHARLES K. DILLAWAY.

"Mr. Epes Sargent Dixwell, a graduate of Harvard College in the class of 1827, and sub-master of the school for a year and nine months, was appointed to fill the place made vacant by the decease of Mr. Leverett. He remained in office till 1851 : he then resigned and established a private school in Boston.

"The successor of Mr. Dixwell was Francis Gardner, himself a pupil of the Latin School, and a graduate of Harvard College in the class of 1831. He was connected with the department of instruction from the time of his graduation to the day of his death, about twenty-five years, during all this long period being absent from the city only one year, which he passed abroad."

The Latin School was begun on School Lane, now School

Street, where City Hall now stands. In regard to its locations we again quote from the article in *Education:*—

"The exact position of the first schoolhouse is not known: but it is matter of record that just ten years after the first employment of Mr. Pormort the town purchased of Mr. Thomas Scottow his dwelling-house and yard, which at this time (the 31st of March, A. D. 1645) was situated on the very lot upon a part of which the City Hall now stands; and that in

FIRST LATIN SCHOOL, SCHOOL LANE.

the October following the constables of the town were ordered to set off six shillings of the rate of Mr. Henry Messenger, the northerly abutter, 'for mending the schoolm' his p' of the partition fence between their gardens.' On this spot stood the first schoolhouse in Boston of which we have any positive knowledge; edging westerly upon the burial-ground, and fronting southerly upon the street which obtained its designation, School Lane, from this fact. As time wore on the old schoolhouse, which had served not only as a place for nurturing the youth of the town but also for the indwelling of the master and his family, fell into decay; and in order to make room for an enlargement of the neighboring chapel, it was taken down in 1748, and another building was erected on the opposite side of the street. 'Master Lovell' opposed the removal; but the town agreed to it in a tumultuous meeting (April 18, 1748), by two hundred

THE ENGLISH HIGH AND LATIN SCHOOL.

and five yeas to one hundred and ninety-seven nays. In the afternoon of the same day this epigram was sent to Mr. Lovell: —

> "'A fig for your learning! I tell you the Town,
> To make the *Church* larger, must pull the School down.
> Unluckily spoken, replied Master Birch, —
> Then *learning*, I fear, stops the growth of the *Church*.'"

Dr. Shurtleff continues his sketch: "In course of time, also, this building yielded to the effects of age and inadequacy, and was renewed about the year 1812," — on the site of the Parker House. "Up to this time the building was designated as the Centre Schoolhouse, after which time it was properly called the Latin Schoolhouse.' This building gave place to the one on Bedford Street, erected in the years 1843-44."

Strange stories are told of the discipline of these old-time schools from fifty to one hundred and fifty years ago.

Good Dr. Johnson, of the "English Dictionary," once had a teacher who wrote a spelling-book and dedicated it "To the *Universe*." Perhaps it was the comprehensive mind of this teacher that made Dr. Johnson a philologist. In speaking of the severe discipline of the schools of the time, Dr. Johnson says that his teacher would punish a boy for not answering a question, whether the boy had any opportunity to know the answer or not.

"He would ask him the Latin for *candlestick*, and if he could not answer he would beat him."

General Oliver, in speaking of the punishments inflicted by one of the teachers in the Latin School, says: —

"He gave me a whipping, but soon after discovered that I was not guilty of the act for which I had been whipped. 'Never mind, Oliver,' he said, 'I will put this to your credit for the next misconduct, and it will not be long before the account will stand all right.'" The General says he soon cancelled the account.

The new Latin School building on Dartmouth Street and Warren Avenue, erected for the use of the High School as well as the Latin School, is the finest structure in America devoted to educational purposes, and the largest in the world as a free public school. It was begun in 1877 and completed in 1880. It is 339 feet long, 220 feet wide, and contains fifty-six school-rooms. It has an elegant exhibition hall 62×82, and a drill hall 130×60. The halls, passages, corridors, and stairways more resemble an academy of art than a school building. Statuary, pictures, and adornments of art meet the visitor on every hand. No one interested in education should visit Boston without seeing this elegant little city of school-rooms, and gaining the inspiration that such a noble structure inspires.

HARVARD COLLEGE.

The beginning of Harvard College in Cambridge, of which we would speak briefly, was similar to that of the Boston Latin School. Boston had been settled six years when, in the autumn of 1636, the General Court voted the sum of £400 towards the erection of a college. In November, 1637, the college was "ordered to be at Newtown," and in the following spring it was enacted that "Newtown shall henceforward be called Cambridge," in honor of the place of education of many of the colonists.

In 1638 Rev. John Harvard of Charlestown died, leaving to the institution one half of his estate and the whole of his library. In return for the benefaction it was ordered that, "The college to be built in Cambridge be called Harvard College."

Mr. Nathaniel Eaton was the first master of this school. He belonged to the old type of teachers. "A mere Orbilius," says Hubbard, "fitter to have been an officer in the inquisition, or master of an house of correction than an instructer of christian youth." We must doubt his fitness even for the position of an officer in a penal institution, for he demeaned himself "in such a scandalous and cruel manner," as a teacher at Cambridge, that he was dismissed. In 1638 commenced the regular course of academic instruction in the new college, and in 1642 nine young men graduated and received their degrees.

The bequest of Harvard amounted to only about £780, but it promoted the establishment of a university which to-day has more than twelve hundred students; a million in endowment; theological, law, medical, and scientific schools of the highest reputation in America; and whose elegant buildings fill a park and would constitute a town.

John Harvard was buried in Charlestown. A monument in the old burying-ground was erected to his memory by Harvard students, and was dedicated in 1828.

COLLEGES IN BOSTON.

Boston University seems destined to be one of the most popular and influential schools in America. It was founded in 1869 by Isaac Rich, Lee Claflin, and Jacob Sleeper. It includes three colleges, four professional schools, and a post-graduate scientific school. It admits females on the same conditions as males, and its standard of admission is very high. Its principal buildings are on Beacon Street, near the Athenæum, but its schools are located in different parts of the city. It is richly endowed, and all of its schools are attended with remarkable success.

The Massachusetts Institute of Technology, a school of industrial science, was founded in 1861. It has forty instructors and three hundred students. The Institute is on the Back Bay, has a noble Greek front, and is one of the finest edifices in the city.

Such were some of the schools of the past, and such are some of the great institutions of learning at the present time. Truly the founders of Boston "built better than they knew." The influence of Boston schools is felt in every State of the Union, and is one of the elements of strength of the Republic.

"When, from the sacred garden driven,
    Man fled before his Maker's wrath,
An angel left her place in heaven,
    And crossed the wanderer's sunless path.
'T was Art, sweet Art! New radiance broke
    Where her light foot flew o'er the ground;
And thus with seraph voice she spoke, —
    'The Curse a Blessing shall be found.'

"She led him through the trackless wild,
    Where noontide sunbeam never blazed;
The thistle shrunk, the harvest smiled,
    And Nature gladdened as she gazed.
Earth's thousand tribes of living things,
    At Art's command, to him are given;
The village grows, the city springs,
    And point their spires of faith to heaven.

"He rends the oak, and bids it ride,
    To guard the shores its beauty graced;
He smites the rock, — upheaved in pride,
    See towers of strength and domes of taste.
Earth's teeming caves their wealth reveal,
    Fire bears his banner on the wave,
He bids the mortal poison heal,
    And leaps triumphant o'er the grave.

"He plucks the pearls that stud the deep,
    Admiring Beauty's lap to fill;
He breaks the stubborn marble's sleep,
    And mocks his own Creator's skill;
With thoughts that swell his glowing soul,
    He bids the ore illume the page,
And proudly scorning Time's control,
    Commerces with an unborn age.

"In fields of air he writes his name,
    And treads the chambers of the sky;
He reads the stars, and grasps the flame
    That quivers round the Throne on high.
In war renowned, in peace sublime,
    He moves in greatness and in grace;
His power, subduing space and time,
    Links realm to realm, and race to race."

                        Charles Sprague.

CHAPTER XXI.

THE ASSOCIATIONS OF BOSTON POETRY.

THE first Boston poet was Rev. John Cotton, whom Cotton Mather calls the " father and glory of Boston." He was the second pastor of the earliest church, a correspondent of Cromwell, and a most conscientious and zealous preacher. He thus alludes to his work in the new colony in one of his poems : —

> " When I think of the sweet and gracious company
> That at Boston once I had,
> And of the long peace of a fruitful ministry
> For twenty years enjoyed."

His skill as a poet may be seen in the following quaint, elegant, and ingenious lines addressed to Rev. Thomas Hooker of Hartford : —

> " To see three things was holy Austin's wish, —
> Rome in her flower, Christ Jesus in the flesh,
> And Paul in the pulpit: lately men might see
> Two first and more in Hooker's ministry.
>
> Zion in beauty is a fairer sight
> Than Rome in flower, with all her glory dight:
> Yet Zion's beauty did more clearly shine
> In Hooker's rule and doctrine : both divine.

> "Christ in the spirit is more than Christ in flesh,
> Our souls to quicken and our states to bless,
> Yet Christ in spirit brake forth mightily
> In faithful Hooker's searching ministry.
>
> "Paul in the pulpit Hooker could not reach,
> Yet did he Christ in spirit so lively preach
> That living hearers thought he did inherit
> A double portion of Paul's lively spirit."

Governor Bradford of Plymouth Colony, one of the Mayflower's pilgrims, was also a poet. We give a single specimen of his verse: —

TO BOSTON.

> "O Boston, though thou now art grown
> To be a great and wealthy town,
> Yet I have seen thee a void place,
> Shrubs and bushes covering thy face,
> And house in thee none were there,
> Nor such as gold and silk did wear,
> No drunkenness were then in thee,
> Nor such excess as now we see,
> We then drunk freely of thy spring,
> Without paying of anything."

A picture of the Golden Age indeed.

The favorite poet of the colony was Anne Bradstreet, daughter of Governor Dudley. She had an English reputation, and was greatly admired and praised by Cotton Mather. She was an ambitious writer and made free use of obscure classical quotations. One of her long poems is entitled "The Four Monarchies of the World."

We have spoken of Mather Byles's poetry. Benjamin Franklin wrote poems, and John Quincy Adams produced several elegant reflective poems which may be found in many collections.

Richard H. Dana, who lately died at the age of more than ninety years, was the first of the generation of poets of the present century. Although he lived to be so old he closed his literary work in middle age. He was a man of excellent influence both in literature and private life.

The fine historic poem found in many school Readers and Speakers entitled "The Dirge of Alaric the Visigoth" was written by Edward Everett at Harvard College.

BENJAMIN FRANKLIN.

We now come to a generation of poets whose works are the classics of American literature.

PIERPONT.

John Pierpont, author of the "Airs of Palestine," and in his day the poet of Boston's great public occasions, was born at Litchfield, Connecticut, 1785. In 1819 he was ordained pastor of Hollis Street Church. He was an eloquent advocate of the temperance and the antislavery cause. At the age of seventy-six he went into the Union army as chaplain of a Massachusetts regiment, and was one of the oldest chaplains in the field. He died at Medford, 1866. As we have spoken of him elsewhere, we give but a brief notice in this connection.

CHARLES SPRAGUE

was known in the city as the "poet-banker." Like Pierpont, he was a descendant of one of the fine old New England families. He was educated in the Franklin School. In 1825 he was elected cashier in the Globe Bank, and he held the office until the time of his death, or nearly half a century.

CHARLES SPRAGUE.

He was a lover of his home, his family, and friends. Nearly all of his best-known poems were inspired by home affection, as for example : —

"We are all here,
Father, mother, sister, brother."

His lines entitled "The Brothers" have the same spirit, and show how sacred to him was his own hearth-stone : —

"We in one mother's arms were locked,
    Long be her love repaid!
In the same cradle we were rocked,
    Round the same hearth we played.

"We are but two : be that the bond
    To hold us till we die;
Shoulder to shoulder let us stand,
    Till side by side we lie."

Next to his family Mr. Sprague loved his native city. We have heard it stated, we know not with what truth, that he only spent one night out of the city for twenty-five years, and that on that occasion, on returning home, he expressed a wish to a friend that twenty-five years might pass ere he should spend a night out of Boston again. His finest poem, with which nearly every schoolboy is familiar, entitled " Ode on Art," and beginning : —

> " When, from the sacred garden driven,
> Man fled before his Maker's wrath,"

was written for the Mechanics' Fair, or the 6th Triennial Festival of the Mechanics' Charitable Association, in 1824. The exhibitions of this Association were way-marks in the progress of Boston's industrial arts ; the Mechanics' Building and Hall, on Chauncy and Bedford Streets, were built from the funds of this society, and the old Mechanics' Fair was a local pride and glory. A permanent building for the exhibition has just been completed on Huntington Avenue.

The old Chauncy Street Church, which Sprague vaguely pictures in the poem entitled " The Winged Worshippers," is gone. The elegant structure on Berkeley Street known as the First Church is its successor. The society, before its removal to Chauncy Street, occupied the Old Brick Church, a quaint structure famous in early history, which stood where is now the Rogers Building, on Washington Street.

HENRY WARE, JR.

We took a walk, on a recent Sunday morning, to the Second Church, on the Boston Back Bay, which stands between the Institute of Technology and the New Old South Church. The beautiful chapel is adorned with mural inscriptions containing the names of the pastors of the church, beginning with John Cotton and Cotton Mather, and ending with Ralph Waldo Emerson. Among the mural epitaphs is that of Henry Ware, Jr. He was pastor of the church as it existed at its most flourishing period in another part of the city, for twelve years.

There are men who come into the world royally endowed with dispositions and graces to exalt the aims and thoughts of those whom they reach by their influence. Such a man was Henry Ware. He was born at Hingham, Massachusetts, 1794, and died in 1843. To live for the good of others was the inspiration of his stainless and prayerful youth. For twelve years one of the most cultivated congregations in Boston was drawn to his church. The edifice where he preached was called the Cockerell Church, from the unchurchly bird on the vane. It stood on Hanover Street. Charlotte Cushman began life as a public singer here.

If a discriminating student of literature were to be asked what he considered the most sublime production of any New-England poet, he would probably answer, The lines to the Ursa Major by Henry Ware, Jr. It is almost the only Miltonic production of the American muse : —

> "Awake, my soul,
> And meditate the wonder ! Countless suns
> Blaze round thee, leading forth their countless worlds, —
> Worlds in whose bosoms living things rejoice,
> And drink the bliss of being from the fount
> Of all-pervading Love. What mind can know,
> What tongue can utter, all their multitudes !
> Thus numberless in numberless abodes,
> Known but to thee, blessed Father ! Thine they are, —
> Thy children, and thy care, and none o'erlooked
> Of thee ! No; not the humblest soul that dwells
> Upon the humblest globe which wheels its course
> Amid the giant glories of the sky,
> Like the mean mote that dances in the beam
> Amongst the mirrored lamps, which fling
> Their wasteful splendor from the palace wall,
> None, none escape the kindness of thy care ;
> All compassed underneath thy spacious wing,
> Each fed and guided by thy powerful hand.

THE "OLD BRICK" CHURCH.

"Tell me, ye splendid orbs! as from your throne
Ye mark the rolling provinces that own
Your sway,— what beings fill those bright abodes?
How formed, how gifted; what their powers, their state,
Their happiness, their wisdom? Do they bear
The stamp of human nature? Or has God
Peopled those purer realms with loftier forms
And more celestial minds? Does Innocence
Still wear her native and untainted bloom?
Or has Sin breathed his deadly blight abroad,
And sowed corruption in those fairy bowers?
Has War trod o'er them with his foot of fire?
And Slavery forged his chains? and Wrath and Hate
And sordid Selfishness and cruel Lust
Leagued their base bands to tread out light and truth,
And scatter woe where Heaven had planted joy?
Or are they yet all paradise, unfallen
And uncorrupt, existence one long joy,
Without disease upon the frame, or sin
Upon the heart, or weariness of life,
Hope never quenched, and age unknown,
And death unfeared; while fresh and fadeless youth
Glows in the light from God's near throne of love?
Open your lips, ye wonderful and fair!

"Speak, speak! the mysteries of those living worlds
Unfold! No language? Everlasting light,
And everlasting silence? Yet the eye
May read and understand. The hand of God
Has written legibly what man may know,—
The glory of the Maker. There it shines,
Ineffable, unchangeable; and man,
Bound to the surface of this pigmy globe,
May know and ask no more. In other days,
When death shall give the encumbered spirit wings,
Its range shall be extended; it shall roam,
Perchance, amongst those vast, mysterious spheres;
Shall pass from orb to orb, and dwell in each
Familiar with its children, learn their laws,
And share their state, and study and adore
The infinite varieties of bliss

> And beauty, by the hand of Power divine
> Lavished on all its works. Eternity
> Shall thus roll on with ever fresh delight;
> No pause of pleasure or improvement; world
> On world still opening to the instructed mind, —
> An unexhausted universe, and time
> But adding to its glories. While the soul,
> Advancing ever to the Source of light
> And all perfection, lives, adores, and reigns
> In cloudless knowledge, purity, and bliss."

We make this copious extract from the poem for the purpose of giving force to an incident that is not well known.

Henry Ware died in the prime of manhood. When the last hour was approaching, the thoughts and visions that had wrapt and entranced his mind when writing the majestic poem seemed to come back to him again. His mind went up, up to the golden circles and zones, and wandered again among the stars. "My mind," he said, "is crowded with precious thoughts of death and immortality. I feel like one who views the parting of the clouds on a dark night. Star after star begins to appear in the space beyond; and the stars I see are but the sentinels of the radiant myriads yet to be revealed."

The origin of another poem — a once popular school poem — illustrates the dignity of the writer's character. Henry Ware's friends were the representatives of wealth and cultured conservatism. But right, to him, was the first consideration, and he stood up grandly for the cause of the slave when antislavery ideas were unpopular in Boston. He believed that the moral sense of America would break the fetters of the bondsman; and he spoke of the coming day of universal liberty with the fire and assurance of an ancient prophet. The press assailed him; the pulpit stood apart from him; but the lamp of his faith burned with a steady flame. At this time, in the last years of his life, the great news of the

East Indian emancipation came ringing over the sea. England had emancipated 800,000 slaves. The abolitionists held a meeting for congratulation and rejoicing at Faneuil Hall. Ware was the poet of the enthusiastic occasion, and his muse caught the spirit of the event. He produced a poem that thrilled the audience and fired the reformers throughout the land. It was a key-note for freedom, and it stood as a prophecy for twenty years. It was the last poem of his life. How grandly it reads in the light of God's providence to-day! We need quote only the opening lines, for it is familiar to all who have had experience in elocutionary exercises: —

> "Oppression shall not always reign,
> There comes a brighter day."

The story of its origin will explain the words which used to be mystical to us: —

> "Old Faneuil echoes to the roar,
> And rocks as never rocked before
> And ne'er shall rock again."

Ware sleeps in Mount Auburn.

HENRY W. LONGFELLOW.

Some time ago, while collecting material for this chapter, we went to Cambridge. The horse-car stopped on a broad, shaded avenue, just outside of Old Cambridge, leaving us under the long, bright archway of October trees. It was a dreamy, hazy afternoon, in whose still, mellow air one might hear the crisp leaves as they dropped among the seared grasses and faded flowers.

A little back from the avenue, garnished with billowy shrubbery which the early autumn had so touched that every hedge seemed to have its burning bush, and among old elms illuminated by spires and turrets of flame, stood an ancient mansion, whose airy porticos and broad, stately appearance reminded the stranger that he looked upon a relic of colonial days. Everything around the mansion seemed quiet, grand, and old. The great elms embraced it with their glowing arms; centennial elms they were, under whose shade Washington and Lafayette had stood.

The house is the residence of Henry Wadsworth Longfellow. All of our readers who love his pure poetry, so full of refreshment and exhilaration, have visited this old mansion, at least, in their dreams.

> "Somewhat back from the village street
> Stands the old-fashioned country-seat.
> Across its antique portico
> Tall poplar-trees their shadows throw.
> And from its station in the hall
> The ancient time-piece says to all, —
> Forever — never!
> Never — forever!"

It was in this old house that the "Psalm of Life," "Excelsior," "Footsteps of Angels," "Hiawatha," and many other poems, familiar as household names, were written.

The house was built for the Vassal family, who were among the most wealthy residents of Cambridge in colonial days. When under the Cambridge elms Washington took command of the American army, in July, 1775, this capacious mansion became his headquarters. Here, more than a hundred years ago, those distinguished persons whose names are associated with the Revolutionary history used to visit him. The house afterwards became the residence of the professors and presidents of Harvard College. In 1835 Mr. Longfellow, having been appointed Professor of Modern Languages and Literature in Harvard College, took up his residence in this historic house.

The poet was born in Portland, Maine, in 1807. In his boyhood he was noted for his studious habits, and such were his brilliancy and industry that he entered Bowdoin College at the early age of fourteen.

It is reported that his first compositions were rejected when offered to a publisher. However this may be, it is true that he wrote in his early years such beautiful poems as the "Hymn of the Moravian Nuns," "The Woods in Winter," and "The Spirit of Beauty."

After his graduation he visited Europe, studying art and the modern languages in the grand old continental cities. His poems have since followed him into all the countries through which he travelled in youth, having been translated into all the principal European tongues.

He made a second visit to Europe in 1835, before assuming the duties of the Harvard professorship. He studied in the old Northern cities, and there laid the foundation of those poems and works associated with Scandinavian history and literature.

Professor Longfellow has lived forty years in the old mansion. With a poet's reverence for old associations, he has refused to have the house altered in any respect, but has filled its antique rooms with books, pictures, statues, and flowers.

We turned from the arched street and entered the open lawn, in whose low grass the late crickets were singing. We were led into the broad hall of the old mansion, through which a wide staircase ascends, and around which are hung pictures and other decorations of art, and where once the form of Washington was often seen.

> "Up and down the echoing stairs,
> Heavy with the weight of cares,
> Sounded his majestic tread."

One of the old rooms occupied by Washington is his study, and to this we were led. It is a fine apartment, richly stored with cabinets of books and with choice works of art. On the table is Coleridge's inkstand, from which was possibly written the "Ancient Mariner." Among numerous relics near at hand are Tom Moore's waste-paper basket, and a small fragment of Dante's coffin. Green plants mingle with the works of art, and the busts of departed friends recall incidents of the years that live only in books or in memory.

In this study stands an old clock, a stately piece of furniture, rising from floor to ceiling, and burnished with the deep, rich color that only age can give. It has sounded the hours in which many of the poet's best compositions have been written, and is made familiar by the poem, "The Old Clock on the Stairs."

Longfellow's poems are as familiar as words of common comfort. Yet, unlike these words, they have not lost their sense of daily use. Nearly every one is acquainted with some of them; most people know many of them; every schoolboy reads and declaims them; and every pulpit quotes them. When a speaker's best thoughts struggle for expression he seeks their help; when bereavement comes into the family these poems are moistened with tears. There are few lives which they have not befriended, and those they have touched, their virtue has refined and elevated.

What a flight of "winged words" has gone out of this old mansion to minister to the refreshment of the world!

ORIGIN OF LONGFELLOW'S POEMS.

It may interest our readers to know the circumstances under which the most familiar of Longfellow's poems were written.

The "Psalm of Life" was written in Cambridge on a fragrant summer morning in 1838. Professor Longfellow was then a young man, hopeful and aspiring; life lay open before him, and the poem but reflected the glow of the poet's spirit and expressed the longing of his heart. He regarded it at first as a personal meditation, like a hopeful entry in one's private diary, and refused to publish it. The poem was printed at last and flew over the world. A portion of it was lately found in Japan, inscribed in Japanese on a fan, which was sent to the poet, who now has it in his possession.

"I was once riding in London," said Mr. Longfellow, "when a laborer approached the carriage and asked, 'Are you the writer of the "Psalm of Life"?'

"'I am.'

"'Will you allow me to shake hands with you?'

"We clasped hands warmly. The carriage passed on, and I saw him no more; but I remember that as one of the most gratifying compliments I ever received, because it was so sincere."

The "Footsteps of Angels," read by so many with tearful memories of the loved and lost, was also an expression of his own feelings. Mr. Longfellow's first wife, a lady of great excellence and loveliness of character, accompanied him to Europe, and died in Rotterdam in 1835. Her decease in the bright morning of life was one of the experiences that make his early poems so tender in their suggestiveness when they speak of bereavement.

> "Then the forms of the departed
>   Enter at the open door;
> The beloved, the true-hearted,
>   Come to visit me once more.
>
> . . .
>
> "And with them the being beauteous,
>   Who unto my youth was given,
> More than all things else to love me,
>   And is now a saint in heaven."

"Excelsior" was written late on an autumn evening in 1841. The poet had received a letter from Charles Sumner, which, we may suppose, was full of noble sentiments. The word "excelsior" caught his eye on a piece of newspaper; a poetic vision rose before him in harmony with the occasion and his stimulated feelings, and he wrote the first draught of the poem on the back of Mr. Sumner's letter.

"The Wreck of the Hesperus" was written in 1839, at midnight. A violent storm had occurred the night before. The distress and disaster at sea had been great, especially on the capes of the New England coast. The poet was sitting in his study late at night, when the shadowy vision of the wrecked Hesperus came vividly before him. He went to bed but could not sleep. He arose and wrote the poem, which came into his mind by stanzas rather than by lines, finishing it just as the "old clock on the stairs" was striking three.

Sir Walter Scott says that he was led to write the romance of Kenilworth because the first stanza of Mickle's famous ballad of Cumnor Hall haunted him.

> "The dews of summer night did fall;
> The moon, sweet regent of the sky,
> Silvered the towers of Cumnor Hall,
> And many an oak that grew thereby."

Longfellow attributes the writing of "The Wreck of the Hesperus" in part to the dreary sound of the words "Norman's Woe."

"The Hanging of the Crane" has a very pleasing history. Longfellow made an evening call on a promising young poet who has since become known to the public. He found him, as the story is told, living in a cosey, humble way, with the tea-table drawn up before the fire, and only the young poet and his newly married wife at the board.

"You are two now," said Longfellow, or words to this effect; "before long little angels will gladden the household, and you will need a larger table. Years will pass and the table will grow; then one by one the loved faces will leave you and you will be two at the table, as you are now. Why do you not write a romance on the Acadian custom of the hanging of the crane, giving distinctness to these family scenes and changes?"

Ten years afterward Longfellow reverted to the subject, and asked the poet if he had attempted the romance. On learning that he had not, he himself wrote the poem which so vividly and elegantly pictures the usual course of domestic history.

The story of Evangeline was first related to Longfellow by Hawthorne, who had been advised to write a romance upon it. But Longfellow gave the Acadian jewel a choicer setting. The story of Hiawatha was related to Schoolcraft by Abraham Le Fort, an Onondaga chief, and may in part be found in Schoolcraft's "Indian Tribes." Longfellow has woven much Indian legendary lore into the warp of the original tradition, which is in itself the poetry of romance. The "Tales of the Wayside Inn" were suggested by the old colonial hostelry at Sudbury, which may still be seen.

The poems of Longfellow touch tenderly on sorrow, for his life has been full of affections and friendships broken by death. His first wife, as we have stated, died in a foreign land. His second wife died young, under very afflicting circumstances. His intimate friends, Hawthorne, Felton, Sumner, Agassiz, are gone. Thoughts of the unseen world seem ever welcome to his mind. One needs to know these facts of his personal history to understand how closely his inner life is reproduced in his poetry. His poems on bereavement are no affected sentiment, but the sincere language of a bereaved, trustful heart.

The shadows were lengthening along the lawn, and the crickets singing plaintively in the hedges, as we turned reluctantly away from the old house in which the spirit of departed days seems to linger, and around which, in the dim future, other memories will gather.

It was evening when we returned to Boston, by way of the old Charles River Bridge, which some thirty years ago suggested to Longfellow the writing of his beautiful poem, "The Bridge," beginning, —

> "I stood on the bridge at midnight,
>   As the clocks were striking the hour,
> And the moon rose o'er the city,
>   Behind the dark church-tower.
>
> . . .
>
> "And far in the hazy distance
>   Of that lovely night in June,
> The blaze of the flaming furnace
>   Gleamed redder than the moon.
>
> .
>
> "How often, O how often,
>   In the days that had gone by
> I had stood on that bridge at midnight,
>   And gazed on the wave and sky!
>
> "How often, O how often,
>   I had wished that the ebbing tide
> Would bear me away on its bosom
>   O'er the ocean wild and wide!
>
> "For my heart was hot and restless,
>   And my life was full of care,
> And the burden laid upon me
>   Seemed greater than I could bear."

ELMWOOD: THE HOME OF LOWELL.

JAMES RUSSELL LOWELL.

Among the living writers of poetry that Boston claims are James Russell Lowell, J. T. Trowbridge, T. B. Aldrich, and W. D. Howells. Though belonging to Boston's literary circle, they, like Longfellow and Whittier, are not, except for brief

JAMES RUSSELL LOWELL.

periods, residents of the city. Lowell lives at "Elmwood," an historic estate near Mount Auburn, associated in literature with his thoughtful work, "My Study Windows." Governor Oliver was mobbed here during the excitement that preceded the Revolution. Mr. Lowell was born in 1819. In 1848 he published "The Vision of Sir Launfal" and "The Biglow Papers." He succeeded Mr. Longfellow as Professor of Modern Languages and Belles-Lettres at Harvard University in 1855. He has travelled extensively and is now U. S. Minister to the Court of St. James. Mr. Trowbridge lives at Arlington, on the borders of Spy Pond. His place is also associated with an incident of the Revolution. It is on Pleasant Street, one of the most beautiful streets in any New England town. Mr. Aldrich has done some of his best literary work at his country residence at Ponkapog, Massachusetts, but his home at present is in Boston. Mr. Howells resides in Belmont in a unique English house commanding beautiful views. He is neighbor to Mr. Trowbridge.

OLIVER WENDELL HOLMES.

The works of Dr. Oliver Wendell Holmes, more than those of any other poetical writer, are associated with Boston's history and with recent public events. He lives in Boston, is a home-poet, and for half a century has usually been invited to celebrate in song notable public occasions. He was born in Cambridge in 1809. He is a medical professor in Harvard College, and has delivered medical lectures before the students in Boston for many years. In 1857 he began to publish in the *Atlantic* one of his most popular works, "The Autocrat of the Breakfast-Table." His poems, "Cambridge Churchyard," "Boston Common," "Under the Washington Elm," &c., are local pictures in verse. One of his poems, "The Dorchester Giant," pretends to explain a sight that any visitor to the Highlands may see, and it is so agreeable as a local fancy that we give it here.

OLIVER WENDELL HOLMES.

THE DORCHESTER GIANT.

THERE was a giant in time of old,
    A mighty one was he;
He had a wife, but she was a scold,
So he kept her shut in his mammoth fold;
    And he had children three.

It happened to be an election day,
    And the giants were choosing a king;
The people were not democrats then,
They did not talk of the rights of men,
    And all that sort of thing.

Then the giant took his children three
    And fastened them in the pen;
The children roared; quoth the giant, "Be still!"
And Dorchester Heights and Milton Hill
    Rolled back the sound again.

Then he brought them a pudding stuffed with plums
    As big as the State House dome;
Quoth he, "There's something for you to eat;
So stop your mouths with your 'lection treat,
    And wait till your dad comes home."

So the giant pulled him a chestnut stout,
    And whittled the boughs away;
The boys and their mother set up a shout;
Said he, "You're in, and you can't get out,
    Bellow as loud as you may."

Off he went, and he growled a tune
    As he strode the fields along;
'T is said a buffalo fainted away,
And fell as cold as a lump of clay,
    When he heard the giant's song.

But whether the story 's true or not,
    It is not for me to show;
There 's many a thing that 's twice as queer
In somebody's lectures that we hear,
    And those are true, you know.

    .   .   .   .   .

What are those lone ones doing now,
    The wife and the children sad?
O! they are in a terrible rout,
Screaming, and throwing their pudding about,
    Acting as they were mad.

They flung it over to Roxbury hills,
    They flung it over the plain,
And all over Milton and Dorchester too
Great lumps of pudding the giants threw;
    They tumbled as thick as rain.

    .   .   .   .

Giant and mammoth have passed away,
    For ages have floated by;
The suet is hard as a marrow-bone,
And every plum is turned to a stone,
    But there the puddings lie.

And if, some pleasant afternoon,
    You 'll ask me out to ride,
The whole of the story I will tell,
And you shall see where the puddings fell,
    And pay for the treat beside.

MRS. JULIA WARD HOWE.

Mrs. Julia Ward Howe, author of the "Battle Hymn of the Republic," is a resident of Boston. She has written much in the interest of the charities of the city and of the social improvement of women. Among her best poems are "Lyrics of the Street."

JAMES T. FIELDS.

The grave has recently closed over James T. Fields, who for years was the central figure among Boston publishers, editors, and literary men. He belonged to the publishing house of Ticknor & Fields.

Mr. Fields was more than an author or a publisher. He was a sympathetic gentleman, who passed beyond the limitations of business and letters, that he might become the friend of the writers whose works he published. Several notable authors, as a tribute to the sympathy of the man, and the generosity of the publisher, dedicated to him their best works. Not a few poems and novels, now ranked among American classics, owed their appearance to Mr. Fields. It is not strange that these authors should become the friend of the man who had discerned their gold while in the ore. They associated themselves heartily with Ticknor & Fields, and helped to make the "Old Corner Bookstore" one of the landmarks of Boston, and famous in the annals of American literature.

No publishing house could show a more brilliant galaxy of authors than Ticknor & Fields. Among American authors whose books bore their imprint were Longfellow, Whittier, Lowell, Holmes, Saxe, Bayard Taylor, Hawthorne, Whipple, Hillard, Stoddard, Stedman, Agassiz, Aldrich, Howells, Trowbridge, Alice Cary, Gail Hamilton, Elizabeth Stuart Phelps, and Mrs. Harriet Beecher Stowe.

Two visits which Mr. Fields made to England, where he was an honored guest, put the firm's name upon the works of De Quincy, Thackeray, Dickens, Tennyson, Kingsley, Reade, and Leigh Hunt.

Mr. Fields, though intimately associated for fifty years with the literary and social life of the city, was a "Boston boy" only by adoption. He was born in Portsmouth, New Hampshire, Dec. 31, 1817, and graduated from its High School at the age of thirteen. He came to Boston, a poor lad, to find a place where he might earn his living. He found it in a bookstore, and began at once to make the use of such talents as God had given him.

His days were given to faithful clerkly service, and his nights to reading and composition. So well did he serve, and such were the taste and discernment which study developed, that within twelve years he became a member of the firm. He made the name of Ticknor & Fields famous. Sagacious in divining the public taste, he was also quick to discern what young authors were likely to become eminent. His genial stimulus so encouraged these that they did their best work for the man who trusted them.

While serving as a clerk, Mr. Fields developed by study and practice the poetical faculty with which he had been gifted. At the age of eighteen, he caught the public ear by a poem delivered before the Boston Mercantile Library Association, on one occasion when Edward Everett was the orator. It was the beginning of a series of occasional poems recited at public commemorations and college commencements. Harvard and Dartmouth recognized the poet's merits, — the former by making him an A. M., and the latter by permitting him to annex, which he seldom did, LL.D. to his name.

Mr. Fields also became favorably known as the contributor to several periodicals, and as the editor of the *Atlantic Monthly*. Subsequent to his retirement from the publishing business, he stood frequently upon the lecture platform. Appreciative audiences greeted him, and listened with pleasure to his reminiscences of the great authors whose works were their favorite reading.

Mr. Fields's merit is not that he was a great poet or great

writer of English prose. His limitations kept him within the circle of minor poets. But what he undertook he did well. His work showed no marks of slovenliness. Good taste dictated what he should and should not say.

Mr. Fields's literary and business life is an example to youth. The poor lad made himself a name in the annals of literature. He did it by a kind heart, an energetic habit, and patient industry. He strove to make the best use of his talents, and to do so thoroughly his work that no carelessness would beget an occasion for apology.

He was a man of the best moral influence. He had no sympathy with those who think it bold to trifle with the claims of religion. In his last years he gave to one of the editors of a popular publication for young people a little poem, saying, "I want to give my testimony to the value of Christian faith," or words of that import. We produce it here : —

A PROTEST.

Go, sophist ! dare not to despoil
   My life of what it sorely needs
In days of pain, in hours of toil, —
   The bread on which my spirit feeds.

You see no light beyond the stars,
   No hope of lasting joys to come?
I feel, thank God, no narrow bars
   Between me and my final home !

Hence with your cold sepulchral bans, —
   The vassal doubts Unfaith has given !
My childhood's heart within the man's
   Still whispers to me, — "Trust in Heaven !"

"Do thou thy work; it shall succeed
　In thine or in another's day,
And if denied the victor's meed
　Thou shalt not miss the toiler's pay."

CHAPTER XXII.

ASSOCIATIONS OF WHITTIER'S POETRY.

JOHN G. WHITTIER.

"Beautiful! beautiful!" exclaimed President Washington, in 1789, as, riding into the town of Haverhill, his eye caught an extended view of the Merrimack. It was autumn. The trees seemed jewelled with rubies and gold, and the streams went winding away like a ribbon amid the unnumbered gems. "Haverhill," said Washington, "is the pleasantest village I ever passed through."

His eye was feasted with a continuous picture of forest-crowned hills, dreamy valleys, shadowy woods, and sparkling waters. He must have felt that such a region deserved to be the birthplace of a true poet, and would be in time.

There are poets who cull flowers from a limited field, and poets who gather blossoms in every land; poets who travel over the world in search of scenes and associations of romance and beauty; and untravelled poets to whom the world brings its riches in the solitude of fameless places. The traveller finds the associations of Moore's poetry on the streams of many lands, but the scenes of Wordsworth's poetry only on the quiet lakes of Grasmere and Windermere.

A like contrast presents itself in two of our own poets. Longfellow, spending the calm decline of life in delicious retirement on the banks of the Charles, has delved in all mines for poetic treasures. He wandered over Europe in his student days, studying her poets in new languages, as he travelled; and his own songs have since gone over the same journey, having been translated into all the languages he then learned. Whittier, in a busy little town on the Merrimack, has found an ample field for poetic thought amid the scenes and associations of home. Though he has temporarily lived in several American cities, his muse has not often wandered from a single rural district in Massachusetts, comprising less than twenty square miles.

To this we must make two exceptions. No "pent-up Utica" confined his muse in those soul-stirring lyrics inspired by his intense love of liberty and hatred of oppression. "Massachusetts to Virginia," with its clarion tones, echoed and re-echoed from every hillside and through every valley, firing anew the patriotism so long dormant in the great and prosperous North. Closely related to this in spirit is his "Pennsylvania Pilgrim." Ready at all times to do justice to the Pilgrims of New England, who have not lacked historian and poet, he felt that the Quaker pilgrims of Pennsylvania, "seeking the same object by different means, had not been equally fortunate." In this little poem he has tried, and not in vain, to erect a simple monument over the unmarked resting-place of one of the two "historical forces with which no others may be compared in their influence on the people."

Whoever reads the "Pennsylvania Pilgrim," with the notes, in which he has rescued a few names from oblivion, will have a picture, though drawn in sober colors, as becomes the subject, in which the figures will stand out from the canvas in bolder relief as the ages glide away and the spirit of Christianity is better understood.

With these exceptions, as we have said, the muse of Whittier seldom wandered beyond the limits of old Essex.

But these twenty square miles of old Essex County are rich with poetic subjects, scenes of rural simplicity, landscapes diversified with river views and sea views, old colonial superstitions, and historic and legendary lore. From the calm hills of East Haverhill, where the poet was born, to the murmurous beaches of Cape Ann, which he has famed in ballad, the region is worthy of a poet, and has found a poet faithful and true to the trusts of home. To this district the genius of Whittier has always turned in its poetic moods, like Goldsmith's to Auburn and Lissory, and like Burns's to the Doon and Ayr. While the poetry of Longfellow shows how thought is enriched by travel, the poetry of Whittier illustrates the wealth of beauty an observant mind may find in restricted limits and native soil. His songs are not the notes of migrations, but native inspirations, attuned to the hills, vales, and rivers of home. If we know less of the world at large by this untravelled culture, we know more of the rich endowments of special places and localities. His estimate of Wordsworth's poetic mission is a just measure of himself: —

> "The sunrise on his breezy lake,
>   The rosy tints his sunset brought,
> World-seen, are gladdening all the vales
>   And mountain-peaks of thought.
>
> " Art builds on sand ; the works of pride
>   And human passion change and fall,
> But that which shares the life of God
>   With him surviveth all."

The localities that have furnished the most frequent subjects for Whittier's pen, and that have helped form the framework, texture, and coloring of nearly all that he has written, are the old towns of East Haverhill, Newbury, Newburyport, Gloucester, the thriving town of Amesbury, the river Merrimack, and the fine Atlantic beaches from Cape Ann to Marblehead.

In the first of these places, East Haverhill, the poet was born, in 1808. He is a descendant of a Quaker family, who early settled upon the banks of the Merrimack, and whose members, from early colonial times, have had a local reputation for piety, good sense, and hospitality. In the perilous times of the Indian war the Whittier family refused to accept the offer of armed protection, though their house was near a garrison, but trusted to the effects of their honor and kind and just dealing with the savages, and were unmolested. Whittier's father, as described in "Snow-Bound," was "a prompt, decisive man." But his energy of character was quite equalled by his benevolence; for he was always charitable to others' failings, and good to the poor. His mother was a patient, loving woman, with a heart to feel for every one, always contented and happy in the affection of her children.

The family library consisted of few books, chiefly of a religious character, and among these "The Pilgrim's Progress" seems to have been the favorite of John's early years. The district school was not favorable to large literary acquirements, being kept by an odd genius, who was sometimes more fond of his toddy than his pupils, and who at these intervals used to have sharp words with his wife, who tended her baby in an adjoining room. The school-room and the queer old pedagogue are described in some lines "To my Old Schoolmaster," with much tenderness of feeling and an evasive deliciousness of humor that makes the smile tremble on the reader's lips : —

THE CARWITHAM VIEW OF BOSTON ABOUT 1730.

> "Through the cracked and crazy wall
> Came the cradle-rock and squall,
> And the goodman's voice at strife
> With his shrill and tipsy wife,
> Luring us by stories old,
> With a comic unction told,
> More than by the eloquence
> Of terse birchen arguments."

The picture of Whittier's early home, which was as hospitable as that which wandering Oliver Goldsmith so much loved to remember, is familiar to all the readers of "Snow-Bound." The very barn is as a familiar place, and all the members of the old family are acquaintances. The reader remembers the kind-hearted uncle, " innocent of books," —

> "A simple, guileless, child-like man,
> Content to live where life began."

the sweet-faced " elder sister," —

> " How many a poor one's blessing went
> With thee beneath the low green tent
> Whose curtain never outward swings."

and even poor crazy Harriet Livermore, whose visits were the one terror to the children of the house.

Whittier speaks with great tenderness of the insanity of this last-named religious enthusiast : —

> "Whate'er her troubled path may be,
>   The Lord's sweet pity with her go !
> The outward wayward life we see,
>   The hidden springs we may not know.
> Nor is it given us to discern
> What threads the fatal sisters spun,
> Through what ancestral years has run
> The sorrow with the woman born ;
> What forged her cruel chain of moods,
> What set her feet in solitudes."

She was a woman of wonderful genius, and with a kindling fancy that startled those around her; but she was harsh and cruel in her darker moods, and sometimes inflicted personal violence on the children, to whom she was an object of awe. She expected to see the coming of the Lord with her own eyes, and, in this confidence, set out for Jerusalem.

> "Through Smyrna's plague-hushed thoroughfares,
> Up sea-set Malta's rocky stairs,
> Gray olive slopes of hills that hem
> Thy tombs and shrines, Jerusalem,
> Her tireless feet have held their way;
> And still unrestful, bowed and gray,
> She watches under Eastern skies,
>   With hope each day renewed and fresh,
>   The Lord's quick coming in the flesh,
> Whereof she dreams and prophesies."

It was in Haverhill that Whittier, in boyhood, wrote his first poems. He was, at the time, an almost unlettered and a very hard-working farmer's boy, upon whom the cares and responsibilities incident to New England farm-life had come early, and who had little home-sympathy in fostering a poetic taste. He sent one of these early rhymes, with much timidity, to William Lloyd Garrison, then an obscure editor of a free-speech paper, published in Newburyport.

It met with a more favorable reception than one of Longfellow's early efforts, which was returned with the gratuitous advice to the author, "to buckle down to the law." Mr. Garrison, on going into the office one day, found the poem under the door. It was written on coarse paper and in blue ink, and, thinking it was doggerel, he was about to throw it into the waste-basket, when some good angel of conscience stayed his hand, and he gave it a reading. In the poem he discovered a poet. Other poems arrived from the same source, and he at last inquired of the postman from what quarter these manuscripts came. The postman believed that they came from a farmer's boy in East Haverhill. "I will ride over and see him," said Garrison; and he made good the generous resolution. He found the young poet at work with his father on the old place. It was the first meeting of the two philanthropists, who were to become so famous in the antislavery contest, and wield so strong an influence in the world.

Young Whittier acknowledged to Garrison the authorship of the poems. The confession may have been hardly pleasing to Whittier's father, who, adhering to plain Quaker principles, did not look upon poetry as a very useful or promising vocation. Garrison urged the duty of sending a boy of such genius to school; but though the Quaker farmer did not seem convinced, John was soon after sent to the academy.

Whittier taught school for a time, and the district trustee thought him "a good tutorer." He came to Boston as an editor in 1829; went to Hartford, in 1830, to take charge of the *New England Weekly;* and afterward returned to Haverhill, to engage in agricultural pursuits. In 1835 he was elected to the Massachusetts Legislature, and afterward went to Philadelphia as an editor of the *Freeman.* These experiences are hardly brought into public notice in his poems. His Indian legends, recounting the old tales he had heard at Haverhill, were only passably successful; his poetic genius was of slow growth, and its recognition was slow.

But his opportunity came at last. The antislavery conflict furnished him a subject that kindled the lyric fire in his soul. His stirring odes, written at this period, which embraced the latter part of the brief portion of his life devoted to editing and politics, are everywhere known, and, as they are not directly connected with our subject, we pass their history.

Whittier's love of retirement led him to the Merrimack again. He settled at Amesbury, where his purely literary life may be said to have begun. Here he wrote "The Chapel of the Hermits," "Snow-Bound," "The Tent on the Beach," "In War Time," "Among the Hills," and nearly all of the domestic ballads which have become household words.

His home is a simple cottage, near the skirts of the town, plain without, but with an air of hospitable comfort within. Near it, on the borders of a tangled grove, is the little Quaker church, looking like an old-fashioned country school-house, standing, as it does, "at the parting of the ways." Here, on Thursdays and Sundays, the poet used to resort, with a few descendants of the old Quaker families, for silent worship. Many of his devout meditations here have doubtless proved the germs of those religious poems which have gone forth with their messages of love and peace to the world.

> "We rose, and slowly homeward turned,
> While down the west the sunset burned;
> And, in its light, hill, wood, and tide,
> And human forms seemed glorified.
>
> "The village homes transfigured stood,
> The purple bluffs, whose belting wood
> Across the waters leaned to hold
> The yellow leaves like lamps of gold.
>
> "Then spake my friend: 'Thy words are true:
> Forever old, forever new,
> These home-seen splendors are the same
> Which over Eden's sunsets came.'"

His house, on his retirement, was in charge of his sister, Elizabeth H. Whittier, a woman richly endowed in mind, with a sweet face and disposition, a pure, loving heart, and an ever conscientious life. The love of the two for each other was like that of Wordsworth for his sister, or of Charles and Mary Lamb. He speaks of this sweet fountain of affection again and again in his poems, and pays a most touching tribute to her memory in "Snow-Bound." She herself was a poet, and he was accustomed to read to her the first copy of what he wrote. He has gathered into "Hazel Blossoms" several of her best poems with his own. "Since she died," he once remarked to a friend, "I cannot tell whether what I have written is good for anything or not."

The years immediately following the establishment of the Whittiers at their home in Amesbury are among the most fruitful in the poet's history. There was a quiet beauty about their home whose charm was its simplicity. The poet had a delightful garden; little animals and pets were ever around him: a bantam now had the freedom of the kitchen, and now a gray parrot talked with him, very profoundly, from the back of his chair.

Eminent people shared the plain hospitality of the sunny rooms. Joseph Sturge found a welcome here. Sturge, like Whittier, was a descendant of a noted line of the gray fathers. Like Whittier, he was born in a rural town, reared in rustic simplicity, and entered *con amore* into the struggle against slavery. He came to this country full of antislavery zeal, and each heart — the poet's and the philanthropist's — knew its mate. After the death of Sturge's wife and child, his sister cared for his home. Both Whittier and his sister made his visit the occasion for verse-writing. When the sister of the reformer died, Whittier wrote to him : —

"Thine is a grief the depth of which another
    May never know;
Yet, o'er the waters, O my stricken brother!
    To thee I go.

"I lean my heart unto thee, sadly folding
    Thy hand in mine;
With even the weakness of my soul upholding
    The strength of thine."

The death of Sturge strongly affected the poet, and was made the occasion of the finest lines that, perhaps, he has ever written, beginning : —

> "In the fair land o'erwatched by Ischia's mountains,
>   Across the charmèd bay,
> Whose blue waves keep with Capri's silver fountains,
>   Perpetual holiday,
>
> A king lies dead," &c.

We have spoken of two of the towns in old Essex most intimately associated with his poetry, — East Haverhill, the scene of "Snow-Bound;" and Amesbury, the scene of his home ballads, and the place in which most of the poems having political reference were written. His muse, with all of its limitations, has a somewhat wider local range. The Merrimack, on which he was born, and from which he has never long wandered, may be considered as his "river of song : " —

> "We know the world is rich in streams
>   Renowned in song and story,
> Whose music murmurs through our dreams
>   Of human love and glory :
> We know that Arno's banks are fair,
>   And Rhine has castled shadows,
> And, poet-tuned, the Doon and Ayr
>   Go singing down their meadows.
>
> "But while, unpictured and unsung
>   By painter or by poet,
> Our river waits the tuneful tongue
>   And cunning hand to show it, —
> We only know the fond skies lean
>   Above it, warm with blessing,
> And the sweet soul of our Undine
>   Awakes to our caressing."

AN OLD-TIME HUSKING FROLIC.

The old towns of Newbury and Newburyport also share the immortality of his verse. The traveller who visits the tomb of Whitefield in the Federal Street Church, in Newburyport, will vividly call to mind the lines entitled "The Preacher."

> "Under the church of Federal Street,
> Under the tread of its Sabbath feet,
> Walled about by its basement stones,
> Lie the marvellous preacher's bones.
>
> . . . . .
>
> "Long shall the traveller strain his eye
> From the railroad car as it plunges by,
> And the vanishing town behind him search
> For the slender spire of the Whitefield Church."

Gloucester, with its fantastic ghost lore, against whose garrison the spirits of the air, in old colonial days, were supposed to wage a warfare; Marblehead, with old-time dialect, more strange when listened to than when seen in print, in the refrain of "Skipper Ireson's Ride;" the curving beaches that sweep away from the mouth of the Merrimack, on which the poet once pitched his summer tent with Fields, the poet and the second *Atlantic* editor, who could decline a MS. so neatly that

> "Bards, whose name is legion, if denied,
> Bore off alike intact their verses and their pride;"

and with Bayard Taylor, who,

> "In idling mood, had from him hurled
> The poor squeezed orange of the world," —

all have a place in the poet's local panorama. The "Songs of Labor," especially "The Shoemakers," "The Drovers," "The Huskers," and "The Fishermen," are all home scenes, as faithfully pictured as they are familiar to the dwellers in "old Essex."

"How beautiful it was, that one bright day
    In the long week of rain!
Though all its splendor could not chase away
    The omnipresent pain.

"The lovely town was white with apple-blooms,
    And the great elms o'erhead
Dark shadows wove on their aerial looms
    Shot through with golden thread.

"Across the meadows, by the gray old manse,
    The historic river flowed:
I was as one who wanders in a trance,
    Unconscious of his road.

"The faces of familiar friends seemed strange:
    Their voices I could hear,
And yet the words they uttered seemed to change
    Their meaning to my ear.

"For the one face I looked for was not there,
    The one low voice was mute;
Only an unseen presence filled the air,
    And baffled my pursuit.

"Now I look back, and meadow, manse, and stream
    Dimly my thought defines;
I only see — a dream within a dream —
    The hill-top hearsed with pines.

"I only hear above his place of rest
    Their tender undertone,
The infinite longings of a troubled breast,
    The voice so like his own.

"There in seclusion and remote from men
    The wizard hand lies cold,
Which at its topmost speed let fall the pen,
    And left the tale half told.

"Ah! who shall lift that wand of magic power,
    And the lost clew regain?
The unfinished window in Aladdin's tower
    Unfinished must remain!"

LONGFELLOW.

CHAPTER XXIII.

THE CONCORD AUTHORS AND THE ASSOCIATIONS OF THEIR WORKS.

LAKE WALDEN, cool and delicious, and full of summer splendor! the memory of it haunts one in midwinter days like a dream. It is indeed little more than a pond; but the circle of hills that surround it exhibit the perfection of New England woods, and few lakelets are always so deep, so clear, and so calm in summer-time.

Away from this sheltered sheet of water on every hand stretch Walden woods, the dark green needles of the pine contrasting with the delicate tints of the oak leaves. The summer winds haunt the pine tops, as Thoreau's flute once haunted the tenantless hills. The shadowy undergrowth is a tangled mass of flowers and ferns, full of sweet odors in the morning, and beautiful with a veiled, half-screened light during the day. The farms of Concord here and there penetrate these woods. It was here that Thoreau

RALPH WALDO EMERSON.

read and wrote, and here Emerson's "Wood-Notes" were inspired.

The literary period of Concord began about the year 1841, or soon after Emerson resigned the charge of the Second Church in Boston, withdrew from society, and went to the borders of Walden woods to live. Few young ministers ever ascended a more popular pulpit than that which Emerson left after a pastorate of two years; he succeeded Henry Ware, Jr., whose life was a powerful influence. Ware had been ten years in training this congregation up to his own ideal of religious culture and devotional living. He had positive views and a positive faith. Emerson was more uncertain and speculative.

He appeared as a literary recluse in the sleepy town of Concord, and finally established himself in the sleepiest part of the town, just on the borders of the green Walden woods. His house is partly hidden with dark pines. It is a lovely spot in summer, but it is somewhat dreary at other seasons, with the wind always moaning through the trees. Some of the trees that surround his mansion were planted by Hawthorne and Thoreau.

"Emerson," says Alcott, his speculative neighbor, "likes plain people, plain ways, plain clothes; shuns egotists; loves solitude, and knows how to use it." He found the old Concord people sufficiently simple in their tastes and habits, and it is said that he always had a kind greeting for the farmers he used to meet in his philosophical walks in Walden woods.

Emerson wrote a poem soon after this self-exile from Boston, which will serve as an excellent photograph of his occupation in retirement: —

> "Good-by, proud world! I'm going home!
> Thou art not my friend, and I 'm not thine.
> Long through thy weary crowds I roam;

A river-ark on the ocean brine,
Long I've been tossed like the driven foam ;
But now, proud world ! I 'm going home.

" Good-by to Flattery's fawning face ;
To Grandeur with his wise grimace ;
To upstart Wealth's averted eye ;
To supple Office, low or high ;
To crowded halls, to court and street ;
To frozen hearts and hasting feet ;
To those who go and those who come ;
Good-by, proud world ! I 'm going home.

" I 'm going to my own hearth-stone,
Bosomed in yon green hills alone, —
A secret nook in a pleasant land,
Whose groves the frolic fairies planned ;
Where arches green, the livelong day,
Echo the blackbird's roundelay,
And vulgar feet have never trod, —
A spot that is sacred to thought and God.

" O, when I am safe in my sylvan home,
I tread on the pride of Greece and Rome ;
And when I am stretched beneath the pines,
When the evening star so holy shines,
I laugh at the lore and the pride of man,
At the sophist schools, and the learned clan ;
For what are they all, in their high conceit,
When man in the bush with God may meet ? "

Alcott followed Emerson's example soon, and left Boston society to live in the rural simplicity becoming a philosopher at Concord. He was a teacher in Boston. The description of the Plumfield school in Miss Louisa Alcott's " Little Men" is evidently drawn from the recollections of early days. Alcott was a radical antislavery man in the days of Boston's most stately conservatism, and when a poor colored girl applied for admission to his school, he followed his conviction of duty, and admitted her. The act so worthy of his manhood proved fatal to the school, and he was glad to seek the cool fringes of Walden woods, and found it a relief to be able to say, like Emerson, —

"Good-by, proud world! I'm going home."

He took a roomy house near Emerson, built the fences around it himself, and began the life of a speculative philosopher, of the transcendental school of thought.

NATHANIEL HAWTHORNE.

Hawthorne and Channing widened the literary circle of Concord literary men, the former occupying the "Old Manse" in which Emerson wrote "Nature," which stood removed from the street, and near the old Concord battle-ground, its monuments, relics, and graves.

Hawthorne was retiring and reticent to an unusual degree even for a literary man. He found the Old Manse full of antique reminders of a departed generation; portraits of New England ministers of Cotton Mather's days, narrow windows, and suspicious shadows, and the traditional accompaniment of all these faded things, the moonlight-haunting ghost.

All of the old colonial mansions had their supposed ghosts; but Hawthorne's ghost, like his house, was a trifle more sombre than the rest, wandering about, and chilling the spirits of the living by the rustle of its (black) silk gown.

Here the Boston poets used to visit, — Longfellow, Fields, and the whole coterie of writers now passing one by one in solemn procession off the stage of literary life. Franklin Pierce was a guest. He was Hawthorne's college-mate, and through his life his most intimate friend.

When Franklin Pierce was elected President he offered Hawthorne the position of U. S. Consul at Liverpool.

THE OLD MANSE.

"Will the man who holds this office have to talk much?" asked Hawthorne of the bearer of the intelligence.

"No," was the answer.

"Thank the Lord," was the fervent rejoinder. His characteristic always discovered itself in the happiest as well as the saddest moments of life.

Hawthorne did not die in Concord, but amid the New Hampshire hills. His old friend, Franklin Pierce, visited him in his last sickness, and was with him on the night of his death.

He was buried in the most beautiful time of the year near the woods and streams he had loved so well. His remains were carried through the blooming orchards of Concord and laid down to an eternal rest beneath a group of pines on a hillside overlooking the Concord battle-field. "All the way from the village church," says James T. Fields, "the birds kept up a perpetual melody. The sun shone brightly, and the air was as sweet and pleasant as though death had never entered the world." Longfellow was there, Lowell, Emerson, Alcott, Holmes, Channing, and Agassiz. Franklin Pierce was true to his early friend to the last, and mingled flowers with the earth in that hillside grave.

We recently visited the site of Thoreau's hut in Walden woods. A noble cluster of pines rises on a ridge of woodland near it, pines that the axe has spared, that loom up like a shadowy cathedral, in which the winds of the seasons make perpetual music. The pond or lake is below it margined with bushes. A simple cross marks the spot where the poet-naturalist lived, and on it is written, "This is the site of Thoreau's Hut."

THOREAU'S HUT.

Thoreau built this hut with his own hands, and here lived more than two years. The birds became his companions; the wild partridge displayed her brood before his door, and the rabbits burrowed under his house, and were there secure from the hound and sportsman. Even the wood-mice came to know him, and one of them would take food from his hand. It was here that his most famous essays, many of which appeared in the *Atlantic*, were written, or had their origin.

Thoreau, in his essay on "Brute Neighbors," describes one of the battles between the black ants and the red ants that took place before his door. He treats the matter in true historical style as though it was an event as great as the Norman Conquest, and conveys the idea that he looked upon the issue with as much interest as he would contemplate one of the old battles of human ambition. The ant-hills in Walden woods still remain much the same as when that remarkable essay was written. It seemed to me like securing an uncommonly choice autograph when I found them.

In his essay on "Economy," he tells us how he lived in the woods during his protracted study of nature. His house cost him twenty-eight dollars. He was a vegetarian, and as he raised his own corn, beans, and potatoes, his expenses for food amounted to about one dollar a month. His books and his flute were his companions, though his literary friends sometimes visited him in his retreat. The Concord farmers used to hear the notes of his flute in the still summer evenings. A beautiful poem entitled "Thoreau's Flute" appeared in print soon after his decease.

Thoreau was a cynic — the same iconoclast in Harvard College as in Walden woods. He held that habits and customs of social life were all unnatural and wrong; that true independence of character was a lost virtue; and that following the customs of the rich made slaves of the poor. The remedy for the ills of society was a disregard to all conventional rules; he himself acted on this theory; but a world of Thoreaus would be a rather dreary place in which to live.

Thoreau died of consumption. His love of nature was strong to the last. He loved to look out of the window in his sickness. He awoke one morning, frost covered the window pane and he had not the strength to scrape it off. "I cannot now even look out of doors," he said sadly, and the world from that time was as lost to him.

The surroundings of Concord have a peculiar charm in summer-time, a rare harmonious blending of grassy meadows, dreamy marshes, noble woods of variegated green, and limpid streams. Emerson, Channing, and Thoreau have all pictured the charms of the Concord River. It is a subtile, ill-defined charm, and one which requires days of delicious leisure among these calm landscapes to appreciate.

" Beneath low hills in the broad interval,
 Through which at will our Indian rivulet
 Winds, mindful still of sannup and of squaw,
 Whose pipe and arrow oft the plow unburies,
 Here, in pine houses built of new-fallen trees,
 Supplanters of the tribe, the farmers dwell."

Emerson.

" The river calmly flows
Through shining banks, through lonely glen,
Where the owl shrieks, though ne'er the cheer of men
 Has stirred its mute repose ;
Still, if you should walk there, you would go there again."

Channing

" I sailed up a river with a pleasant wind,
 New lands, new people, and new thoughts to find.
 Many fair reaches and headlands appeared,
 And many dangers were there to be feared ;

" But when I remember where I have been,
 And the fair landscapes that I have seen,
 THOU seemest the only permanent shore,
 The cape never rounded nor wandered o'er."

Thoreau.

The poetry of Thoreau is evasive and peculiar. " His poetry," says Emerson, " might be bad or good ; he no doubt wanted a lyric faculty and technical skill, but he had no source of poetry in his spiritual perception." There is a pleasure in getting at the quaint meanings of many of his rhymes : —

> " If, with fancy unfurled,
>   You leave your abode,
> *You may go round the world*
> *By the old Marlborough road.*

> " The respectable folks —
>   Where dwell they ?
> They whisper in the oaks,
>   And they sigh in the hay."

Some of his lines are as mysterious as Emerson's " Brahma " was to the country editor, who failing to find any meaning in it after reading it in the usual way, began at the last line and read it backwards, and thought he received light.[1]

---

[1] BRAHMA.

If the red slayer thinks he slays,
  Or if the slain think he be slain,
They know not well the subtile ways
  I keep and pass and turn again.

Far or forgot to me is near,
  Shadow and sunlight are the same,
The vanished gods to me appear,
  And one to me are shame and fame.

They reckon ill who leave me out,
  When me they fly I am the wings,
I am the doubter and the doubt,
  And I the hymn the Brahman sings.

The strong gods pine for my abode,
  And pine in vain the sacred seven ;
But thou, meek lover of the good,
  Find me, and turn thy back on heaven.

For example : —

> "Give me an angel for a foe,
>   Fix now the place and time,
> And straight to meet him I will go,
>   Above the starry chime.
>
> "And with our clashing bucklers' clang
>   The heavenly spheres shall ring,
> While bright the northern lights shall hang
>   Beside our tourneying."

The solitude of Thoreau's life gave him a strong sense of his own personality : —

> "My life is like a stroll upon the beach
>   As near the ocean's edge as I can go ;
> My tardy steps its waves sometimes o'erreach ;
>   Sometimes I stay, and let them overflow.
>
> "My sole employment 't is, and scrupulous care,
>   To place my gains beyond the reach of tides, —
> Each smoother pebble, and each shell more rare,
>   Which ocean kindly to my hand confides."

One by one the old Concord poets and romancers have departed, as Thoreau saw Walden woods falling around him before he died. The axe was ever busy in his forests, and death has been as busy among his friends. "Thank God they cannot cut down the sky," he once said, as he heard of the wood-choppers' work. The skies remain, and trees sprout again, while even genius proves a wandering and uncertain light, and fades and disappears.

The Concord writers have been proverbially unsocial, but there appeared among them in the best days of their literary efforts a new Corinne, who more than any other American woman distinguished herself for her social charms. We refer to Margaret Fuller, Countess Ossoli, who had met nearly all the Concord philosophers and poets at Brook Farm, where she had enchanted other dreamers with the peculiar brilliancy of her own dreams. "When she came to Concord," says Emerson, "she was already rich with friends, rich in experience, rich in culture. She was well read in French, Italian, and German literature." She entered the cold intellectual atmosphere of Concord like a nun, and she came and went like a social queen. She had a nature formed for friendship, and absorbed the feelings and affections of others, and influenced them by an intense personality that it was almost impossible to resist. Emerson says that she wore her circle of friends like a diamond necklace. "They were so much to each other that Margaret seemed to represent them all. She was everywhere a welcome guest. The houses of her friends in town and country were all open to her. Her arrival was a holiday."

MARGARET FULLER (COUNTESS OSSOLI).

"I knew her ten years," says Emerson (1836-1846), "and never without surprise at her new powers." She became an intimate friend of Mrs. Emerson: she flitted like a sunbeam among the shadows of the Old Manse after Hawthorne came to occupy it, and was a frequent guest at Channing's. "The Concord stage coachman," says Emerson, "distinguished her by his respect, and the chambermaid was pretty sure to confide in her on the second day her homely romance."

Concord River and Walden woods were a delight to her at this most happy period of her life. She was a lover of nature as well as of art and sentiment; and these variegated woods, hills, and calm waters were among the teachers that formed her tastes, and enriched her mind and character.

We have spoken of the last scenes of the life of Hawthorne and of Thoreau. The going-out of life of few people has been so sad and tragic as that of this brilliant woman, whose tall monument rises over a tenantless grave on one of the hill-slopes in Mount Auburn.

It was an Italian spring. The Apennines had put their mantles of snow aside, and fruit was swelling among the blossoms on the Arno. "The Italian spring," said Madame Ossoli, "is a paradise. Every old wall and ruin puts on a festoon or garland, and the heavens stoop daily nearer, till the earth is folded in an embrace of light."

But her heart amid these scenes turned homeward, and she resolved to return with her child. Her husband, Count Ossoli, was to accompany her. Her last days in Italy were very happy, and yet the joy was tinged with sadness, as of a shadow of some unseen fate into which life was entering. "The world is indeed a sad place," she said, "despite its sunshine, buds, and crocuses. But I never felt as happy as now, when I always find the glad eyes of my little boy to greet me. I find the tie between him and me so deep-rooted that nothing but death can part us. Nothing but a child can take the worst bitterness out of life."

She sailed from Italy at this happy period of her life, and the rest is well known. The ship was wrecked in sight of the American shore. The wreck was twelve hours in breaking up, rocking on the reef off Long Island, the high wind rushing over it and the huge waves dashing around it. For twelve hours, in her night-robes and with dishevelled hair, this gifted woman, to whom the shores already in sight promised so much if she could but reach them, sat face to face with death. They offered to attempt to rescue her, but in a way that would separate her from her husband and child. She refused each offer for aid that involved a separation. She would be saved with them, or would perish with them. At length a tremendous wave shattered the wreck, and the brave woman perished with her husband and child, true to the last to her family as she had ever been true to her friends.

Old Wright's Tavern, a quaint relic of Revolutionary days, where Pitcairn, just before the Concord fight, stirred his brandy, declaring "I hope to stir the —— Yankee blood so before night!" stands on the Walden side of Concord, not far from Emerson's, and is a link between a generation gone and the generation now passing away. Thoreau's birthplace is seen on the old Virginia road, and the Old Manse retains its quaintness, and strangers run out from Boston to visit it on delicious summer days, and there dream over the old dreams of the vanished novelist, romancer, and enchanter.

But the literary summer of Concord has passed, and the song birds have fled before the dropping leaves, and the association of Concord River and Walden woods will ere long be a romance. Emerson alone survives these mysterious singers of other days, though Alcott still talks the poetry he does not write.

When Emerson shall have followed on in this procession of vanishing lights, Concord, it would seem, will be a place of literary memories, like the English lake district of Cumberland and Westmoreland when Wordsworth was gathered to the poets in Grasmere church-yard, and the rapid Rotha was left to sing the poets instead of being sung by the poets on its shaded banks. But though the singers may be gone, the poetry of nature will long linger on the quiet banks of the Concord, and amid the breeze-haunted, blossom-haunted shadows of Walden woods.

" THE air is full of farewells to the dying,
    And mournings for the dead ;
 The heart of Rachel, for her children crying,
    Will not be comforted !

" Let us be patient !   These severe afflictions
    Not from the ground arise,
 But oftentimes celestial benedictions
    Assume this dark disguise.

" We see but dimly through the mists and vapors ;
    Amid these earthly damps
 What seem to us but sad, funereal tapers
    May be heaven's distant lamps.

" There is no Death !   What seems so is transition ;
    This life of mortal breath
 Is but a suburb of the life elysian,
    Whose portal we call Death."

                                      LONGFELLOW.

CHAPTER XXIV.

MOUNT AUBURN.

ON the 24th of September, 1831, a large concourse of people assembled in a deep, picturesque valley, near the Charles River, in Old Cambridge, to consecrate a rural cemetery. The leaves were just beginning to change; the sky was unclouded, and the cool air, purified by the showers on the preceding night, seemed a broad mirror of sunlight, here and there rimmed with vermilion hills and golden woods. Out of the valley or deep glen like a finger of faith rose Mount Auburn, jewelled with autumn fringes.

The literary men of a generation gone were there. Henry Ware, Jr., John Pierpont, and Charles Sprague, at that time the poetic lights of Boston, all contributed to the exercises. Mr. Pierpont's grand original hymn was taken up by a thousand voices and was echoed among the hills on the mellow, breezeless air: —

> "Decay! decay! 't is stamped on all;
> All bloom in flower and flesh shall fade;
> Ye whispering trees, when ye shall fall,
> Be our long sleep beneath your shade!
>
> "Here to thy bosom, Mother Earth,
> Take back in peace what thou hast given,
> And all that is of heavenly birth,
> O God, in peace recall to heaven."

A half century has passed away since that bright, calm September day, when first were thrown open these tranquil streets and shaded avenues of Boston's city of the dead. One by one the scholars, jurists, artists, and philanthropists, who gathered there, have returned again to share the unbroken companionship of the tomb. As the visitor threads the winding ways of the hill and dale he is everywhere reminded of the literary and philanthropic lights of the past, and is made to feel how early falls the twilight and the evening of fame. Here rest Bowditch, Binney, Appleton, Thayer, Ashmun, Whiting, Buckingham, Story, and Lawrence,

OSSOLI MEMORIAL.

and a long generation of scholars and benefactors, whose names we have not even the space to recall. Here sleeps Hannah Adams, a once famous historical writer, and Frances Osgood, an admired poetess in her day, whose monument is a broken harp. Here is seen the elaborate monument of Margaret Fuller (Countess Ossoli), — "By birth, a child of New England; by adoption, a citizen of Rome; by genius, belonging to the world."

ENTRANCE TO MOUNT AUBURN CEMETERY.

We enter the enclosure through a broad granite gateway, the design of which was taken from an ancient Egyptian temple. The scene which meets the eye in summer time has few equals in quiet loveliness and harmony of beauty in New England. An immense parterre, some 130 acres in extent, now shadowy with trees, now silvery with jetty fountains, comes into view, and makes one feel that this is affection's holy ground.

As we pass up Central Avenue, which is margined with beds of rare flowers and works of art, we first come to the monument of

GASPARD SPURZHEIM,

whose name is associated with Gall in the early discoveries in phrenological science. He came to this country from Prussia to lecture, but died soon after his arrival in Boston in 1832.

SPURZHEIM MONUMENT.

His body was given to science, and his heart and brain may still be seen in Dr. Warren's collections of specimens of anatomy. His remains were among the first interred in the cemetery.

460   *Young Folks' History of Boston.*

Turning to the left into Chapel Avenue, the steps of the visitor are next arrested by the celebrated bronze statue of

DR. NATHANIEL BOWDITCH,

the first full-length bronze statue ever cast in this country.

We never pass this monument without recalling an incident that furnishes a healthy and helpful lesson to the young. Dr. Bowditch was remarkable for his simplicity and moral

BRONZE STATUE OF DR. NATHANIEL BOWDITCH.

energy of character, and he rose in science mainly by his own efforts. Once in youth, being very fond of music, he made the acquaintance of some music-loving fellows of the aimless and profitless sort, but full of warm, friendly feeling, and he found their society so pleasing that he seemed likely to follow their unthrifty habits.

At length the conduct of some of his companions showed the real danger of his position. He resolved to abandon his new friends at once. "What am I doing?" he said. "Forgetting my studies in order to be with those whose only

THE CHAPEL.

recommendation is that they love music. I shall fall into their habits if I continue. I will do so no longer." It was a turning point in life. His abandoned fiddle was always kept, and is still owned by one of his family.

His last days were serene and happy, and were passed in the companionship of books and children. Looking back on a well-employed youth, he once said, "Every morning when I awoke and saw the sun I thanked God that he had placed me in this beautiful world."

Passing the grave of Dr. Daniel Sharp, of blessed memory, we come to the Lawrence monument, one of the most lofty and beautiful in the grounds. The name of

AMOS LAWRENCE,

like that of Bowditch, has its lessons. He was a poor boy, but had the strong moral purpose that compels success. "I spent my first Sunday in the city at church," he once said.

THE STORY STATUE.

"I determined to begin life just right." Out of that church, which he entered a poor country lad, he was carried at last amid the tears of the city and brought here to fill a benefactor's grave.

We now come to the chapel, which contains the fine statues of Joseph Story, John Winthrop, John Adams, and James Otis. It is lighted by a beautiful oriel window in front, where cherubs brighten in the sunlight and lose half their beauty in the shadow. It is always open to visitors.

Near the chapel has recently been erected one of the most beautiful works of art in Boston's cemeteries, an Egyptian monumental statue of colossal size, called

THE SPHINX.

It is designed to commemorate the conservation of the American Republic, the destruction of Slavery, and the heroes who fell in the Union war. It was cut from a single block of granite. It was executed by Martin Milmore, who designed the Soldiers' Monument in Boston, as well as the famous bust of Sumner, and many local works of art.

We might branch off from the central route to the tower, and visit the monuments of Lucius Bolles, of saintly memory; of Ballou, who had many virtues and many friends; or Cleveland of Revolutionary fame. But proceeding to the hill and tower we pass the plain tomb of Rufus Choate, standing like a rock on the steep hillside, buried in cool shadows. At a little distance from the way, in a lot margined with evergreen, is the grave of "Fanny Fern." It is marked by a beautiful cross surrounded with delicately wrought fern leaves in pure marble. Her father, Deacon Nathaniel Willis, and her brother, N. P. Willis, the poet, sleep in another part of the cemetery.

We now come to the base of Mount Auburn, and in its circle repose the remains of Charles Sumner, Louis Agassiz, Edward Everett, and Noah Webster, the lexicographer. In fact, the whole base is circled with places that strangers love to visit, from the associations of bright and precious memories, and no spot is now so much inquired after as the grave of

CHARLES SUMNER.

It is on Arethusa Path, near Walnut Avenue, at the foot of the tower. The lot has no fence, no margin of flowers or evergreens, and no memorial stones, except a row of small slabs of white marble, just rising out of the ground, and bearing the names and dates of the Sumner family who are buried there. A tall gnarled oak stretches one broad arm above it, which we always associate with one of the last remarks of the statesman. "A great man," said Mr. Sumner, at a last interview with a friend, "when under the shadow of defeat, is taught the uses of adversity, and *as the oak-tree's roots are strengthened by its shadow*, so all defeats in a good cause are but resting-places on the road to victory at last."

We well remember the mild March day when at sunset, amid the tolling bells of all the surrounding towns, the great funeral procession wound along the avenues, and, to the music of trombones, and to the singing of Luther's majestic choral, his body was lowered into a grave of flowers. The terraced hillside was full of people. Tears flowed on all cheeks, and the mourning was sincere. Flowers from Southern soil were piled upon the coffin; in the gathering shadows the sexton did his work, and an immense cross of calla lilies was set at the head of the new-made grave. That grave has never wanted for floral tributes. Though the humblest it is the most often visited grave of all.

The grave of

LOUIS AGASSIZ

is in the long procession of illustrious sleepers that encircles the dells below the tower. A red stone cross, mantled with vines, stands in the centre of the lot, a fit emblem of the

CHARLES SUMNER'S SARCOPHAGUS.

great naturalist's faith. The monument of Agassiz is striking for its appropriateness and simplicity. It is a granite boulder

LOUIS AGASSIZ.

rising as though naturally out of the grave, and bears on one of its sides simply

JEAN LOUIS RODOLPHE AGASSIZ.
BORN AT MOTIER, SWITZERLAND,
MAY 28TH, 1807; DIED AT CAM-
BRIDGE, MASS., DEC. 14, 1873.

The funeral of Agassiz took place on a mild afternoon on the 18th of December, — a day out of season, as mellow as the changing days of winter to spring, or September to the coolness of fall. Like his great teacher, Cuvier, he had requested that he might be buried in the most simple possible manner. The request was in the main regarded, but his friends resolved to bury him in flowers. The coffin, over

THE AGASSIZ BOULDER.

which Cherubini's sweet requiem was sung in the college chapel, seemed an immense floral offering; the lot where the grave was made was carpeted with evergreen; the earth thrown up by the sexton was hidden by ivy, japonicas, azalias, carnations; the grave itself was wholly lined with green boughs and creamy flowers, and the stone cross held aloft in the wintry silence the greenest of ivy and the whitest of blooms.

The scene was in harmony with the great naturalist's character,— the cross, the floral offerings. Flowers were to him God's alphabet, and the Christian world had looked to him as the defender of their faith against materialism. Agassiz never forgot the religious instruction he had received from his pious parents in the Alp-walled Oberland and the beautiful Pays de Vaud. "'These are the thoughts of God," he once said of mountains. Nature to him was God's thoughts in the past.

At the foot of the tower, on a green slope overlooking the Charles River and "Roxbury" fields, rises a plain monument, on one side of which is inscribed, —

POET.
PATRIOT.
PREACHER.
PHILOSOPHER.
PHILANTHROPIST.
PIERPONT.

It marks the resting-place of the venerable author of "The Airs of Palestine," "Napoleon at Rest," "The Pilgrim Fathers," and "Passing Away." Hollis Street Church, where he preached for many years, is seen in the far distance from the beautiful spot.

Pierpont in selecting the lot wrote a poem entitled "My Grave," in which he thus pictures the resting-place : —

> "My grave! I've marked thee on the sunny slope,
> The warm dry slope of Auburn's wood-crowned hill,
> That overlooks the Charles and Roxbury's fields,
> That lie beyond it, as lay Canaan's green
> And smiling landscape beyond Jordan's flood,
> As seen by Moses.

> Standing by thy side
> I see the distant city's domes and spires.
> There stands the church within whose lofty walls
> My voice for truth and righteousness and God —
> But all too feebly — has been lifted up
> For more than twenty years, but now shall soon
> Be lifted up no more."

The monument of Anson Burlingame may be seen near the fountain at the foot of the hill, — a beautiful marble block, covered on the top by an immense bundle of wheat, — a not inappropriate emblem of a fruitful life.

THE TOWER

Ascending the stone tower, which rises some sixty feet from the top of Mount Auburn, we obtain an extended view of the environs of Boston,— a scene of enchantment on a clear day in summer or early fall. Below lies the city of the dead ; just beyond is Elmwood, the residence of James Russell Lowell, with its green acres of grand old trees ; on one side runs the placid Charles, like a picture of beauty ; on the other are hills, woods, spires, and towns, and white lines of houses, like outstretched arms joining one town to another; while in the distance rise the three hills and the brick city of Boston, the gilded dome of the State House glimmering in the sun.

JARED SPARKS.

Among the new graves that the visitor should see are those of Charlotte Cushman and James T. Fields. The former, which is near the tower, is marked by a noble monolith.

The stranger, on leaving the enclosure, may like to visit the grave of Jared Sparks, which is on Garden Avenue near the bell and the well-house. It is among the last objects usually visited, from its nearness to the gate. Passing out of the enclosure, "Auburn, Sweet Auburn" fades like a vision, but no one can fully understand or appreciate the Christian culture of Boston until he has exchanged the scenes of her activities for a thoughtful walk in the city of the dead.

FOREST HILLS CEMETERY.

As beautiful as Mount Auburn, though not as historic, is "Forest Hills." The entrance to this blooming park that hides the dead is through a gateway which is most elegant and impressive. In golden letters on the arch above it are the words: "I am the Resurrection and the Life." As one passes the gate he seems in a vast garden of flowers and statuary. Here are pleasant sheets of water, rocky eminences, cool clusters of trees. General Joseph Warren, who fell at Bunker Hill, is buried here, on the summit of a hill called Mount Warren. The receiving tomb here is the largest, or one of the largest, in the country. Its portico is massive and imposing. Within are two hundred and eight catacombs.

At one side of this cemetery is the Strangers' Burying-Ground, or ground of single graves, called the Field of Manoah.

And here, at the Strangers' Burying-Ground, we will take leave of the reader, who has followed us in these pages through the events of two hundred and fifty years.

THE FIELD OF MANOAH.

I see afar the sun's red lustres, burning
    On skeletons of woods,
And hear the lone bird haplessly returning
    To wintry solitudes.

Around me stand white monuments in clusters,
    An open space before,
Whose tombs reflect few monumental lustres, —
    The sad Field of Manoah.[1]

It is the field in which the stranger slumbers,
    Where ferns untrod are found;
Yet many a grave, without a history, numbers
    That unfrequented ground.

[1] Judges xvi. 31. "Manoah" — rest.

The Field of Manoah.

Amid the graves one lone shaft there arises —
    I seek the spot alone —
A name, familiar, memory surprises
    Upon the tapering stone.

'T is Owen Marlowe. This is all the history
    That on the shaft appears;
All else is vanished into endless mystery
    And unfamiliar years, —

Save that his genius many throngs delighted,
    And won its meed of fame,
And love his kindly sympathies requited,
    And chiselled here his name.

A few brief years he spoke to throngs applauding
    Before the footlights' blaze,
And read as long the chronicles recording
    His triumphs and his praise.

And, far from scenes where life's young dream had perished,
    And happy days had flown,
And from the kindred that his heart had cherished,
    He died, and died alone.

And here he sleeps, where balmy June's returning
    Touches with green his bed,
And bright years pass, with golden harvests burning,
    Unheeded by the dead.

Like *her* whose life with long applause was sated,
    Who was the world's glad guest,
But finds a grave in Auburn isolated,
    The actor went to rest.

Beside this grave the other graves seem lonely;
    Yet all these graves are lone,
Removed from kindred, and surrounded only
    By dust of the unknown.

Sad are the homes whose hearths are half deserted,
  Or, from the fireside's blaze
The feet of loved ones, by the world perverted,
  Take solitary ways.

But sadder far than partings made by trial,
  By distance or the wave,
Is that lost hope, that remediless denial
  Of kinship in the grave.

Yet many here their roof-tree left for others,
  Their hearth and lattice vine,
To earn some easier life for toil-worn mothers,
  By Yarrow or the Rhine.

And some are gathered in this spot retired,
  Where deeds are fragrant yet,
Who in death's silent chamber, faith inspired,
  The waiting angels met;

Who walked alone the city's thronging highway,
  Like the celestial road,
And sought in other lives, in mart and by-way,
  The brotherhood of God.

Here piteous hands that duty led from pleasure
  Laid them beneath the blooms,
But the Escurial holds no nobler treasure
  In all its golden tombs.

Gone to the city of unshaded splendor,
  Gone from life's harvest field,
They gave the world the best their hearts could render,
  The best that life can yield.

The twilight near, the cool winds o'er me stealing,
  The city's spires before,
I leave to-night, with sweet and chastened feeling,
  The lone Field of Manoah.

INDEX.

ADAMS, SAMUEL, 206; at Lexington on the morning of the fight, 226.
Agassiz, Louis, grave of, 464; monument, 467, 468.
Agassiz Museum, 353.
Alcott, A. Bronson, 441; in Concord, 442.
Aldrich, T. B., 409, 410.
Allston, Washington, his personal character, 304; intimate with Washington Irving, 305; buried by torchlight, 304; a story of, 339; poem by, 29.
American Revolution begun, 222.
Ancestors, our, the monuments to, 37.
Andrew, Governor, responds to President's call for troops, 317; address to Legislature in 1864, 318.
Andros hated by Boston people, 146.
Antislavery struggle, the, 309; meetings in Faneuil Hall, 313, 314; societies, 314.
Anville's, Admiral d', fleet destroyed, 190.
Arbella, the, why so named, 48; voyage of, 49; reaches Salem harbor, 50; in Boston harbor, 52.
Argyle, Duke of, married in the Frankland House, 199.
Arlington, 353; Arlington Heights, 349.
Arlington Street Church, 240.
Arms sold to the Indians by Thomas Morton at Merry-Mount, 67.
"Art," poem by Charles Sprague, 387.
Art Square and buildings near, 338.
Aspinet, first enemy of the Pilgrims, 75; restores a lost boy, 79.

BALTIMORE regiment at Bunker Hill centennial, 335, 336.
Bates, Joshua, founder of the Public Library, 324.
Beaches near Boston, 356.
Bells of Christ Church, 239.
"Belshazzar's Feast," Allston's, 305.
Bjarne, son of Heriulf, voyage and discoveries of, 360.
Blackstone, William, sole inhabitant of Boston, 39; invited Winslow and his friends to Boston, 40; removed to Rehoboth, 43; married late in life, 43.
Blue Hills at Milton, 349.
Boston founded by gentlemen, 31; growth of, 65, 85; invested by the Provincials, 257; assault planned, 258; bombardment of, 261; evacuated by the British, 262; occupied by Washington, 266;
becomes a city in 1822, 293; to-day, 323; its territory and population, 323; valuation, 324; schools and churches, 324; Public Library, 324; Public Latin School, 375.
Boston Bay, 354.
Boston Common a cow-pasture, 369.
Boston, England, ancient name of, 16; description of, 31; resembles Rotterdam, 31; proud of her daughter, 31.
Boston massacre, 214.
Boston News-Letter, the first newspaper published in America, 177.
Boston poetry, associations of, 389.
Boston University, 385.
Botolph, or Botulph, derivation of the name, 16. See St. Botolph.
Bowditch, Dr. Nathaniel, bronze statue of, 460.
Boy, the lost, 75.
Boys' books in 1720, 178.
Boys of Boston and General Gage, 215.
Bradford, Gov., lines "To Boston," 390.
Bradstreet, Anne, the favorite poet of the colony, 390.
Breakfast to officers of French fleet, 230.
Brick houses built, 137.
"Bridge, The," Longfellow's poem, 406.
British army in Boston reinforced, 243.
British open fire on Bunker Hill, 244.
Bromfield's Lane, 369.
Bunker Hill fortified, 243; battle of, 244; centennial celebration of battle, 332.
Bunker Hill Monument, corner-stone of laid by Lafayette, 293, 294; the celebration, 294; Ray Palmer's memories of the occasion, 296; the grounds, 302; description of the monument, 303.
Burnet, Gov., cost of his reception, 177.
Burns, Anthony, arrest, 314; surrender, 317.
Byles, Mather, first pastor of Hollis Street Church, 287; a tory, 287; guards himself, 288; his wit, 289; specimen of his poetry, 290.

CAMBRIDGE church-yard, 303; verse from Holmes's poem on, 305.
Cambridge, how it had its beginning, 62.
Cape Cod, the Keel Cape, Kialarness of the Northmen, 362.
Cape Cross, or Krossanes, probably Plymouth, or Nantasket Beach, 365.

Carwitham view of Boston about 1730, 425.
Castle Island, 354.
"Catechism," the, 372.
Centennial celebration of Battle of Bunker Hill, 332.
Charles II. proclaimed king in Boston, 138.
Charles River settlements Arcadias, 43.
Charlestown settled from Salem, 40, 62.
Charter of Charles I. revoked, 145; a new one granted, 146.
Chauncy Street Church, 393.
Children bewitched, 116.
Choate, Rufus, tomb of, 463.
Christ Church, story of a visit to, 234; oldest church in Boston, 236.
Chronicles of John of Tynemouth, extracts from, 20.
"Church, the, hath no place left to fly into but the wilderness," 47.
Chimes of Christ Church, 234, 240.
Coleridge's inkstand, 402.
Common, the, a part of Blackstone's farm, 43; gallows on the, 103.
Conant, Roger, one of first settlers of Salem, 50.
Concord authors, 439; unsocial, 448.
Concord, Provincial Congress at, 219; battle of, 221; literary period of, began, 440.
Coote, Richard, the second royal governor, 174.
Copp's Hill Burying-ground, 234, 239.
Copp's Hill, guns from the battery on, set fire to Charlestown, 239.
Corey Hill, Brookline, 349.
Corey, Martha, hanged as a witch, 123.
Cotton, John, Vicar of Boston, 32; flight to New England, 35, 48; memorial chapel to, 36; the first Boston poet, 389.
Cushman, Charlotte, monument to, 471.

DANA, RICHARD H., 391.
Dante's coffin, Longfellow has a fragment of, 402.
Dark day of 1780, 289.
Deer Island used as a place of confinement for Indians, 131.
Demons put to flight by St. Botolph, 23.
Diaz, Mrs., on the old-time primary schools, 371.
Dillaway, Charles K., master of the Latin School, 379.
"Dirge of Alaric the Visigoth," written by Edward Everett, 391.
Dissenters persecuted, 47; find a place of refuge, 66.
Dixwell, Epes Sargent, master of the Latin School, 379.
Dorchester, first settlers at, 62.
"Dorchester Giant, The," Holmes' poem, 410.
Dorchester Heights seized by the British, 257; fortified by the Americans, 261; a storm prevents a British attack on, 262; view from, 350.
Dudley, Deputy-Governor, letter to the Countess of Lincoln, 62; angry with Winthrop, 65.
Dudley, Joseph, president of the provisional government, 146; an unpopular governor, 174.
Duel, first in Boston, 128, 160.
Dyer, Mary, story of, 103.

EAST Indian emancipation, 399.
Easty, Mary, executed as a witch, 123.
Eaton, Mr. Nathaniel, first master of Harvard College, 384.
"Eberhard," poem, 340.
Edwards, Jonathan, in New England, 190.
Elm, the Old or Great, on the Common, 103, 124; Quaker graves near, 104; inscription on the gate of the enclosure, 127; Indians executed on, 128.
Elm, the Washington, on Cambridge Green, 257.
Emerson, Ralph Waldo, 439; a literary recluse, 440; his poem, "Brahma," 447; alone survives of the Concord authors, 451.
Emigrants, dispersion of the, 62.
Endicott, John, settles at Salem, 50; governor, 92; cuts red cross from English flag, 95; opposition to Quakers, 95.
England, dark times in, 47.
English laws of trade resisted, 142.
Episcopal Church, origin of its existence in Boston, 145.
Eric, the Red, in Greenland, 360.
Estaing, Count d', at Madam Hancock's reception, 230; entertains Boston ladies on ship-board, 233.
Esquimaux, called Skraellingar, by the Scandinavians, 362.
Eutaw, the flag of, in Boston Music Hall, 336.
Evangeline, story of, related to Longfellow by Hawthorne, 405.
Everett, Edward, and others restored chapel at St. Botolph's Church, 36.
Everett, Edward, 391.
"Excelsior," Longfellow's poem, inspired by a letter from Charles Sumner, 404.

FAMILY, the lost, 71.
Faneuil, Andrew, mansion of, 193.
Faneuil Hall, 194.
Faneuil, Peter, 194.
"Fanny Fern," grave of, 463.
Federal Street Church, 240.
Feather Store, the old, 137.
Fields, James T., 415; his first poem, 416; an example to youth, 417; his poem, "A Protest," 417; his grave, 471.

Index.   477

Field of Manoah, or Strangers' Burying-ground at Forest Hills Cemetery, 472.
Fire in Boston in 1679, 137; the great one of November, 1872, 328.
First Brick Church, 395.
First Church, the, 65, 240.
Food scarce in Boston, 258.
"Footsteps of Angels," origin of the poem, 403.
Forest Hills Cemetery, 471.
Fort Independence, 354.
Fort Sumter, fall of, 317.
Franklin, Benjamin, his birthplace, 177; story of his early struggle, 181; 390, 391.
Frankland's Palace, 197.
Frog Pond, the, 127.
Fugitive Slave Law, 314.
Fuller, Margaret (Countess Ossoli), 448; her tragic death, 450; monument to, 456.

GALLOWS erected, 132.
Gardner, Francis, Master of the Latin School, 379.
Garret, Richard, and others lost, 71.
Garrison, William Lloyd, in Baltimore, 309; mobbed in Boston, 310; visit to Whittier, 428.
General Court to be held in Boston, 65; members of the, elected by the people, 141; the governing power, 145.
George II., bells of Boston tolled at his death, 206.
George III., the sad king, 266; insanity of, 267; kindness to the poor, 272; fond of children, 272; at death-bed of his daughter, 275; blindness of, 275; death, 276; popularity, 276.
Goodwin, John, children of bewitched, 116.
Gould, Benj. Apthorp, Master of the Latin School, 378.
Governors, the democratic, under the charter, 169.
Governors, the eleven royal, 169.
Governor's Island once called Governor's Garden, 354.
Granary Burying-ground, 160.
Grapes found by the Northmen in Massachusetts, 361.
Greenland, Northmen in, 360.
Groton, England, birthplace of John Winthrop, 57.
Gunpowder, three tons sent to Washington from Rhode Island, 258.
Gyanough, the courteous sachem, 76.

HALE, SIR THOMAS, the adventurer, 156.
Hancock's, Dorothy, reception, 230.
Hancock, John, 206; marries Dorothy Quincy, 225; at Lexington on the morning of the fight, 226; President of the Continental Congress, 229; Governor of Massachusetts, 230, 293.
Hancock, Thomas, 206.

"Hanging of the Crane," history of the poem, 404.
Harvard College, 384.
Harvard, John, bequest of, 385.
Harvard Memorial Hall, 353.
Haverhill, Washington's praise of, 421.
Hawthorne, Nathaniel, Longfellow's poem to, 437; 442; his death and burial, 443, 444.
Hayslop, Mr., the pedagogue, 369.
Hiawatha, story of, related to Schoolcraft by an Onondaga chief, 405.
Hollis Street Church, 283; first pastor, Mather Byles, 287.
Holmes House, Washington's first headquarters, 257; "Old Ironsides," written in, 257.
Holmes, Oliver Wendell, 410.
Hooker, Rev. Thomas, lines to, by John Cotton, 389.
Hopkins, Matthew, witch-finder general, 110; his methods of torture, 111; his death, 112.
House, Wm. Blackstone's, the first built in Boston, 39.
Houses demolished for fuel, 258.
Howe, General, at Bunker Hill, 244; evacuates Boston, 262.
Howe, Mrs. Julia Ward, 414.
Howells, W. D., 409, 410.
Hunnewell's Gardens, 349.
Husking Frolic, an old-time, 433.
Hutchinson, Anne, banished, 87.

ICELAND settled by Northmen, 360.
Ikanho, or Ykanho, ancient name of Boston, 16, 32.
Increase of the early settlements, 66.
Independence declared, 293.
Indian a faithful, 72.
Indians friendly to the settlements on the Charles River, 43; kidnapped, 75; many noted, brought to Boston for execution, 128.
Ingolf and Leif in Iceland, 360.
Irving, Washington, friend of Allston's, 305.

JAMAICA PLAIN, 350.
Jethro, story of old, the Indian missionary, 128.
John of Tynemouth, Rector of St. Botolph, extracts from chronicles of, 20.
Johnson, Isaac, a gentleman of wealth, 48; selects his abode in Boston, 50; death, 52; his grave the first in King's Chapel Burying-ground, 52.
Johnson, Lady Arbella, the story of, 47; guest of John Endicott, 50; her death, 51; a stone church erected on her grave, 52.
Jones, Margaret, the first victim of witchcraft in New England, 112.
Jubilee, musical, of 1869, 327; 1872, 398.

KIALARNESS — Keel Cape — Cape Cod, 362.
King George's War, 189.
King, Starr, 283.
King's Chapel, 50; the royal governors worshipped in, 177.
King's Chapel Burying-ground, 52, 57.

LABRADOR, the old Hella-land, 361.
Lafayette visits Boston, 293; lays the corner-stone of Bunker Hill Monument, 294.
Lancaster, a family at, murdered by Indians, 131.
Lantern in St. Botolph's Church went out forever when Cotton left the town, 35.
Latimer, George, arrested without a warrant as a fugitive slave, 313.
Latin School building, the new, 385.
Laud, Archbishop, imposed the ritual, 32; his iron rule, 47.
Lee, General Fitz Hugh, in Boston Music Hall, 336.
Leif, story of, 356.
Leif's Booths, 361.
Leonard, Marm, the schoolma'am, 371.
Leverett, Frederic P., master of the Latin School, 379.
Leverett, Governor John, 137.
Lewis, minister, hung for witchcraft, 112.
Lexington, battle of, 220.
Liberty, spirit of, aroused, 214.
Lincoln Cathedral, 15.
Lincolnshire County, England, 15.
Lisbon, earthquake at, 198.
Longfellow, Henry W., 399; visited Europe, 401; his study, 402; in retirement, 422.
Longfellow's poems, origin of some of, 402; characteristics of, 405.
Lovell, John, master of the Latin School, 377.
Lowell, James Russell, 409; Elmwood, the home of, 407, 471.
Lynn, 353.

"MAGNALIA," stories of gross superstition in Cotton Mather's, 115.
Maine given to Sir Ferdinando Gorges, 142; purchased by Massachusetts, 142.
Malden, the hills of, 349.
"Manoah, Field of," poem, 472.
Marblehead, 355, 435.
Massachusetts Bay Colony, the leaders of came from Lincolnshire, England, 15.
Massachusetts Institute of Technology, 385.
Massachusetts Sixth Regiment attacked in Baltimore, 317.
Mastodon giganteus, skeleton of in the Warren Museum, 342; discovery of the skeleton, 344.
Mather, Cotton, and the witchcraft delusion, 116.

Mather, Cotton, Increase, and Samuel, willow at tomb of, cut from tree at Napoleon's grave, 239.
Mattakees, fishing huts of the, 76.
Mayflower, the, one of Winthrop's fleet, 49; arrives in Charlton harbor, 61.
May-pole set up by Thomas Morton and cut down by Endicott, 67.
Mechanics' Charitable Association, 393.
Medford, first settlers at, 62.
Merrimack, the, Whittier's "River of Song," 432.
"Merry Monarch," Charles II. called the, 145.
Merry-Mount, the revellers at, 67.
Mickle, Samuel, the cynic, 181.
Milton Lower Mills, 350.
Monument grounds at Bunker Hill, 302.
Moore's, Tom, waste-paper basket in Longfellow's study, 402.
Morton, Thomas, the rioter, 66.
Mount Auburn Cemetery, 353, 455; entrance, 457; the chapel at, 461, 463; the sphinx, 463; the tower, 470.
Muddy River lands granted for school purposes, 376.
Mural inscriptions, 393.
Museum of Fine Arts, 338.

NAHANT, 355.
Napoleon at Rest, poem by Pierpont, 284.
Newburgh, skeleton of mastodon found at, 344.
Newbury and Newburyport in Whittier's verse, 435.
Newfoundland probably discovered by Leif, 361.
New Old South Church, 393.
New York Seventh Regiment at Centennial of Bunker Hill, 335.
Nix's Mate, story of, 151.
Nonconformity could not be overlooked, 32.
Non-representation in parliament an argument of the magistrates, 142.
Nook's Hi'l fortified, 265.
Normandy subjected by the Northmen, 359.
Northmen, expeditions of the, 359.
North Meeting-house, signal lanterns in steeple, 219.
Nova Scotia discovered by Leif, 361.

"O COUNTRY FAIR," poem, 347.
Old Brick Church, the, 393.
Old Goody Glover, story of, 116.
Old Manse, the, 442, 443.
Old North Church, see Christ Church.
Old South Church stands in Winthrop's garden, 58; the church of the people, 189, 240.
"Old South stands, The," poem, 331.
Oliver, General H. K., on the early schools of Boston, 369.

Ossoli, Countess, see Margaret Fuller.
Otis's, Harrison Gray, anecdote of Master Lovell, 378.
Otis, James, 205.

PALFREY, PETER, one of the first settlers of Salem, 50.
Palmer's, Rev. Ray, memories of Bunker Hill, 296.
Parker, Theodore, 314, 317.
Peace declared, 293.
"Peace Jubilee" of 1869, 327.
People independent under the charter, 141.
Phillips, Samuel, the duelist, 160.
Phips, Sir William, governor, 146; the story of Sir William and his great good fortune, 170.
Pierpont, John, 283; poem at laying corner-stone of Bunker Hill Monument, 291; pastor and poet, 391; original hymn at dedication of Mount Auburn, 455; monument of, 469.
"Pilgrims, The," motto from Longfellow, 55.
Pitcairn, Major, interred in Christ Church, 236.
Pormort (Portmorte), Philemon, the first "schulemaster" of Boston, 376, 380.
Prayer, Thomas Prince's, 190.
Prescott, General, leads the farmer soldiers to Charlestown, 243.
President's call on Governor Andrew for militia, 317.
Primer, the New England, 372.
Prospect Hill fortified, 257.
"Protest, A," poem by James T. Fields, 417.
Province House, the, 174.
Provincial Congress organized, 216.
Provincials, the, rally at Concord, 221.
Provisional government for the colony, 146.
"Psalm of Life," anecdote of the poem, 403.
Puritans, Macaulay on the, 45.
Putnam, General, at Bunker Hill, 247.

QUAKER books burned, 95.
Quaker graves near the Old Elm, 104.
Quakers, opposition to, 95; whipped, 99; law for capital punishment of, repealed, 100.
Quincy's, Dorothy, wedding, the story of, 225; reception of the French officers, 230.
Quincy, President, quotation from, 37.

RAIN brought by the bones of St. Botolph, 19.
Randolph, Edward, "the evil genius of New England," 142.
Rawson's Lane, now Bromfield Street, 155.

Rawson, Rebecca, story of, 155; lost at Port Royal, Jamaica, 159.
Red-coats in Boston, 216.
Relic, a gigantic, 341.
"Resignation," motto from Longfellow's poem on, 453.
Revere's, Paul, ride, 219.
Roxbury, first settlers at, 62.

STS. ADULPH AND BOTOLPH, educated in Belgic France, 20
St. Adulph, governs church of Maestricht in Belgium, 20; his body moved, 24.
St. Botolph's Church, 31; the tower a lighthouse, 32.
St. Botolph, the good abbot, 16; founder of Old Boston, 19; his bones influence the rain, 19; incidents in life of, 20; puts demons to flight, 23; death, 23; miracles performed at his tomb, 24.
St. Edmond's Monastery, Bury, England, 19.
St. Ethelwold transfers the bodies of saints, 24.
Salaries paid the governors, 174.
Salem, first settlers in, 50; 355.
Salem Street, ancient and modern, 234.
Saltonstall, Sir Richard, 49.
"School Committee," the, 373.
Schoolhouse, the first, 380; called the Centre, and afterwards the Latin, 383.
School Punishments, 370.
Schools, the old Boston, 369; influence of Boston, 385.
Second Church, 393.
Shawmut, old name of Boston, 40.
Shenhan, John, a poem, 161.
Sickness among settlers at Salem and Charlestown, 40.
Slaves and slave-pens, 309.
Soldiers' and Sailors' Monument, 319; dedication of, 337; description, 337.
South Carolina regiment at Bunker Hill centennial, 335, 336.
Southern regiments, reception of at the Bunker Hill centennial, 335.
Sparks, Jared, grave of, 471.
Sphinx, the, at Mount Auburn, 463.
Sprague, Charles, the poet-banker, 392.
Spring Lane, why so named, 58.
Springs of pure water, 39; led to the settlement of Boston, 40.
Spurzheim, Gaspard, his brain, heart, and skull in the Warren Museum, 342, 459.
Stamp Act, passed in 1765, 205; effect of, 209; repealed, 209.
Standish, Miles, sent to arrest Thomas Morton at Merry-Mount, 67.
Steamers, excursion, 354.
Stories, fireside, 151.
Story Statue, the, at Mount Auburn, 462.
Stranger's Burying-ground, 472.
Sturge, Joseph, the reformer, 431.
Suburbs of Boston, 349; gray and venerable, 354.

Sumner, Charles, on the Fugitive Slave law, 314; grave of, 464; his sarcophagus, 465.
Surriage, Agnes, the tavern maid of Marblehead, 197.

"TALES OF THE WAYSIDE INN," how suggested, 405.
Tea, tax imposed on, 213; destruction of, 216.
"Ten Hills," Winthrop's farm, 72.
Thanksgiving, first day of, 61.
Thompson, Pishey, his "History and Antiquities of Boston" (England), 20.
Thoreau, Henry D., 444; friendship with animals and birds, 444; a cynic, 445; his death, 445; his poems, 447.
Thoreau's hut, 444.
Thorwald, story of, 359, 362.
Tileston's, Madame, school, 371.
"Tom of Lincoln," the old bell, 15.
Tories, effigies of hanged, 132.
Treasures sunken in the Spanish main, 173.
Tremont Street, follows the windings of William Blackstone's cow, 43.
Trimountain, early name of Boston, 40.
Trinity Church, 338.
Troops, British, stationed on the Common, 214; start for Concord, 220; retreat to Boston, 222.
Trowbridge, J. T., 409, 410.
"Two Brothers," stones marking bounds of Winthrop's and Dudley's lands, 66.

VANE, HENRY, arrives in Boston, 85; a leader in England, 87; jealous of Cromwell, 87; executed, 88.
Vassal family, tomb and tablet, 304; family mansion, Longfellow's residence, 400.
Virginia regiment at Bunker Hill centennial, 335.

WALDEN, LAKE, 439.
Waltham, river excursions from, 349.
Wampanoags, favorite resort of, 79.
War, the civil, begun, 317.
Ware, Henry, Jr., 393; his "Ursa Major," 394; his antislavery ideas, 398; his last poem, 399.
Warren, Dr. John Collins, 341.
Warren, General Joseph, 206; sends out Paul Revere, 219; death of, 248; statue of, 303; now buried at Forest Hills, 303.

Warren Museum, 341.
Washington, George, first monument and bust of, 236; appointed commander-in-chief, 253; arrival at Cambridge, 253; took command of the army, 257; headquarters, 257; elected president, 293; visits Boston, 293.
Washington Street, follows the windings of William Blackstone's cow, 43.
Water supply of Boston, 327.
Watertown, first settlers at, 62.
"We are One," poem by Washington Allston, 29.
Webster, Daniel, oration of at Bunker Hill, 295, 300.
Wellesley College, 349.
Whitefield, George, in Boston, 193; tomb of at Newburyport, 435.
Whittier, John G., 421; his love of liberty, 422; the poet of old Essex County, 423; energy of character, 424; his boyhood, 428; antislavery odes, 429; his home, 430.
Whittier's poetry, associations of, 421.
Williams, Roger, comes to Boston, 88; banished for his opinions, 92.
Wilson, John, pastor of the First Church, 65.
Wineland, 362.
Winslow, Edward, searches for a lost boy, 76.
Winter Hill fortified, 257.
Winthrop, Henry, drowned at Salem, 61.
Winthrop, John, decides to leave England, 47; carries the king's charter, 49; some incidents of his life, 57; extracts from his journal, 61; fording a stream, 67; visits Plymouth, 68; lost for one night, 72; death of, 92.
Winthrop statue in Scollay Square, 61.
Witchcraft, account of the Salem, 109.
Witches, belief in, in England and Scotland, 109; methods of discovering, 110; in the Hebrew nations, 124.
Wollaston, Captain, settles a company at Mount Wollaston, now Braintree, 66.
Woodbridge, Benjamin, killed in a duel, 160.
"Wreck of the Hesperus," origin of the poem, 404.
Wright's Tavern, 451.

YKANHO, St. Botolph's monastery at, destroyed, 23.

Cambridge: Printed by John Wilson & Son.

www.ingramcontent.com/pod-product-compliance
Lightning Source LLC
Chambersburg PA
CBHW051237300426
44114CB00011B/768